ALTERNATIVE
HEALTH
THERAPIES

ALTERNATIVE HEALTH THERAPIES

DENISE WHICHELLO BROWN
& SANDRA WHITE

**Eagle
Editions**

A QUANTUM BOOK

Published by Eagle Editions Ltd
11 Heathfield
Royston
Hertfordshire SG8 5BW

Copyright ©MMI
Quantum Publishing Ltd.

This edition printed 2001

ISBN 1-86160-422-X

QUMAIBU

This book is produced by
Quantum Publishing Ltd.
6 Blundell Street
London N7 9BH

Printed in Singapore by
Star Standard Industries Pte Ltd

contents

introduction to
Aromatherapy

The aim of this section is to introduce you to the fragrant world of 'Aromatherapy' a word which derives from 'aroma', meaning fragrance or smell and 'therapy' meaning treatment. This ancient healing art combines the aromatic essence of plants, known as essential oils, with relaxing massage.

A versatile holistic treatment, Aromatherapy is based on the ancient principle that the spirit and the body should be in harmony. By using a subtle combination of different essential oils, aromatherapy promotes both physical health, and mental and emotional well-being.

This section is intended to provide an introduction to the main essential oils, and to promote an understanding of how they are extracted, stored and used. A useful directory provides vital information on the properties of each oil, together with guidelines for safe usage, and effects and contra-indications to be aware of. The other key element of aromatherapy – massage – is then explained and demonstrated in the following two sections.

A full Aromatherapy treatment is a truly wonderful experience, combining, as it does, the beneficial properties of the essential oils with the warm relaxing atmosphere of a well prepared massage and possibly the enjoyment of soothing music which can appeal to the whole 'Mind, Body and Spirit'. However, this is not the only way that Aromatherapy can find a place in our busy lives. From fragrant baths to scented candles or oil burners, it can and does benefit and improve our day to day attitude to living.

Although it is one of the most ancient of the healing arts, Aromatherapy has only really become widely popular in the last few years. This increased popularity is largely due to people's growing awareness of the advantages of following a 'natural' path to health and fitness, rather than relying on conventional medicine. The effects of this new awareness can be felt in all areas

Making your own aromatherapy blends can be very satisfying

Oils can be extracted from many different parts of the plant or fruit.

of our lives today. More and more people have changed their diets as new information has become available regarding the benefits of fresh, natural foods, rather than the convenience or 'junk' foods favoured until recently. At the same time there has been growing appreciation and respect for what have often been termed as 'alternative' therapies, but which are more accurately described as 'complementary' therapies. These are the ancient and traditional treatments and remedies such as Aromatherapy and Reflexology that are now widely accepted as a complement to modern medicine, rather than as a replacement. By combining what is best from both the ancient healing arts and modern technology, we can truly achieve a healthy balance in both our physical and emotional lives.

Creating a relaxing atmosphere is an essential part of aromatherapy

IMPORTANT NOTICE

This book must not be used as a substitute for treatment of medical conditions when it is important that the help of a doctor is sought. The information is not intended to diagnose or treat and any safety guidelines covered throughout the book must be adhered to.

It is of particular importance that essential oils are not to be taken internally and all other contra-indications regarding the oils are closely observed.

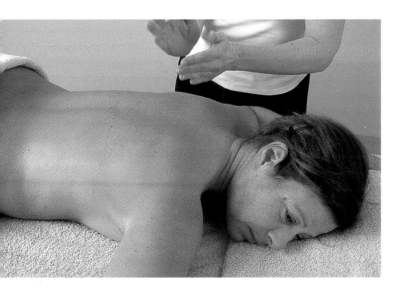

Aromatherapy combines the healing properties of essential oils with a relaxing massage.

history of
Aromatherapy

Aromatherapy is reputed to be at least 6000 years old, and is believed to have been practised by most of the world's ancient civilisations. Early man lived closely with his surroundings and was in tune with nature. His sense of smell was highly acute and herbs and aromatics were commonly used in the preservation of food, as aids to digestion or to treat a variety of ailments.

It is widely accepted that the Aromatherapy we know today can trace its origins back to ancient Egypt. A medical papyri believed to date back to around 1555 BC contains remedies for all types of illnesses, and many of the methods of application described are similar to those used in Aromatherapy and herbal medicine today.

The Egyptians used a method known as infusion (this process is described in a later chapter) to extract the oils from aromatic plants. One of the earliest ways of using aromatics was probably in the form of incense. For example, frankincense was commonly burned at sun rise as an offering to the sun god, Ra, while myrrh was offered to the moon. The Egyptians were also experts at embalming, and used aromatics to help preserve flesh. Yet aromatics had their place in pleasurable practices also, as the Egyptians enjoyed being massaged with fragrant oils after bathing.

There is evidence that the ancient Chinese civilisations were using some form of aromatics at a similar time to the Egyptians. Shen Nung's herbal book is the oldest surviving medical reference in China and dates back to around 2700 BC. This book contains information about over 300 plants. Like the Egyptians, the ancient Chinese also used aromatics in religious ceremonies, by burning aromatic woods and incense to show respect to their Gods. Their practice of using aromatics was linked to the equally ancient therapies of massage and acupressure.

Aromatherapy of some kind has also been in use for many centuries in India. The traditional Indian medicine, known as Ayurveda, has been practised for over 3000 years and this too, incorporates aromatic massage and the use of dried and fresh herbs as important aspects of the treatment.

The ancient Chinese are believed to have been among the first practitioners of herbal medicine.

The Greeks continued the practice of using aromatic oils begun by the Egyptians, and used them both medicinally and cosmetically. A Greek physician, Pedacius Dioscorides, wrote a definitive book about herbal medicine, and for at least 1200 years this was used as the Western world's standard medical reference. Many of the remedies he describes are still in use today.

The Romans took much of their medical knowledge from the Greeks, and they went on to refine and improve the use of aromatics, to the extent that Rome eventually became known as the bathing capital of the world. The popularity of scented baths followed by massage with aromatic oils is well documented, with public bath houses taking prominent positions in most towns. The popularity of aromatics lead to the opening up of extensive trading routes which enabled the Romans to import 'exotic' oils and spices from such far-away places as India and Arabia.

As the glory of the Roman Empire faded, the use of aromatics declined, with the knowledge of their use eventually being lost throughout Europe during the so-called dark ages. However, herbal and aromatic skills were still practised by some. One of the few places where the use of herbal medicine continued was in the monasteries, where the monks used plants from their herbal gardens to produce infused oils, herbal teas and medicines.

During the Middle Ages and the time of the plague, it was realised that certain aromatic substances seemed to help prevent the spread of infection, and aromatic woods such as cedar and pine were burnt to fumigate homes and streets.

The modern revival of the use of essential oils is thought to be due to a Persian physician and philosopher known as Avicenna who lived from AD 980 to AD 1037.

The Arabs began to use a method of distillation, and study of the therapeutic use of plants became popular in their Universities. During the Crusades this knowledge of distillation spread to the invading forces, and the lost process was brought back to Europe once more. By 1200 AD, essential oils were being produced in Germany, based mainly on herbs and spices brought from the Far East and Africa.

The invasions of South America by the conquistadors brought about the discovery of more medicinal plants and aromatic oils as the Spanish discovered the wealth of plant lore and remedies that had been used by the Aztecs for many centuries. Indeed, the vast range of medicinal plants found in Montezuma's botanical gardens formed the basis of many new and important remedies and treatments.

The Romans were famous for their practice and enjoyment of massage and bathing with scented oils.

The healing power of lavender was one of the first to be re-discovered.

Native American Indians throughout the northern continent also used aromatic oils and produced their own herbal remedies. These were discovered when the early settlers began to make their way across the plains and prairies of the 'New World'.

However, despite their use in many other world cultures for centuries, it was not until the 19th century that scientists in Europe and Great Britain began researching the effects of essential oils on bacteria in humans. A French chemist, Rene Maurice Gattefosse, began his research into the healing powers of essential oils after burning his hand in his laboratory. Almost without thinking he immersed the burn in lavender oil and was immediately impressed by how quickly the burn healed. In 1937 he published a book about the anti-microbial effects of the oils

and it was he who actually coined the word 'Aromatherapy'. He went on to set up a business producing oils for use in fragrances and cosmetics. At around the same time another Frenchman, Albert Couvreur, published a book on the medicinal uses of essential oils.

A French medical doctor, Jean Valnet, discovered Gattefosse's research and began experimenting with essential oils. At about the same time Margaret Maury, a French biochemist, developed a unique method of applying these oils to the skin with massage. Micheline Arcier, now living in London, studied and worked with Maury and Valnet and their combined techniques created the form of Aromatherapy that is now used all over the world.

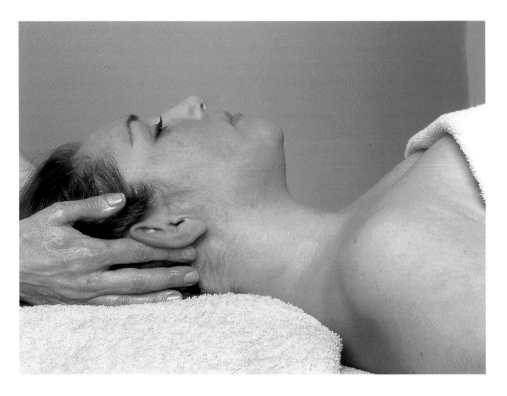

Today aromatherapy is valued throughout the world.

Approach to health

The holistic approach to keeping healthy is not new. The ancient healing traditions of India and China are based on the idea that the body, mind and spirit form an integrated whole and are inextricably connected with the environment. These traditions further maintain that to be healthy, all of these elements must exist in a dynamically balanced state of well-being.

"The cure of the part should not be attempted without treatment of the whole. No attempt should be made to cure the body without the soul. If the body and head are to be healthy you must begin by curing the mind. Let no one persuade you to cure the head until he has first given you his soul to be cured."
Plato 427-347 BC

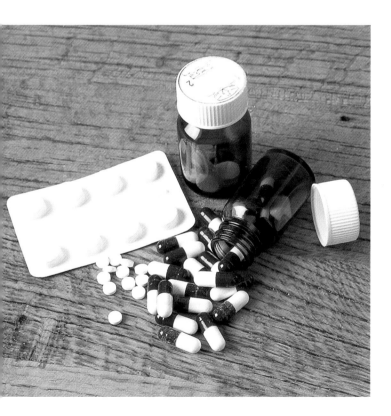

Aromatherapy complements conventional medicines, which generally only treat a specific area or set of symptoms.

The human organism can, in theory, be divided into three levels: physical, emotional and mental. However, in reality these are not separate and there is constant interaction between them. If there is imbalance in one level, then the others can not be in harmony. This is in direct contrast with conventional medicine, which treats a particular part of the body, or a particular set of symptoms to cure an ailment, and which normally uses chemical intervention or surgery.

A physical symptom such as a headache may be related to an underlying psychological problem and although dealing with the physical symptom alone may well relieve the pain temporarily, it will not necessarily bring about a long-term solution.

Today, more and more people are returning to a holistic lifestyle, as they find that the traditional methods and practises help them to enjoy a higher level of vitality and well-being. Aromatherapy is one holistic practice that can easily be incorporated into our everyday lives to help us achieve a state of well-being.

Although some stress is essential in our lives, the stress created in today's environment is often extreme, and detrimental to our well-being.

STRESS

The word stress is one which is familiar to most of us. It is an almost expected part of daily life, and it is hardly surprising to learn that an estimated 75% of visits to GPs are due to stress-related problems.

However, we cannot avoid stress as it is essential to life. It is the dynamic, creative force which makes us sit, walk, run etc. and is therefore vital for our very existence. Stress is the adaptive response of the body to demands made on it. We are all unique and what may be creative stress for one person may be destructive to another. Creative stress can be defined as stress that we can use to inspire us, or to drive us to greater heights or successes, whether

personal or professional. Destructive stress on the other hand makes us ill, ruins our concentration and makes us feel as if life is too much for us to deal with.

Although it is true, therefore, that we all need a certain amount of stress in our lives, it is our response to stress that dictates whether a positive or negative effect on our well-being.

In times of fast-moving, constantly changing lifestyles, we are being expected to cope with any demands placed on us and illness or disease is often the only way for our body to tell us that it cannot cope with such pressure. When stress becomes a regular feature in our lives, our energy reserves become rapidly depleted, and if we do not take the time to 'recharge our batteries', then nature often steps in, manifesting some form of illness that forces us to stop and review our lives.

High blood pressure, strokes and heart disease are often considered to be related to stress and other disorders such as rheumatism, cancer, skin disorders and digestive problems are more likely to develop when our resistance is low.

Any change in our lives is potentially stressful as change requires us to adapt. Major changes such as marriage, divorce, new job, redundancy, financial problems or a birth or death in the family are just some of the most common life changes that force us to make major adjustments. If more than one of these changes occur within a short space of time we may overlook the need to take time to adjust. Our response to increased pressure, whether external or self-imposed usually makes us force ourselves to keep going, even when our bodies may be telling us we need to rest or relax. It is this denial of our physical and emotional needs that often results in unpleasant consequences, such as illness, depression or exhaustion.

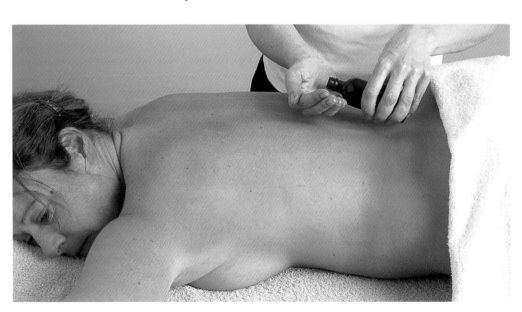

Massage is one of the most effective relaxation techniques. Combined with soothing aromatherapy oils its benefits are increased.

It is therefore very important that we equip ourselves with ways of managing stress. One of the most effective and agreeable methods of doing this is the practise of Aromatherapy, where the use of essential oils plays a vital role.

Conventional medicine often has little to offer when it comes to dealing with stress-related conditions as it usually only treats the symptoms of such problems – emotional distress or insomnia are common examples – with the use of tranquillisers or sleeping tablets. These may help in the short-term, but they are not a long-term solution to the problem.

Chamomile

As a holistic form of treatment, aromatherapy aims to deal with the underlying cause of the complaint, as well as the symptoms, and this form of treatment is very important when dealing with stress-related problems, as a physical symptom is more often than not a manifestation of an underlying psychological or emotional problem. Essential oils have many properties which make them ideal for helping you to cope with stress. Oils such as chamomile help to relax the body and improve sleep. Neroli is ideal for helping with anxiety and depression, while lavender is helpful for high blood pressure, insomnia and depression. These oils can be used in different ways to help with stress related problems, although one of the easiest, yet most enjoyable methods is to simply relax in a warm bath with essential oils.

Certain oils such as lavender, sandalwood and tea-tree have a positive effect on the immune system, making our bodies more able to cope with the demands and pressures of everyday life. Using these oils on a regular basis can help to prevent stress-related ailments. It is clear, then, that with the help of these wonderful oils, managing the stress in our lives can become easier.

Neroli

an introduction to
Essential Oils

Aromatherapy essential oils can be used in a number of different ways, from healing to cosmetic.

Each of the essential oils used in Aromatherapy can be used in a number of different ways, and can be used either alone or combined with other oils to enhance our health and sense of well-being. Before beginning to use Aromatherapy treatments, it is important to understand how each oil works, and which can be used most effectively to ease or prevent specific ills, or to promote a particular feeling.

Essential oils are highly fragrant, non-oily plant essences. The term oil is somewhat inappropriate as these essences have a consistency which resembles water more than oil. They are volatile and evaporate easily so they must be stored in a cool place, in dark coloured bottles away from direct sunlight.

The essences are insoluble in water but dissolve in vegetable oils, wax and alcohol.

The essential oils can be found in different parts of the plant such as the flowers, twigs, leaves and bark, but also often in the rind of the fruit. Each oil originates in special sacs in the plant material.

Essential oils are antiseptic as well as having their own individual properties and have many complex chemical constituents. Due to its many different components one oil can have a variety of uses.

The oils work in various ways on the body. If applied to the skin they are absorbed quickly through the hair follicles due to their molecular structure. They diffuse into the blood stream or are taken up by the lymphatic fluids and transported throughout the body. Different oils are absorbed at different rates and this can vary between 20 minutes to two hours or even more so it is best not to shower for a time after applying the oils.

The essential oils are extracted from various parts of the plant. In fruit, oils generally come from rinds or seeds

Before using an oil, it is always very important to note the contra-indications for each oil and to stick closely to these recommendations.

A general rule when choosing oils is to select and use those whose scents you find particularly appealing. The whole principle of Aromatherapy is that it should be a pleasurable experience, and choosing an oil whose aroma is unpleasant to you will not be beneficial. There will generally be more than one oil you can use for a particular purpose, so you shoud be able to find one you like.

The nose plays an important part in Aromatherapy. When inhaling essential oils the odour molecules are transmitted to the emotional centre of the brain known as the limbic system. This system is connected to other parts of the brain involved with memory, breathing and blood circulation as well as the endocrine glands which regulate hormone levels in the body.

The effect on the memory is important as it can help bring back recollections of the past, not all of which will be pleasant. If you do not like the smell of a particular oil, for example, it could well be that it reminds you of something in your past that you would prefer to forget. This is another reason it is a good idea to avoid the use of this oil.

Essential oils are often described as having top, middle or base notes and this relates to the amount of time that the aroma of each oil will last.

• Oils with base notes have the longest lasting aroma, with scents that can last up to one week.

• Oils with middle notes have a shorter span, with aromas lasting about two to three days.

• Oils with top notes have the shortest-lasting aromas, with scents which only last for up to 24 hours.

In terms of creating a balanced perfume, a combination of top, middle and base notes will produce the best results. However, when it comes to making aromatherapy blends, it is not necessary to stick to any fixed rules. As you become familiar with the different oils you will be able to create blends which are right for you. Experimenting with these wonderful essences will be an enjoyable and educational experience, as you learn which oils combine the best, and produce the best effects.

There are many scents to choose from, so finding an aroma that suits you should be easy.

Once you have found the scents you prefer, you can use them in your everyday life in pot pourris for example.

SAFETY PRECAUTIONS

Although essential oils are generally considered to be safe to use they are very powerful, highly concentrated substances which should be treated with a certain amount of respect. It is important to take note of the following safety guidelines before proceeding:

- Do not use any oil that you are not familiar with.

- The following oils should not be used during pregnancy or when breast feeding:
  Thyme, Sage, Wintergreen, Basil, Clove, Marjoram, Cinnamon, Fennel, Jasmine, Juniper, Rosemary, Aniseed, Peppermint, Clary Sage, Oregano, Nutmeg, Bay, Hops, Valerian, Tarragon, Cedarwood.

- The following should be avoided during the first 3 months of pregnancy:
  Chamomile, Geranium, Lavender and Rose.

- If there is history of previous miscarriage do not massage.

- The following oils may cause slight skin irritation:
  Basil, Rosemary, Fennel, Verbena and Lemon Grass.

The only essential oils which can be used undiluted on the skin are Lavender and Tea Tree but care should be taken as some people have a sensitivity to these oils.

- The following oils should NOT be applied to the skin before sunbathing or using a sun-bed:
  Bergamot, Orange, Lemon or other citrus oils.

- If you or anyone you are considering treating, suffer from epilepsy, great care should be taken as certain oils could aggravate the condition. The following oils should NOT be used:
  Fennel, Hyssop, Sage, and Rosemary.

- Do NOT take essential oils internally, although herbal teas can be used in moderation.

- Keep oils away from children and if any essential oil gets in the eye, rinse immediately with water.

- If you are taking homeopathic remedies, check that the essential oil will not interfere with their effectiveness.

- If you have sensitive skin or are prone to allergies you should do a skin patch test before using a particular oil. First wash and dry the forearm, then add a few drops of the blended oil to the gauze of a large plaster. The plaster should be placed on the forearm and left for 24 hours. The plaster should then be removed and if the area appears irritated or red do not use that particular blend. This test does not guarantee that there will not be an adverse reaction but it will give a good indication.

- If you dislike the smell of a particular oil, this is a good indication that the oil is not right for you and a suitable alternative should be used.

- Do not use steam inhalations if you suffer from asthma.

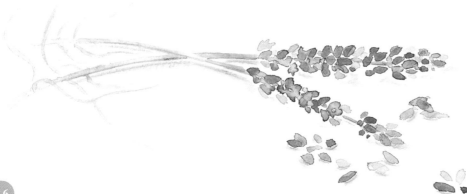

The following pages cover 35 of the most commonly-used Essential oils. Each plant is listed alphabetically by its botanical name, which is shown in brackets after the common name.

CHAMOMILE, ROMAN (*ANTHEMIS NOBILIS*)

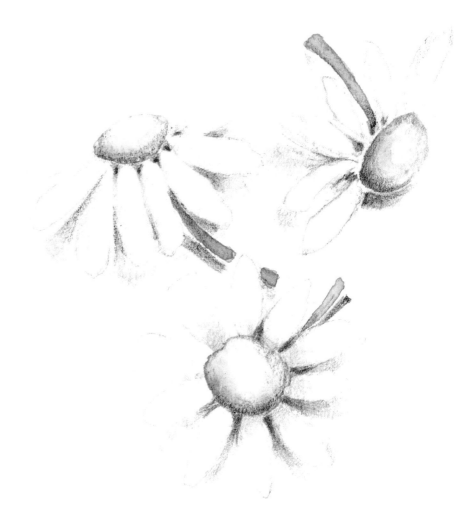

Effects: Soothing and harmonising
Aroma: Middle note

This small plant, native to Europe, has a daisy-like flower. It is mainly cultivated in Italy, England, France and the USA. Chamomile tea is renowned worldwide for its calming effect.

Properties
- Tonic
- Soothing
- Pain reliever
- Antibacterial
- Antiseptic
- Digestive stimulant

Contra-indications
Not to be used during early pregnancy. May cause skin irritation.

Extraction
Steam distillation of the flower heads.

Uses
- Rheumatism
- Gout
- Skin conditions
- Inflammations such as eczema
- Nervous tension
- Neuralgia
- Digestive problems such as colitis and gastritis
- Headaches
- Depression

Chamomile also promotes relaxation and eases tension, anxiety and fear. It has a soothing effect on skin conditions such as ulcers, boils and blisters and may help in conditions such as psoriasis, dermatitis and acne.

Massaging the abdomen is helpful when treating indigestion and flatulence. May help with Irritable Bowel Syndrome.

Chamomile is also very helpful when used in massage to alleviate nervous tension and headaches and lower back pain.

Scent
Sweet, herbal , fruity scent.

Combines with:
- Bergamot
- Geranium
- Lavender
- Clary Sage

FRANKINCENSE (*BOSWELLIA CARTERI*)

Effects: Uplifting

Aroma: Base/middle note

This small tree is native to the Red Sea area and the oil is produced in China, Somalia and Ethiopia. The spice is used during religious ceremonies and an ingredient in cosmetics.

Properties
- Analgesic
- Anti-inflammatory
- Antiseptic
- Antidepressant
- Expectorant

Contra-indications
None.

Extraction
Steam distillation of the gum resin obtained from the bark of the trees.

Uses
- Skin care
- Respiratory conditions
- Urinary infections
- Nervous conditions

Frankincense also has a beneficial effect on mature skins.

It can be used blended as a chest and back massage for respiratory conditions including asthma, bronchitis and colds, and helps wounds to heal.

It is a uterine tonic and can be helpful for heavy periods and also as a massage after birth.

It is helpful as a blended massage oil for those who are frightened and nervous and is very comforting for those who feel isolated and alone.

Scent
Sweet, warm and balsamic.

Combines with:
- Rose
- Sandalwood
- Lavender
- Neroli

YLANG YLANG (CANANGIUM ODORATUM)

Effects: Stimulating
Aroma: Base/middle note

This tall tree is native to the Philippines and the Far East. The large distinctive flowers can be various colours but the yellow ones are considered to produce the best oil.

Properties
- Antiseptic
- Antidepressant
- Calming
- Sedative

Contra-indications
May be an irritant to sensitive skins and should not be used on inflammatory skin conditions. The strong scent can cause headaches.

Extraction
Steam distillation of the flowers.

Uses
- Intestinal infections
- High blood pressure
- Stress

Ylang-Ylang is helpful in dealing with anxiety, panic and shock as it has a relaxing effect on the nervous system. It is also believed to help feelings of resentment, guilt and jealousy.

It has a balancing effect on the hormones and is a tonic for the uterus.

Ylang-Ylang oil has a balancing effect on oily and dry skins.

Scent
Powerful, sweet, balsamic, floral, exotic.

Combines with:
- Clary Sage
- Geranium
- Lavender
- Lemon
- Cedarwood

CEDARWOOD (CEDRUS ATLANTICA)

Effects: Strengthening and powerful
Aroma: Base note

This tree grows in southern Europe, the Orient and North America. Cedarwood gum was used by the Egyptians many years ago as an important ingredient in the mummifying process.

Properties
- Antiseptic
- Sedative
- Expectorant
- Antifungal
- Astringent

Contra-indications
May irritate sensitive skins. Do not use during pregnancy.

Extraction
Steam distillation of the wood as well as the sawdust.

Uses:
- Bronchitis

- Nervous tension
- Cellulite
- Cystitis
- Certain skin conditions such as eczema.

Cedarwood is good for acne, and oily skin and when blended with rosemary and eucalyptus is used as a treatment for dandruff. It has a calming effect on the nervous system. May be helpful for arthritic and rheumatic pains.

Scent
Woody.

Combines with:
- Bergamot
- Rosemary
- Sandalwood

NEROLI/ORANGE BLOSSOM *(CITRUS AURANTIUM)*

Effects: Calming and peaceful

Aroma: Top note

An evergreen tree with fragrant white blossom which originated in the Far East. It is now grown in the Midi region of France, Southern Italy, Spain, Mexico, California and South America.

Properties
- Antidepressant
- Antiseptic
- Antispasmodic
- Sedative

Contra-indications
None.

Extraction
Steam distillation of the flowers.

Uses
- Flatulence
- Headaches
- Nervous tension
- Depression
- Insomnia.

Neroli is also used in skin preparations.

Due to its very soothing effect, Neroli is very helpful in stress-related conditions such as panic attacks and irritable bowel syndrome when used diluted in massage.

It has a calming effect on the heart and has a beneficial effect on dry, sensitive skin and broken capillaries. Being antispasmodic it is helpful in digestive problems such as colitis.

Scent
Rich, floral, refreshing.

Combines with:
- Lavender
- Chamomile
- Sandalwood
- Citrus oils

ORANGE *(CITRUS AURANTIUM)*

Effects: Calming and energising
Aroma: Top note

This is the same tree that produces Neroli oil — an evergreen tree with fragrant white blossom which originated in the Far East. The orange tree is a familiar sight in the Mediterranean regions with blossom appearing in Spring and Autumn.

Properties
- Antidepressant
- Antiseptic
- Antispasmodic
- Digestive
- Detoxifying
- Sedative
- Tonic

Contra-indications
May irritate skin and is photo toxic.

Extraction
Expression of the rind of the fruit.

Uses
- Anxiety
- Mature skins
- Indigestion
- Muscular pains
- Cellulite

Orange has a beneficial effect on the nervous system, as it calms and relaxes and may help insomnia.

Orange is beneficial for digestive problems such as constipation, diarrhoea and flatulence, and helps the system eliminate toxins through the skin. Orange can also relieve muscular aches and pains.

It is beneficial for dry skin and dermatitis but should only be used in very low dilutions.

Respiratory conditions can be alleviated, and orange is a useful oil for depression and sadness.

Scent
Fresh and light. Fruity and sweet.

Combines with:
- Frankincense
- Sandalwood
- Lavender
- Rosemary
- Ylang-ylang

BERGAMOT (*CITRUS BERGAMIA*)

Effects: Uplifting and refreshing
Aroma: Top note

This small tree is native to Morocco and parts of Asia. The name comes from a small town in Italy called Bergamo where the oil was first sold. Bergamot belongs to the same family as the orange tree and one of its more familiar uses is as the flavouring in Earl Grey tea.

Properties
- Antiseptic
- Antispasmodic
- Antidepressant
- Uplifting

Contra-indications
Bergamot is photo toxic so should not be used with exposure to sunlight.

Extraction
Expression of the outer part of the peel from the small orange-like fruit.

Uses
- Sore throat
- Loss of appetite
- Flatulence
- Its antiseptic properties are helpful in the treatment of acne and also for boils and abscesses.
- It can also help to ease shingles, chicken pox and cold sores.
- It has a positive effect on the immune system and is helpful for colds, flu, mouth infections and sore throats.
- It is a useful air freshener when used in a vaporiser.
- It can be added to a bath in a well-diluted form to alleviate both cystitis and thrush.

Bergamot is also widely used in perfumes and the confection industry. It is used to flavour Earl Grey Tea and has a positive effect on anxiety and depression.

Scent
Fruity with slightly balsamic, spicy undertone. Fresh and sharp.

Combines with:
- Chamomile
- Juniper
- Neroli

PETITGRAIN (*CITRUS BIGARDIA*)

Effects: Restoring

Aroma: Top note

This is yet another oil produced from the Orange tree.

Properties

- Antibacterial
- Antifungal
- Antiseptic
- Antispasmodic
- Stimulant

Contra-indications

None.

Extraction

Steam distillation of the twigs and leaves.

Uses

- Respiratory infections
- Skin conditions such as acne.

Petitgrain is also beneficial in digestive conditions such as flatulence.

It has a positive effect on the nervous system and is helpful in cases of stress, depression, nervous exhaustion and stress-induced insomnia.

Scent

Fresh, sweet, floral.

Combines with:

- Other citrus oils

LEMON (CITRUS LIMONOM)

Effects: Cleansing and stimulating
Aroma: Top note

This evergreen tree is thought to have originated in India, and now grows extensively in southern Europe, particularly in Portugal and Spain.

Properties
- Antiseptic
- Astringent
- Antiviral
- Stimulant

Contra-indications
May irritate sensitive skin. Photo toxic.

Extraction
Expression of the outer part of the rind of the fruit.

Uses
- Sinusitis
- Sore throat
- Tonsillitis
- Inflammation of the gums
- Migraine
- Chilblains
- Verrucae

Lemon is also a good first aid treatment for snake and insect bites. Also has a great use in skin and beauty care as a skin tonic and helps clear warts, corns and verrucae.

It has a general cleansing effect on the body. Lemon may be effective in relieving headaches and rheumatic pains.

It can be used in a vaporiser but should NOT be inhaled and sun and sun beds should be avoided for several hours after use on the skin.

Scent
Refreshing, clean, lively.

Combines with:
- Chamomile
- Frankincense
- Lavender
- Sandalwood
- Ylang-Ylang
- Other citrus oils

GRAPEFRUIT (*CITRUS PARADISI*)

Effects: Refreshing
Aroma: Top note

A tree native to the West Indies and Asia and cultivated in California, Brazil and Israel.

Properties
- Antiseptic
- Astringent
- Diuretic
- Stimulant

Contra-indications
Grapefruit is photo toxic.

Extraction
Expression of the peel of the fruit.

Uses
- Digestive problems
- Water retention
- Depression
- Anxiety, self doubt

Combined with lemon, grapefruit can make a refreshing and revitalising morning bath.

Scent
Sweet, fresh, citrus-y.

Combines with:
- Lavender
- Other citrus oils

MYRRH (*COMMIPHORA MYRRHA*)

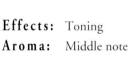

Effects: Toning
Aroma: Middle note

This bush is native to Africa and Arabia. The oil has been used since ancient times.

Properties
- Analgesic
- Astringent
- Antiseptic
- Expectorant

Contra-indications
None.

Extraction
Steam distillation of the gum resin.

Uses
- Arthritis
- Coughs and colds
- Bronchitis
- Stimulates digestive system

Scent
Warm and spicy.

Combines with:
- Frankincense
- Orange
- Geranium
- Pine

CYPRESS (*CUPRESSUS SEMPERVIRENS*)

Effects: Refreshing
Aroma: Middle/base note

This is a tall evergreen tree native to the Mediterranean regions. It is now cultivated in France, Spain and Morocco. It was used as a natural remedy by many of the ancient civilisations.

Properties
• Astringent
• Antispasmodic
• Diuretic
• Expectorant

Contra-indications
Due to its effect on the menstrual cycle, cypress should be avoided in pregnancy.

Extraction
Steam distillation of both the needles and twigs.

Uses:
• Rheumatism
• Muscle and nervous tension
• Haemorrhoids
• Spasmodic coughs

Cypress is helpful as a massage oil to treat rheumatic aches and pains as well as swollen joints.

Used as an inhalant, its antispasmodic properties help alleviate coughs, bronchitis, asthma and sore throats.

Cypress is very helpful for regulating the menstrual cycle and treating oedema. It also has a beneficial effect on menopause symptoms such as hot flushes and irritability.

It can be used in treating oily skin and hair.

Scent
Refreshing and sweet.

Combines with:
• Citrus oils
• Lavender
• Sandalwood
• Rose
• Juniper

EUCALYPTUS (*EUCALYPTUS GLOBULUS*)

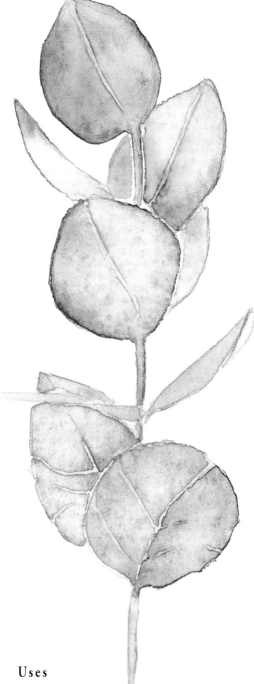

Effects: Balancing and stimulating
Aroma: Top/middle note

This tall evergreen is also known as the Gum Tree and originated in Australia. There are hundreds of varieties, many of which are now found in Southern Europe, Brazil and California.

Properties
- Stimulant
- Antiseptic
- Analgesic
- Antiviral
- Anti-inflammatory
- Decongestant, particularly useful for respiratory as well as urinary tract infections.
- Insect repellent

Contra-indications
Eucalyptus is a powerful oil and should be avoided by sufferers of high blood pressure or epilepsy. It can prove fatal if taken internally.

Extraction
Steam distillation of the leaves and twigs.

Uses
- Sinusitis
- Flu
- Bronchitis
- Sore throat
- Asthma
- Other pulmonary conditions.
- Rheumatism and aching muscles
- Skin problems such as burns, cuts, wounds and ulcers

Eucalyptus is also very useful as an air disinfectant. Burning the oil helps to purify the air in sickrooms.

Used as an inhalant it is beneficial for respiratory conditions and as a chest massage oil using the diluted oil.

Its anti-inflammatory properties are helpful when used as a massage oil to relieve pains and aches associated with rheumatism and arthritis. It is helpful for neuralgia and headaches.

It can be used to alleviate urinary infections such as cystitis when added to a bath.

Scent
Camphorous, woody, clear.

Combines with:
- Lavender
- Rosemary
- Marjoram
- Juniper

CLOVE (*EUGENIA CARYOPHYLLATA*)

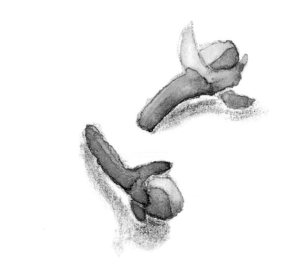

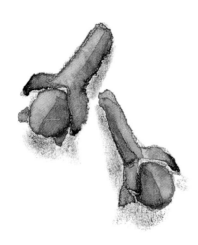

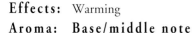

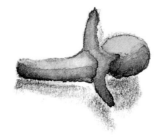

Effects: Warming
Aroma: Base/middle note

This is a small evergreen tree which grows in the West Indies and Madagascar. Cloves are commonly used in cooking and dental preparations.

Properties
- Analgesic
- Expectorant
- Stimulant

Contra-indications
Clove is a very potent oil and should be used with great care. Used for massage it could cause skin irritation. Only use in very low dilutions less than 1%.

Extraction
Steam distillation from both the stalks and stems.

Properties
- Antiseptic
- Analgesic
- Antispasmodic
- Disinfectant
- Insecticide

Uses
- Toothache
- Muscular and nerve tension
- Infected wounds
- Indigestion

Clove also relieves respiratory conditions and has been used to treat bronchitis, laryngitis and colds.

It is an excellent room disinfectant and insect repellent.

Clove is also used in natural toothpastes.

Scent
Sweet, spicy and fresh.

Combines with:
- Lavender
- Orange
- Bergamot
- Ylang-ylang

FENNEL (FOENICULUM VULGARE)

Effects: Clearing
Aroma: Middle note

This herb has yellow flowers and originates from Spain and Eastern Europe. It belongs to the carrot family.

Properties
- Antiseptic
- Anti-spasmodic
- Diuretic
- Stimulant

Contra-indications
May irritate sensitive skins. Do not use in pregnancy or with epilepsy sufferers.

Extraction
Steam distillation of the seeds.

Uses
- Indigestion
- Flatulence
- Nervous tension

Its diuretic properties make fennel helpful in the treatment of gout, particularly when combined with juniper.

Useful in digestive problems such as constipation and flatulence. (Fennel tea helps colic and diarrhoea).

Scent
Sweet but earthy.

Combines with:
- Geranium
- Lavender
- Sandalwood

JASMINE (JASMINUM GRANDIFLORUM)

Effects: Soothing
Aroma: Base note

This is a shrub native to Asia and India and which is cultivated in China and the Mediterranean regions. It is an evergreen with small, fragrant flowers.

Properties
- Antidepressant
- Antiseptic
- Antispasmodic
- Expectorant

Contra-indications
Generally none but allergic reactions have been known.

Extraction
Solvent extraction of the flowers.

Uses
- Headache
- Anxiety
- Lack of confidence

Jasmine is also helpful for respiratory conditions such as laryngitis, catarrh and coughs.

It can help with uterine disorders such as period pains and labour pains.

It has a beneficial effect on the nervous system and may help ease tension and anxiety.

It is used in skin care and has a beneficial effect on dry or sensitive skins.

Scent
Warm and floral.

Combines with:
- Sandalwood
- Rose
- Chamomile
- Ylang-ylang
- Citrus oils

JUNIPER *(JUNIPERUS COMMUNIS)*

Effects: Cleansing
Aroma: Middle note

This small hardwood bush thrives in Arctic regions and can be found in Sweden, Canada and central Northern Europe. It has been used for many years as an antiseptic.

Properties
- Analgesic
- Astringent
- Diuretic
- Expectorant

Contra-indications

Juniper should not be used by people with severe kidney disease, as it can over-stimulate the kidneys. Avoid use during pregnancy.

Extraction

Steam distillation of the berries.

Uses

- Eczema
- Acne
- Sores and ulcers
- Rheumatism and gout
- Cystitis.

Juniper is also a useful disinfectant.

Use diluted as a massage oil for aches and pains and rheumatism.

Juniper has a calming effect and is helpful to ease stress when used as a massage oil.

It is very helpful in treating gout as it helps with elimination of toxins. Due to its diuretic effect, Juniper is helpful in conditions of the genito-urinary tract such as cystitis.

It may be helpful for acne, dermatitis and weeping eczema and can sometimes help cellulite.

Juniper is very cleansing emotionally as well as physically and helps revitalise.

Scent

Fresh, woody and sweet.

Combines with:
- Lavender
- Rose
- Rosemary
- Frankincense
- Sandalwood

LAVENDER *(LAVENDULA ANGUSTIFOLIA)*

Effects: Calming and healing
Aroma: Middle note

This flowering shrub is native to the Mediterranean regions and is now cultivated worldwide. Its lovely violet-blue flowers are a familiar sight in many English gardens. The highest quality lavender is found growing at high altitudes. Lavender was very popular with the Romans who used it in connection with bathing. Lavender is one of the mildest yet most effective of all the essential oils and probably the most widely used. It is a must for any first aid kit.

Properties
- Analgesic
- Anti-inflammatory
- Antiseptic
- Diuretic
- Sedative
- Calming
- Insecticide

Contra-indications
Avoid use during the early stages of pregnancy. Lavender should be used with caution in cases of low blood pressure.

Extraction
Steam distillation of the flowering tops.

Uses
- Rheumatism
- Skin conditions
- Headaches
- Colds and flu
- Sinusitis
- Bronchitis
- Insomnia
- Burns
- Dandruff
- Wounds and sores, such as leg ulcers and acne.

Lavender is also very useful for treating insect and snake bites. Undiluted lavender oil can be added to burns and is a very effective treatment.

Due to its sedative properties, lavender is very helpful for relieving insomnia and can be used for this purpose diluted in a massage oil, added to a bath or a few drops put on a pillow.

It can be used in a massage blend to ease aches and pains and also added to a bath for this purpose.

It is very helpful in easing headaches by massaging the oil on the temples and the feet.

As an inhalant it relieves respiratory problems such as bronchitis, catarrh, and throat infections.

It is helpful for circulatory conditions such as chilblains.

It has a beneficial effect on tension and anxiety.

As already stated, lavender is very helpful in dealing with minor burns and sunburn, and may also be useful in treating psoriasis and eczema.

Massaging the lower back and abdomen with lavender oil eases period pains. Hot compresses also help.

Scent
Floral, woody, sweet, herbaceous.

Combines with:
- Clary Sage
- Marjoram
- Geranium
- Juniper
- Frankincense

TEA-TREE (*MELALEUCA ALTERNIFOLIA*)

Effects: Cleansing
Aroma: Top note

This tree is a species of the Melaleuca tree found in Queensland and New South Wales in Australia.

Properties
- Powerful antiseptic
- Antifungal
- Antiviral
- Antibiotic
- Detoxifying
- Stimulant
- Insecticide

Contra-indications
May irritate sensitive skins.

Extraction
Steam distillation of the leaves and twigs.

Uses
- Helps the immune system attack infections, viruses, fungi and yeast
- Helpful in colds, flu and catarrh

It is useful for the treatment of athletes foot, corns etc. A few drops can also be added to a foot bath.

Adding the diluted oil of tea tree to a bath will help alleviate urinary problems such as cystitis, and fungal infections such as Candida albicans which is related to thrush.

It has a beneficial effect on skin problems such as spots, burns, warts, sunburn, boils.

Scent
Spicy, fresh, medicinal.

Combines with:
This oil is best not mixed with other essential oils.

CAJEPUT (*MELALEUCA LEUCODENDRON*)

Effects: Clearing

Aroma: Top note

This is a tall tree which grows abundantly in Malaysia and the Philippines. The name means 'white tree'. It comes from the same family as tea-tree.

Properties
- Pain reliever
- Antiseptic
- Expectorant
- Insecticide

Contra-indications
Cajeput may be a skin irritant in high concentrations.

Extraction
Steam distillation of the fresh leaves.

Uses
- Neuralgia
- Rheumatism
- Lung congestion
- Toothache
- Earache
- Colds
- Skin conditions such as acne.

Cajeput is also good for massaging tired muscles and joints.

It can be used as an inhalation for laryngitis and bronchitis.

Scent
Medicinal camphorous smell.

Combines with:
- Eucalyptus
- Rosemary
- Tea-tree

MELISSA/LEMON BALM (*MELISSA OFFICINALIS*)

Effects: Calming

Aroma: Middle note

A bushy herb with pink or white flowers, native to the Mediterranean regions.

Properties
- Antidepressant
- Antispasmodic
- Sedative

Contra-indications
May cause skin irritation so always use well-diluted. It is difficult to find pure .

Extraction
Steam distillation of the leaves and tops.

Uses
- Colds and flu

Melissa has a beneficial effect on the nervous system and is helpful in stress related conditions.

Scent
Fresh, sweet, herbaceous.

Combines with:
- Bergamot
- Geranium
- Eucalyptus

PEPPERMINT (*MENTHA PIPERITA*)

Effects: Stimulating
Aroma: Top note

This herb has been used for many centuries as a medicine, particularly in the treatment of digestive problems. It is grown widely in France, Italy, America and England. The leaves can be used to make peppermint tea which is believed to aid digestion.

Properties
- Antiseptic
- Antispasmodic
- Analgesic
- Astringent
- Decongestant
- Expectorant
- Digestive aid

Contra-indications
Peppermint could irritate sensitive skins, and is not ideal for use in full body massage. However, it can be helpful in localised areas.

Extraction
Steam distillation of leaves and the flowering top.

Uses
- Asthma
- Bronchitis
- Sinusitis
- Migraine
- Indigestion and other digestive problems.

Peppermint is also useful as an insect repellent, and is particularly effective against mosquitoes.

Massage the diluted oil into the temples to ease headaches. Steam inhalations are helpful for respiratory problems.

Massaging the abdomen will help relieve colic and indigestion.

Added to a bowl of water, peppermint is excellent for refreshing tired feet.

Helpful in treating muscular and joint pains.

Scent
Fresh, strong, grassy, minty.

Combines with:
- Eucalyptus
- Rosemary

BASIL *(OCIMUM BASILICUM)*

Effects: Uplifting and stimulating
Aroma: Top note

This herb originated in Asia and is used extensively in the traditional Indian medicine known as Ayurveda. The plant is very aromatic and is a popular ingredient in cookery, particularly Italian dishes.

Properties
- Antidepressant
- Antiseptic
- Uplifting
- Analgesic
- Antispasmodic
- Emmenagogue

Contra-indications
May cause irritation to sensitive skins so always use well-diluted. Not to be used during pregnancy.

Extraction
Steam distillation of the leaves and flowering tops.

Uses
- Migraine
- Mental fatigue
- Nervous tension
- Sinus congestion
- Bronchitis
- Colds
- Constipation
- Rheumatism.

Can also be used in the first aid treatment of wasp stings and snake bites.

Scent
Fresh, sweet and spicy.

Combines with:
- Frankincense
- Geranium
- Citrus oils

MARJORAM *(ORIGANUM MAJORANA)*

Effects: Soothing and warming
Aroma: Middle note

A bushy plant native to France, Spain, Hungary and Yugoslavia. It has very small white flowers.

Properties
- Analgesic,
- Antiseptic
- Antispasmodic
- Diuretic

Contra-indications
Not to be used during pregnancy.

Extraction
Steam distillation of the leaves and flowering tops.

Uses
- Anxiety
- Bronchitis
- Insomnia
- Aches and pains
- Sinusitis
- PMT

Marjoram has a beneficial effect on rheumatism, arthritis, sprains and cramp.

It can also help relieve digestive problems such as colic, flatulence and constipation, and can be used to relieve skin problems and bruises.

Respiratory conditions such as bronchitis can be alleviated.

Scent
Warm, spicy, woody.

Combines with:
- Bergamot
- Cedarwood
- Lavender
- Rosemary

GERANIUM (*PELARGONIUM GRAVEOLENS*)

Effects: Comforting and healing
Aroma: Middle note

This shrub originated in Algeria, Madagascar and Guinea. There are hundreds of different species of the Geranium family. It has a colourful flower in varying shades of pink and is a familiar sight in window boxes, particularly in the Mediterranean regions.

Properties
- Antiseptic
- Antifungal
- Anti-spasmodic
- Diuretic

Contra-indications
Geranium oil may irritate sensitive skins. It is best avoided during pregnancy.

Extraction
Steam distillation of the flowers, stalks and leaves.

Uses
- Neuralgia
- Tonsillitis
- Inflammation of the breasts
- Slow circulation
- Burns
- Oedema of the legs
- Rheumatism

Geranium is also helpful in dealing with PMT and menopause symptoms. Its diuretic properties make geranium useful for helping with fluid retention.

Used in massage or inhalations, geranium has a beneficial effect on nervous tension and depression. Massaging with the diluted oil also helps poor circulation. It has a soothing effect on inflamed tissue and can ease swollen legs and oedema. Its astringent quality makes geranium ideal as a skin tonic and conditions such as burns and eczema may respond well to it.

Scent
Floral, earthy and sweet.

Combines with:
- Lavender
- Chamomile
- Rosemary
- Sandalwood
- Cypress
- Juniper

PINE (PINUS SYLVESTRIS)

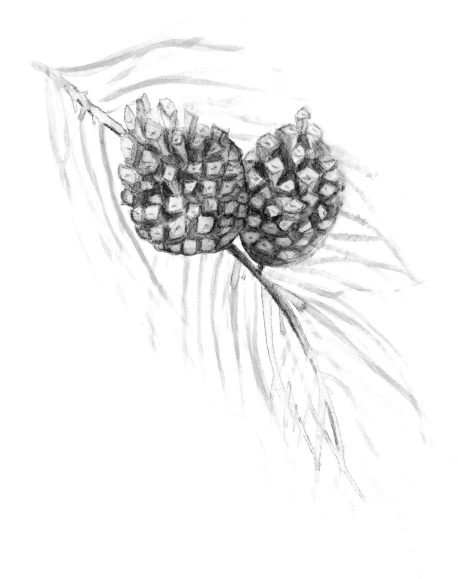

Effects: Clearing
Aroma: Middle note

This tall evergreen is found extensively in Scandinavia, the former Soviet Union and Europe. There are many species of pine but the needles of the Scotch Pine are considered to produce the best oil.

Properties
- Antiseptic
- Expectorant
- Tonic

Contra-indications
May cause irritation to sensitive skins.

Extraction
Steam distillation of the needles.

Uses
- Respiratory tract infections
- Flu
- Sinusitis
- Rheumatism
- Gout

Pine is also useful as a disinfectant.

It is ideal as an inhalation for the treatment of respiratory problems such as bronchitis and laryngitis.

As a massage oil, use diluted to ease aches and pain such as gout and rheumatism. It can also be used as a compress in these conditions.

Burnt in a vaporiser pine is ideal as a room disinfectant.

Scent
Balsamic, woody.

Combines with:
- Eucalyptus
- Sandalwood
- Lavender
- Geranium
- Rosemary

BLACK PEPPER (*PIPER NIGRUM*)

Effects: Stimulating
Aroma: Middle note

This is a woody climbing vine native to India. The oil is also produced in Malaysia and China.

Properties
- Expectorant
- Diuretic
- Stimulant

Contra-indications
Use in low dilutions as this oil may irritate sensitive skins. Avoid during the first three months of pregnancy.

Extraction
Steam distillation of the black peppercorns.

Uses
- Indigestion
- Sinus congestion
- Helpful for chilblains
- Colds and flu
- It is beneficial for digestive problems such as heartburn, flatulence and constipation and can also help in cases of loss of appetite.
- Muscular aches and pains

Scent
Warm and peppery.

Combines with:
- Lavender
- Sandalwood
- Rosemary

PATCHOULI (POGOSTEMON CABLIN)

Effects: Soothing
Aroma: Base note

A flowering herb native to Asia.

Properties
- Antiseptic
- Anti-inflammatory
- Astringent
- Diuretic
- Sedative
- Antidepressant

Contra-indications
None.

Extraction
Steam distillation of the dried leaves.

Uses
- Anxiety
- Skin conditions such as eczema, acne, scar tissue and chapped skin

Patchouli can have a beneficial effect on athlete's foot.

Due to its diuretic effect, patchouli may be an effective treatment for water retention and cellulite.

Scent
Sweet, woody.

Combines with:
- Lemon
- Neroli
- Lavender
- Ylang Ylang

ROSE *(ROSA CENTIFOLIA /ROSA DAMASCENA)*

Effects: Comforting

Aroma: Base/middle note

We are all familiar with this beautiful plant. Roses are cultivated in Bulgaria, Turkey and Morocco. It is one of the most useful essential oils but unfortunately it is extremely expensive. Distillation of roses originated many years ago in ancient Persia.

Properties

- Antidepressant
- Antiseptic
- Antispasmodic
- Astringent
- Diuretic
- Sedative
- Antibacterial

Contra-indications

Avoid using rose during the early stages of pregnancy.

Extraction

Distillation of the flower petals.

Uses

- Headache
- Sore throat
- Insomnia
- Depression

Rose water is used extensively in skin care.

Massage with the blended oil will help depression, pre-menstrual tension and regulation of the menstrual cycle.

It has a beneficial effect on mature, dry and sensitive skins as well as broken thread veins.

Scent

Warm, rich, floral, intense.

Combines with:

- Chamomile
- Lavender
- Sandalwood
- Jasmine
- Bergamot
- Geranium

ROSEMARY (ROSEMARINUS OFFICINALIS)

Effects: Restoring
Aroma: Middle note

This shrub-like herb is grown in Italy, Spain, the South of France and Tunisia. It is widely used in cooking.

Properties
- Analgesic
- Antidepressant
- Antirheumatic
- Antispasmodic
- Diuretic
- Stimulant
- Decongestant
- Antiseptic

Contra-indications
As rosemary is highly stimulating, it should not be used in cases of epilepsy, high blood pressure and pregnancy.

Extraction
Steam distillation of the flowering top.

Uses
- Rheumatism
- Gout
- Liver and gall bladder problems
- Colds and flu
- Wounds and burns
- General fatigue
- Digestive problems

Rosemary is also used extensively in cooking. Rosemary is said to help memory and is often used by students during exams by adding a drop to a tissue.

Used as a blend in massage it helps relieve aches and pains and improves circulation. As a rub before and after sports activities Rosemary helps maintain suppleness. Massaging the chest with diluted oil alleviates cold symptoms.

Due to its diuretic effect, Rosemary may help with water retention, cellulite and menstrual cramps. It has an astringent effect on the skin.

Scent
Refreshing, herbaceous, woody.

Combines with:
- Cedarwood
- Geranium
- Juniper

CLARY SAGE (SALVIA SCLAREA)

Effects: Soothing and warming
Aroma: Top/middle note

Clary Sage is a herb with small purplish-blue flowers, and is a native of Southern Europe.

Properties

- Antispasmodic
- Antiseptic
- Calming
- Anti-inflammatory
- Sedative, uplifts the spirit

Contra-indications

Due to its highly sedative effect, Clary Sage should not be used before driving. Do not use during pregnancy.

Extraction

Steam distillation of the flowering tops and leaves.

Uses

- Respiratory problems
- Asthma
- Sore throat
- Depression
- Skin preparations

Clary Sage can be used as a massage blend or diluted in the bath. It is an ideal treatment for both nervous exhaustion and depression.

Massaging the abdomen gently will help relieve period pain and other uterine problems. It regulates hormones and may help PMT symptoms. Clary Sage is also good for relieving digestive problems such as wind by massaging the abdomen.

Its general soothing action is excellent for cramp and muscle spasm and it acts like a tonic to the whole body.

It can also be useful for inflamed, puffy skin and dandruff.

Scent

Sweet, spicy, herbaceous smell.

Combines with:

- Lavender
- Geranium
- Rose
- Rosemary
- Ylang-Ylang

SANDALWOOD (SANTALUM ALBUM)

Effects: Balancing
Aroma: Base note

This evergreen tree comes from Australia and the East Indies. In India the Sandalwood tree is widely considered to be sacred.

Properties
- Antiseptic
- Antidepressant
- Antispasmodic
- Anti-inflammatory
- Diuretic
- Calming
- Astringent

Contra-indications
Do not use for depressed people as it may lower their mood even more.

Extraction
Steam distillation of the wood.

Uses
- Bronchitis
- Urinary infections
- Fatigue

In powdered form, Sandalwood is burned during religious ceremonies.

It helps nervous tension and anxiety either as a blended massage oil or in a vaporiser or burner.

Added to a bath or massaged on the lower back as a blended oil it may help alleviate cystitis.

Sandalwood helps to improve the immune system.

Massaged into the chest or throat as a blend it helps sore throats and bronchitis.

Sandalwood is widely used in beauty preparations and has a beneficial effect on eczema, acne and dry and chapped skin.

Scent
Sweet, woody, warm.

Combines with:
- Frankincense
- Jasmine
- Rose
- Geranium
- Ylang-Ylang

VETIVER *(VETIVERIA ZIZANIOIDES)*

Effects: Grounding
Aroma: Base note

This is a scented grass native to India and Indonesia. It is from its abundant roots that the oil is produced.

Properties
- Antibacterial
- Anti-fungal
- Calming

Contra-indications
None.

Extraction
Steam distillation of the roots.

Uses
- Arthritis
- Nervousness
- Insomnia
- Stress
- Mature skins

Vetiver has a very calming effect and is used to treat anxiety and nervous tension.
It is used in the perfume industry.

Scent
Heavy, sweet, woody, earthy.

Combines with:
- Sandalwood
- Geranium
- Lavender
- Ylang-Ylang

GINGER *(ZINGIBER OFFICINALE ROSCOE)*

Effects: Warming
Aroma: Top note

This plant originates from India, China, Africa and Australia. Ginger root is used extensively in cooking, as it is an excellent digestive aid.

Properties
- Analgesic
- Antidepressant
- Expectorant
- Stimulant
- Digestive aid

Contra-indications
Ginger may irritate sensitive skins.

Extraction
Steam distillation of the dried and ground roots.

Uses
- Catarrh
- Colds and flu
- Arthritis
- Indigestion
- Constipation

Ginger is also helpful for stimulating poor circulation.
It can be used to ease arthritis, rheumatism and sprains either as a blended massage oil or as a compress.
It is useful in respiratory conditions such as bronchitis, sinusitis etc.
It can be helpful in digestive problems such as flatulence, colic, diarrhoea. It has a positive effect on the nervous system and can help nervous exhaustion.

Scent
Woody, warm spicy.

Combines with:
- Eucalyptus
- Cedarwood
- Citrus oils

Terminology

A guide to descriptions found in the essential oil directory.

Analgesic – this means pain - relieving
(Chamomile, Lavender, Rosemary)

Antidepressant – this lifts the mood
(Bergamot, Geranium)

Antifungal or fungicidal – this inhibits mould and fungi growth
(Lavender, Tea-tree)

Antibiotic – This kills pathogenic bacteria
(Tea-tree)

Antiseptic – this is cleansing and prevents the development of microbes
(Bergamot, Eucalyptus, Lavender, Tea-tree)

Anti-inflammatory – this helps to reduce and prevent inflammation
(Clary Sage, Patchouli, Sandalwood)

Antispasmodic – this relieves muscle spasm in smooth muscle
(Chamomile, Ginger, Lavender)

Antiviral – this destroys certain viruses
(Tea-tree)

Astringent – this contracts blood vessels and body tissue
(Lemon, Sandalwood, Myrrh)

Antibacterial or bactericidal – this inhibits bacteria growth
(Bergamot, Lavender, Lemon, Rosemary, Tea-tree)

Carminative – this reduces intestinal spasm
(Chamomile, Lavender. Peppermint)

Decongestant – this reduces congestion
(Eucalyptus, Rosemary)

Detoxifying – this helps the body to get rid of waste products
(Juniper, Lemon)

Diuretic – this aids urine production
(Cypress, Geranium, Lemon, Patchouli)

Emmenagogue – this encourages menstruation and is therefore not to be used during pregnancy
(Chamomile, Clary Sage, Jasmine, Juniper, Lavender, Marjoram, Rose, Rosemary)

Expectorant – this encourages coughing -up of mucus
(Bergamot, Eucalyptus, Sandalwood)

Fungicide – prevents and combats fungal infection
(Tea-tree, Geranium)

Phototoxic – These oils skin pigmentation on exposure to UV light so must not be used before going in the sun or using sunbeds.
(Bergamot, Lemon, Orange, Grapefruit)

Sedative – this slows down functional activity and lessens excitement, calming
(Chamomile, Clary Sage, Lavender, Rose)

Stimulant – this has an uplifting effect on the body
(Geranium, Peppermint, Rosemary)

Essential Oils

The following are simply guidelines for making oil blends for specific conditions, and as you become more familiar with the oils you will doubtless find that you prefer to make up your own combinations. You will find many different combinations recommended for specific conditions as some oils appeal to one person more than another, and some are more appropriate for particular individuals.

ACNE

This is usually caused by excessive secretion of sebum caused by hormonal stimulation.
Essential Oils
Chamomile, Geranium, Lavender, Frankincense, Tea-tree.
- Add to a carrier oil suitable for face massage and gently massage the face.
- Combine with a skin lotion and apply.
- Apply a toner such as rose flower water. (If the face is inflamed do NOT massage).

ANXIETY

Essential Oils
Bergamot, Cedarwood, Chamomile, Geranium, Lavender, Sandalwood, Ylang-Ylang.
- Add to a carrier oil for massage.
- Add to a bath and soak for up to 15 minutes.

ASTHMA

Essential Oils
Cedarwood, Eucalyptus, Lavender.
- Add a few drops to a bath.
- Combine with a carrier oil for massage. Massaging a few drops of diluted oils on the sternum (breast bone) can help bring relief from the feeling of tightness.
- Do not use inhalations.

ATHLETE'S FOOT

This is caused by a fungal infection.
Essential Oil
Tea-tree.
- Add a few drops to a footbath or dab the area with impregnated cotton wool.

BRONCHITIS

Oils that help bring up mucus will be beneficial.
Essential Oils
Cedarwood, Cypress, Marjoram, Pine.
- Massage the chest and back with the diluted oil.
- Add a few drops in the bath.
- Use as an inhalation.

BURNS AND SUNBURN

Essential Oil
Lavender.
- This can be added to the skin without a carrier oil to treat minor burns.
- Add to a bath.
- Use as a cold compress.

BRUISES

Essential Oil
Lavender.
- Add to a bath.
- Dab the area with 1-2 drops on cotton wool.
- Use as a cold compress.

CATARRH

Essential Oils
Cedarwood, Eucalyptus, Lavender, Lemon, Rosemary, Sandalwood, Tea-tree.
- Add a few drops to the bath.
- Use as an inhalation or compress.

CELLULITE

Essential Oils
Rosemary, Geranium, Lemon, Juniper, Fennel.
- Add to a carrier oil for massage.
- Skin brush regularly with the essential oils.
- Add a few drops of the oils to a bath.

CHILBLAINS

Essential Oils
Rosemary, Lavender, Chamomile, Marjoram.
- Add to a bath or a foot bath.
- Apply as a compress.
- Dab the affected area with the mixed oil.

COLD SORES

Essential Oils
Tea-tree or Eucalyptus.
- Apply 1-2 drops to the affected area with cotton wool.

COLDS

Essential Oils

Eucalyptus, Lavender, Lemon, Marjoram, Pine, Peppermint, Tea-tree.

- Add several drops to the bath.
- Use as an inhalation or in a vaporiser.
- Massage the throat and chest with diluted oils.

CONSTIPATION

The main causes are low roughage, lack of exercise, hurried meals and stress.

Essential Oils

Rosemary, Marjoram, Orange, Black Pepper.

- Add to a carrier oil for massage of the abdomen.
- The use of physillium husks or linseed in the diet is very helpful.

Bran is not recommended as it can irritate the digestive tract. Regular meal times and adequate exercise are also important.

CORNS

Essential Oils

Lemon.

- Dab with a few drops added to cotton wool.

CYSTITIS

This is an infection of the urinary tract.

Essential Oils

Bergamot, Juniper, Lavender, Sandalwood, Tea-tree, Chamomile.

- Add to carrier oil and massage the abdomen and lower back. (If the person has a temperature or is passing blood in the urine they must visit their doctor).
- Add a few drops of the oil to a bath.
- Use as a hot compress on the lower back.

DANDRUFF

Essential Oils

Rosemary, Lavender.

- Use as a hair tonic massaged into the scalp a few times a week.
- To make the tonic add a few drops of each oil to 200 ml of distilled water and 2 teaspoons of cider vinegar in a dark glass bottle. Make sure that you give it a good shake.

EARACHE

Essential Oils

Chamomile, Lavender.

- Use as a compress.

ECZEMA

Essential Oils

Chamomile, Lavender, Sandalwood, Geranium.

- Add a few drops to a bath.
- Combine with a carrier oil and massage gently. (Take care as the skin may be very sensitive).
- The use of Evening Primrose Oil as a supplement or face cream can be beneficial.

EMOTIONAL STATES

The following can be used as a massage blend or added to a bath.

Depression

Chamomile, geranium, lavender, sandalwood, ylang-ylang.

Insecurity

Sandalwood, frankincense.

Loneliness

Marjoram.

Poor Memory

Rosemary.

Panic Attacks

Lavender, ylang-ylang, frankincense.

Low Self-esteem

Sandalwood, ylang-ylang.

EXHAUSTION AND FATIGUE

Essential oil

Lavender, Geranium, Rosemary.

- Add to a carrier oil for general massage.
- Add to bath water and soak for about 115 minutes.

ACHING FEET

Essential Oil

Peppermint.

- Add to a bowl of warm water and soak feet for 10 minutes.
- Add to a carrier oil for foot massage.

FLATULENCE

Essential Oils

Basil, Fennel, Rosemary.

- Add to a carrier oil and massage the abdomen.

HAEMORRHOIDS

These normally occur due to constipation and can cause great discomfort.

Essential Oils

Cypress, Frankincense.

- Add a few drops to a bath.

HAY FEVER

Essential oil

Juniper.

- Combine with a carrier oil and massage the sinus areas.
- Add a few drops to a tissue and inhale.

HEADACHE

Essential Oils

Chamomile, Rosemary, Lavender, Peppermint.

- Add to a carrier oil and massage around the temples, the base of the skull and anti-clockwise on the solar plexus. Massaging the neck and shoulders can also be helpful as some headaches are caused by tension in these areas.
- If the person is suffering from a migraine headache then massage should not be given.
- Use as a compress or inhalation.
- Add a few drops to a bath.

IMMUNE SYSTEM (TO BOOST)

Essential Oils

Lavender, Lemon, Tea-tree.

- Use as an inhalation or in a vaporiser.
- Combine with a carrier oil for massage.
- Add a few drops to the bath.

INDIGESTION

Heartburn and indigestion are very common problems and can be eased by the use of the following oils. If the symptoms last for several weeks then the person should visit their doctor.

Essential Oils

Chamomile, Peppermint, Lemon, Fennel.

- Add to a carrier oil and massage the stomach and anti-clockwise on the solar plexus.
- Drinking chamomile, peppermint or fennel herbal tea is also helpful.

INFLUENZA

Flu is a viral infection which can have unpleasant symptoms such as aching muscles and fever. Fever is a sign of the body trying to rid itself of the problem and should be left to run for up to 48 hours providing it is not too high.

Essential Oils

Lavender, Peppermint, Tea-tree, Marjoram, Lemon, Cypress, Eucalyptus.

- Peppermint oil will help to reduce the problem and ease congestion. (Do not use for babies oryoung children).
- Muscular aches can be eased by baths or rubs using marjoram and lemon which will help eliminate toxins. (Do not massage in cases of high temperature).
- Use as an inhalation.

INSECT BITES

Essential Oils

Lavender, Chamomile, Tea-tree, Lemon.

- Add the oil to two tablespoons of a carrier oil and apply to the affected area. Lavender or Tea-tree oil can be used neat.
- To ease swelling apply a cold compress containing a few drops of chamomile and lavender.
- Add a few drops to a bath.

INSOMNIA

Essential Oil

Chamomile and Lavender.

- Add to a carrier oil and give a relaxing back massage.
- Add a few drops of lavender oil to the bath or one drop to a pillow.

IRRITABLE BOWEL SYNDROME

Essential Oil

Chamomile.

- Add to a carrier oil for an abdomen massage.
- Add a few drops to a bath.

MENOPAUSE SYMPTOMS

Essential Oils

Clary Sage, Geranium and Sandalwood, Lavender.

- Add a few drops to a carrier oil to give a relaxing full body massage.
- Add a few drops of oil to the bath.

MOUTH ULCERS AND GUM INFECTIONS

Essential Oils

1 drop of Tea-tree, Geranium and Lemon added to half a glass of water for use as a gargle.

- Dab the ulcer with 1-2 drops of tea-tree added to cotton wool.

MUSCULAR SPASM

Essential oil

Clary sage.

- Massage the area with the diluted oil.

PAINFUL PERIODS

Essential Oils

Chamomile, Clary Sage, Rosemary.

- Add to a carrier oil and give full body massage.
- Add to a bath or use as a compress.

IRREGULAR PERIODS

Essential Oils

Chamomile, Clary Sage, Geranium, Lavender.

- Add to a carrier oil for massage.
- Add to a bath.

HEAVY PERIODS

Essential oil

Cypress.

- Add to carrier oil for massage.
- Use as a compress or add to a bath.

POSTNATAL DEPRESSION

Essential Oils

Bergamot, Chamomile and Neroli.

- Add to a carrier oil and give a full body massage.
- Add a few drops of oil to a bath.

PREMENSTRUAL SYMPTOMS

Essential Oils

Lavender, Chamomile and Geranium.

- Add to a carrier oil and massage the whole body using relaxing strokes.
- Add a few drops of the oil to a bath.

RHEUMATISM AND ARTHRITIS

Essential Oils

Rosemary, Chamomile, Lavender, Juniper.

- Add to a carrier oil and massage into the affected area. (Do not massage over any swollen areas or inflamed joints).

- Add 10- 15 drops to a warm bath and soak for 15 minutes.
Rheumatic conditions benefit from cleansing diets containing plenty of fresh fruit and vegetables and grains. Stimulants such as tea and coffee are best avoided.

Arthritis also benefits from diets which help clear toxins from the body. Gentle exercise and keeping the joints warm are also helpful.

SINUSITIS

This can be extremely painful around the top of the nose and across the cheeks. If the problem persists a doctor should be visited.

Essential Oils

Lavender, Eucalyptus and Tea-tree, Peppermint (for inhalations), Rosemary, Bergamot and Juniper (for massage).

- Add to a bowl of hot water and inhale. (Do NOT use this method if an asthma sufferer).
- Using a few drops added to a of carrier oil massage around the base of the skull using circular movements, press on the acupressure points at the base of the nostrils and at the inner corners of the eyebrows and gently work along the eyebrows using a pinching movement.

SKIN CARE

Blackheads

Essential Oils

Pine, Eucalyptus, Lavender

- Use as a facial steam adding the Oils to a bowl of hot water.

Broken capillaries /thread veins

Essential Oils

Chamomile, Neroli, Rose.

- Use combined with facial oil, cream or lotion.

Dry skin

Essential Oils

Chamomile, Sandalwood, Rose, Lavender, Neroli.

- Use combined with facial oil, cream or lotion.

Mature skin

Essential Oils

Frankincense, Geranium. Rose.

- Use combined with facial oil, cream or lotion.

Normal / combination skin

Essential Oils

Chamomile, Lavender, Neroli, Rose.

- Use combined with facial oil, cream or lotion.

Oily Skin

Essential Oils

Cedarwood, Frankincense, Geranium, Bergamot, Ylang-ylang, Lemon, Rosemary.

- Use combined with facial oil, cream or lotion.

Sensitive Skin

Essential Oils

Geranium, Lavender, Rose, Chamomile

- Use combined with facial oil, cream or lotion, but in very weak mixture.

Wrinkles

Essential Oils

Neroli, Frankincense

- Use combined with facial oil, cream or lotion.

SORE THROAT

Essential Oils

Tea Tree,Lavender, Sandalwood, Lemon.

- Add to a carrier oil and gently massage the neck and shoulder area using downward strokes.Massaging the chest can also be helpful.
- A compress can also be used.
- A few drops can be added to a bath.

STRESS

Essential Oils

Sandalwood, Chamomile, Lavender, Clary Sage, Bergamot.

- Add to carrier oil and give a full body massage or if time is limited massage the back, shoulders, neck and face as these areas hold a lot of the tension.
- Add a few drops of the essential oil to the bath.

SPRAINS

Essential Oils

Rosemary, Chamomile and Lavender.

- Add to a carrier oil and gently massage around the effected joint with light strokes, but do not massage swollen areas.
- Apply a cold compress to the swollen area.

TOOTHACHE

Essential Oils

Clove, Peppermint.

- Use as a compress.

VAGINAL THRUSH

Essential Oils

Bergamot, Rose and Lavender or Tea-tree oil.

- Add to a carrier oil and massage the abdomen and lower back.
- Add several drops of oil to a bath.

VERRUCAE AND WARTS

Essential Oils

Lemon, or Tea-tree.

- Dab the affected area with neat oil.

ROOM DISINFECTANT

Essential Oils

Eucalyptus, Lavender, Lemon.

- Use in an oil burner.

Extraction

There are a variety of ways that essential oils can be extracted, although some of these are less commonly used today. The most common method currently in use is steam distillation, although there are various more efficient and economical processes being developed all the time.

Steam Distillation

The plant material is placed into a still which is similar to a very large pressure cooker. Steam under pressure is passed through the plant material. The heat causes the globules of oil in the plant to burst open and the oil will evaporate quickly.

The essential oil vapour and the steam then pass out of the top of the still into a water-cooled pipe. The vapours are condensed back to liquids and the essential oil separates from the water and floats to the top. These oils must be stored in dark-coloured bot-tles in a cool place as they are adversely affected by heat, oxygen, light and moisture.

If stored under the correct conditions, as described, oils should last quite some time. However citrus oils such as lemon and orange are best kept for about six months only.

Some essential oils, notably rose and jasmine, are very expensive due to the fact that the petals of these flowers produce quite a low yield. It has been estimated that more than eight million jasmine flowers are required to produce one kilogram (2.2 lb) of jasmine oil.

Maceration

This process produces what is known as an 'infused oil' rather than an essential oil. Plant material is soaked in a vegetable oil, heated and strained. The oil mixture can be used for massage.

Maceration is a good method for extracting oils for massage purposes.

Before cold pressing, rinds are chopped and ground.

Enfleurage

This method uses wooden frames with a plate glass top which are covered with warm lard. Flower petals are spread over the layer of grease and replaced at regular intervals until the lard is saturated with the essence. Alcohol is then used to wash the grease away and obtain the essence. Any remaining lard can be used in soap making. Although this method is useful for essences which tend to disappear in the process of distillation it is used very rarely these days.

Cold Pressing

This process is used for obtaining essential oils from citrus rinds such as orange, lemon, grapefruit and bergamot. The rinds are ground or chopped and then pressed. The resulting liquid is a mixture of essential oil and watery components which, if left, will separate. In the past the rinds were squeezed into sponges. Oils produced by cold pressing have a relatively short shelf life.

Oils should be stored in a cool, dark place.

Solvent Extraction

A hydrocarbon solvent is added to a drum containing plant material to help dissolve the essential oil. The solution is then filtered and concentrated by distillation and we are left with a substance containing resin known as a resinoid or a combination of wax and essential oil known as concrete. The oil is finally obtained by a process of extraction using pure alcohol.

The alcohol then evaporates and the residual solution is called absolute. Oils produced by this method are not ideal as the solvents are toxic substances and there is always a small residue left behind in the oil which could cause allergies and affect the immune system. Rose and jasmine are extracted by this method.

Carbon Dioxide

This is a recently developed method. Carbon Dioxide or butane, can extract the essential oil from the plant when liquefied under pressure. The resulting liquid is drained and allowed to depressurize and the carbon dioxide returns to a gas. The pure essential oil remains.

The same plant can sometimes be treated by different methods to obtain different oils. For example, orange essence is produced from the skins of oranges by the method of cold pressing, while neroli essential oil is produced from the orange blossom by solvent extraction.

Oil can also be extracted from different plants, fruit and seeds for use as a carrier oil.

The different extraction methods and various parts of the plant used will produce varying strengths of each essential oil.

A few drops of essential oils can be added to bath water to help relaxation and improve the skin. The essential oil should be mixed with a little carrier oil before adding to the bath and then stirred well. This is a particularly enjoyable way to relax whilst benefiting from these wonderful oils.

The oils can be used as an inhalation by adding about 2-3 drops to a bowl of almost boiling water and inhaling for around 10 minutes to ease blocked sinuses, chest complaints and colds. (This method is NOT to be used by asthma or allergy sufferers). Facial steaming with essential oils is often used in beauty treatments for deep cleansing and moisturising of the skin.

Gargles and Mouthwashes

These are an excellent way of dealing with throat infections, mouth ulcers and gum problems. Add two drops of the oil to a glass of water and use as a mouthwash.

Herbal Teas

These teas are an excellent way of taking herbs and plants internally to improve bodily functions. However they should be used in moderation as they do have medicinal properties. In some countries such as France, doctors give essential oils by mouth but this could have certain dangers as the oils are very potent and is NOT to be recommended unless administered by a medically qualified practitioner. Herbs can also be used in cooking.

Compresses

These can be hot or cold and are prepared by adding 2-5 drops of the oil or oils to a bowl of water. A flannel is used to skim the top of the water and applied to the affected area for about 15 minutes. If hot and cold compresses are used alternately, hot should be applied first, followed by the cold compress. Compresses are ideal for treating swollen joints, backache and headache.

A few drops of essential oil can be added to bath oils and creams to enhance relaxation.

Room Sprays

A clean plant spray is filled with water and a few drops of essential oil added. Shake well and spray in the room. Lavender is ideal for this purpose.

Vaporisation

With this method a few drops of oil are added to a bowl of water which is placed over a small candle. Special oil burners are widely available and make attractive ornaments. The essential oil gradually evaporates into the room. Care should be taken to ensure that the water does not boil dry. This is an ideal way of scenting a room.

Foot Bath

This is wonderful way to relax after a tiring day and is ideal for easing aching feet. Simply add a few drops of essential oil to a bowl of hot water and soak the feet. Peppermint oil is particularly good for this.

Skin and Hair Care

Essential oils can be used as skin moisturisers when added to a carrier oil such as Jojoba.

You can also add them to fragrance-free and lanolin-free creams or lotions to create your own skin care products.

Essential oils can also improve the condition of your hair as well treating as scalp disorders. A few drops of essential oil added to a jug of warm water can be used as a final hair rinse. Chamomile is excellent for fair hair while rosemary is recommended for darker hair.

Herbal teas can be helpful, but should only be used in moderation.

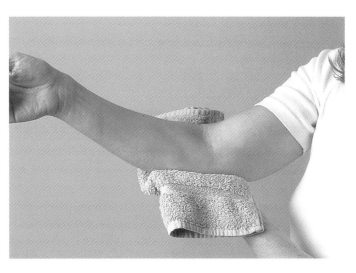

A hot or cold compress can ease swollen or aching joints.

A couple of drops of oil in a glass of water makes an effective mouthwash.

Another way to scent a room is to add a few drops of your favourite oil to a pot pourri mixture.

introduction to Theraupeutic Massage

A BRIEF HISTORY

The ancient healing art of massage is undoubtedly the oldest form of physical medicine. In China there are references to massage in the oldest recorded medical text the Nei Ching written by the Yellow Emperor.

Historical records show that massage therapy was practised widely amongst the Greeks and Romans.

In ancient Rome, Julius Caesar, who suffered from neuralgia and

"Rubbing can bind a joint which is too loose and loosen a joint that is too rigid."

(Hippocrates, the 'Father of Medicine,' 5 BC)

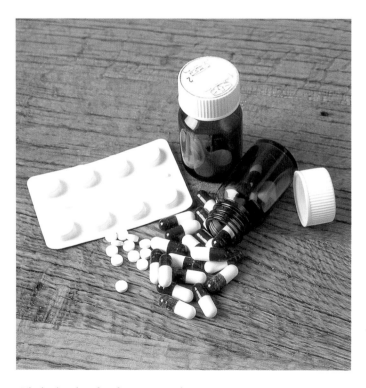

The healing benefits of massage complement orthodox medicine.

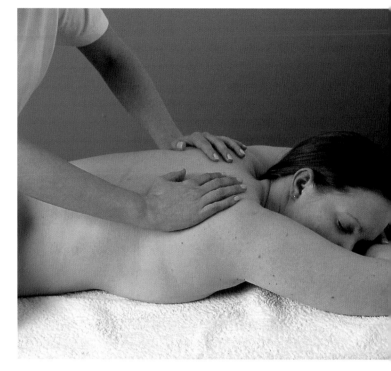

Therapeutic massage is today much in demand

headaches, received daily massage. Pliny, the renowned Roman naturalist was treated for his asthma. Galen, the Roman Emperor's physician, prescribed massage to prepare the gladiators for combat and to treat their injuries.

After the decline of the Roman Empire there is very little physical medicine recorded until the Middle Ages. Fortunately interest was revived by the French physician Ambrose Paré, who established the credibility of massage amongst the medical profession.

The classical technique known as 'Swedish massage,' which is described in this book, was developed by the Swedish Professor, Per Henrik Ling (1776-1839). He established a school of massage in Stockholm and in 1877, Swedish massage was introduced to the United States by Doctor Mitchell. Massage began to increase in popularity.

At the present time there is a rapidly growing demand for therapeutic massage. It is widely practised in clinics, health clubs

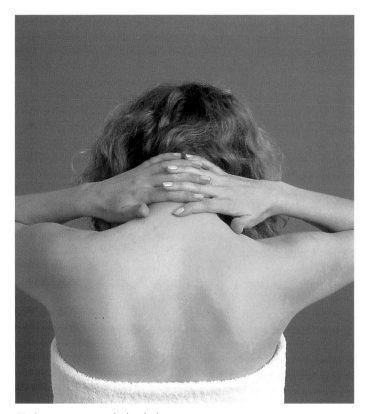

Neck massage can soothe headaches

and even in many hospitals and hospices. Thousands of therapists have trained, including lay people as well as doctors, nurses, midwives, osteopaths, chiropractors and physiotherapists who incorporate therapeutic massage into their work. The healing language of touch may complement all forms of orthodox medicine. We ALL have the power in our hands to massage and help others using the simple techniques described in this section.

THE BENEFITS OF MASSAGE

Therapeutic massage has an enormous impact on all the systems of the body.

THE NERVOUS SYSTEM

Massage can have a very powerful sedative effect on the nerves, melting away the stresses and strains of everyday life. Headaches can be relieved, patterns of insomnia broken and states of anger, impatience and irritation are soothed.

THE MUSCULAR SYSTEM

Muscular aches and pains, fatigue and stiffness can all be successfully treated with the healing art of massage. Cramp is reduced; old scar tissue broken down and good muscle tone can be induced.

THE SKELETAL SYSTEM

Disorders of the skeletal system, such as arthritis, benefit enormously from massage. Stiffness of the joints is alleviated and pain can be reduced considerably.

THE CIRCULATORY SYSTEM

Massage is excellent for improving the functioning of the heart and circulation. After a series of treatments, poor circulation improves sometimes dramatically and blood pressure falls.

THE LYMPHATIC SYSTEM

Accumulated waste substances are rapidly eliminated by the action of massage. Swellings, which may accumulate around an injury, can also be dispersed.

THE RESPIRATORY SYSTEM

Mucus and bronchial secretions can be loosened and eliminated from the lungs by performing percussive movements over the upper back and opening the chest.

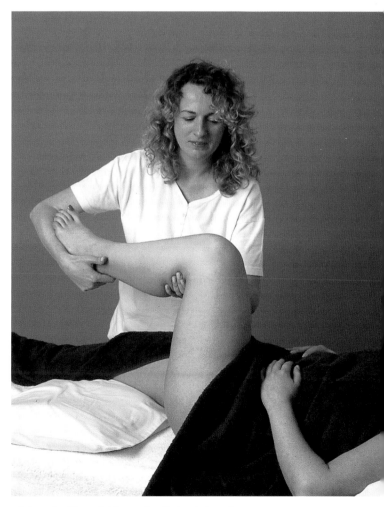

Joint pain, like arthritis, can be alleviated through massage.

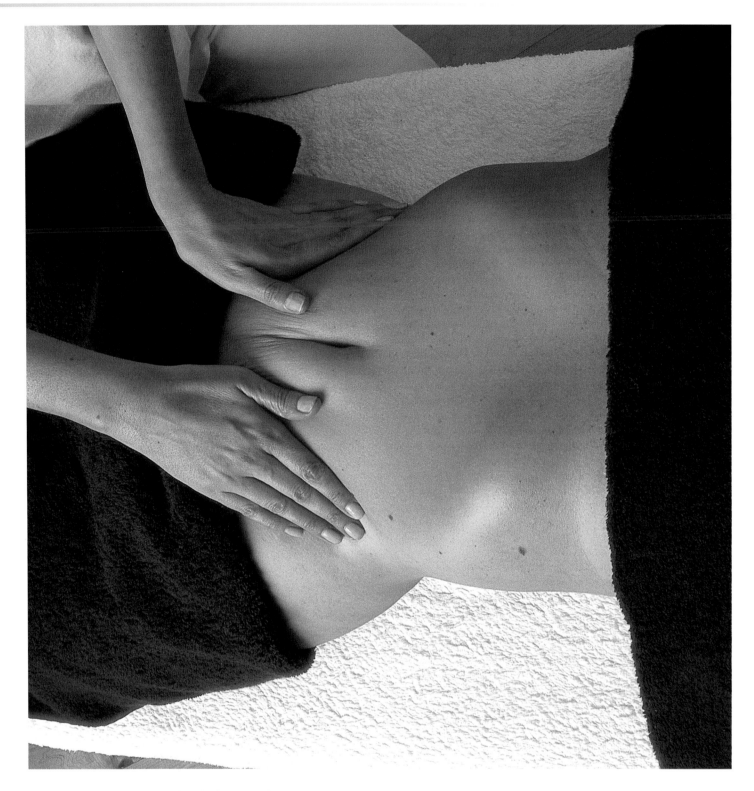

Gentle abdominal massage is excellent for digestive problems.

THE DIGESTIVE SYSTEM

Massage encourages the elimination of waste matter from the colon. Constipation is relieved and digestion improved.

THE REPRODUCTIVE SYSTEM

Menstrual problems such as PMT, period pain, irregular menstruation and the menopause will all improve with regular therapeutic massage.

getting
Started

Massage can be performed by anyone with very little equipment. The basic requirements are a firm massage surface, towels, cushions, a bottle of oil and of course a pair of hands. However if you can create the right atmosphere then maximum benefit can be derived from the treatment.

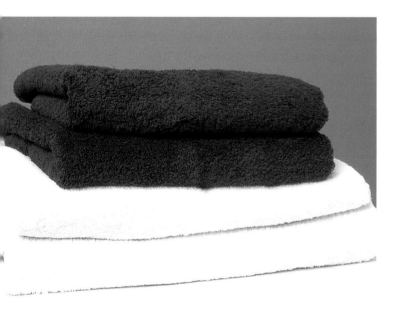

Make sure you have plenty of towels to hand to cover the receiver.

ENVIRONMENT
Your room should be warm and cosy, as relaxation is impossible if you feel cold. As the body temperature will drop during the massage, a good supply of spare towels and blankets is essential. Areas that are not being treated should always be covered up.

Soft and subdued lighting will create the perfect setting. Dim the lights or light a few candles around the room. Fresh flowers or essential oils add a pleasant aroma to the atmosphere and crystals such as rose quartz enhance the ambience.

It is vital to choose a time when you will not be disturbed. Take the telephone off the hook and tell your family and friends not to enter the treatment room. You may like to play some relaxing music or alternatively you may prefer silence.

PERSONAL PREPARATION
1. It is essential to wear comfortable and loose fitting clothes preferably something with short sleeves as you will get very warm and you need to be able to move around easily.

2. Take off all jewellery as rings, bracelets and watches can scratch the receiver.

3. Make sure that you trim your fingernails down as far as possible - digging the nails in is hardly therapeutic. Always wash your hands prior to the treatment and check that nails are scrupulously clean.

4. Spend a little time prior to the treatment consciously relaxing yourself. A calm state of mind is very important since if you are feeling angry or depressed it is highly likely that these feelings will be communicated to the receiver. Allow all your tension to float out of the body so that the healing energies can flow through your hands.

Carrier oils or essential oils should be used during a massage treatment.

A face ring brings added comfort for the receiver when they are lying on their front.

MASSAGE SURFACE

You will need a firm yet well-padded surface. If you are massaging on the floor, place a thick duvet or two or three blankets down onto the floor. You will require a cushion to kneel on so that your knees do not get sore. If the receiver is lying on their back place one pillow under the head and another one under the knees. If the receiver is lying on the front one pillow should be placed under the head and shoulders and another under the feet. Do not use a bed for your therapeutic massage, as these are never the correct height and therefore could make your back ache.

A professional therapist will work on a massage couch. If you find that you are doing lots of massage then it might be a good idea to invest in a portable couch. They are reasonably priced and can be erected anywhere in the house and folded away after use taking up little space. Use plenty of cushions to keep the receiver comfortable. A face ring is ideal to support the receiver's head when they are lying on their front. The massage techniques are much easier to perform on a couch and you will not tire so quickly. The massage techniques in this book are demonstrated using a massage couch.

Always ensure that you cover up any part of the receiver that is not being treated.

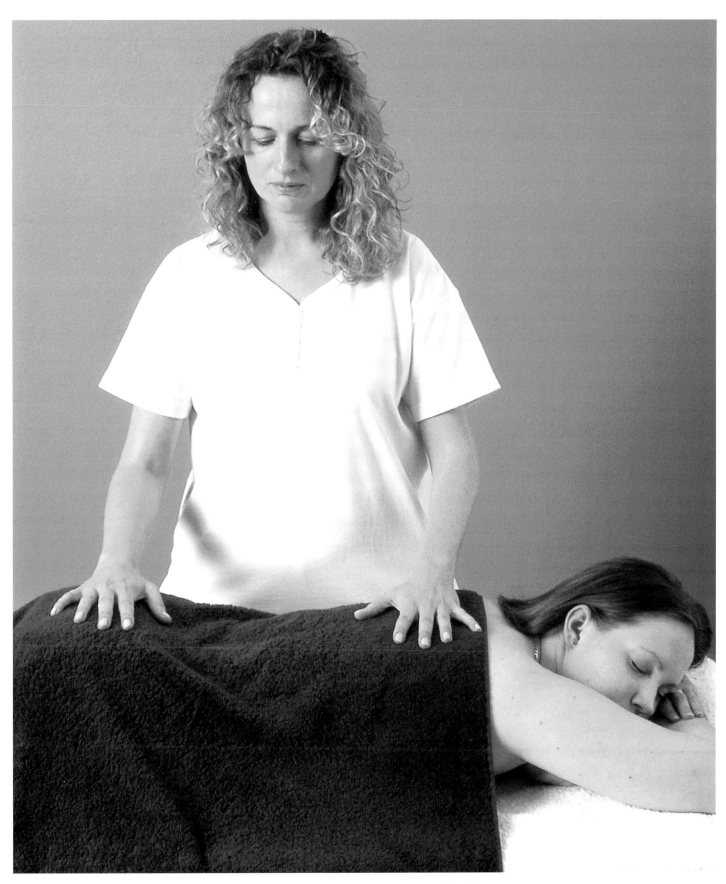

A massage couch is a useful tool as it is the correct height to allow the masseur/masseuse to work comfortably

CONTRA-INDICATIONS

WHEN NOT TO MASSAGE AND WHEN TO EXERCISE CAUTION

Although therapeutic massage is an extremely safe complementary therapy, there are times when massage is inappropriate or even dangerous. If you are at all unsure then always seek the advice of a medically qualified doctor. Please observe the following contra-indications at all times:

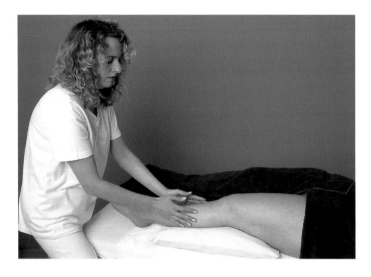

1. PHLEBITIS AND THROMBOSIS

Phlebitis is the formation of a clot in a vein that causes it to inflame. This gives rise to severe pain, redness, heat and swelling. If a thrombosis (i.e. a clot) forms in a vein, massage could dislodge the clot causing a fatal stroke or a heart attack.

2. SEVERE VARICOSE VEINS

Massage is a wonderful therapy for the prevention of varicose veins. However, if they are severe they should be avoided since you may cause a great deal of pain and further damage to the vein. Massage should be given above and below the affected area.

3. INFECTIOUS DISEASES

If the receiver has an infectious or contagious disease such as scabies, ringworm, chicken pox or shingles, then massage is not advisable. A rise in temperature is an indication that the body is fighting off toxins and massage should be avoided so that more toxins are not released into the system.

4. AREAS OF SEPSIS

Never massage over an area in the presence of pus – e.g. a boil or a carbuncle.

5. RECENT SCAR TISSUE AND WOUNDS

Massage is highly beneficial over old scar tissue since it helps to break it down and increase mobility. However, massage over a recent scar or wound can cause it to open up or become infected. Only when the site has fully healed should massage be performed.

6. INFLAMMATORY CONDITIONS

Areas of inflammation should never be massaged whether it is inflammation of a joint, muscle, skin or organ. Inflammatory conditions include bursitis (housemaid's knee), tendonitis, gastro-enteritis and nephritis (inflammation of a kidney).

7. PREGNANCY

Massage is invaluable during pregnancy since it induces deep relaxation, relieves aches and pains, improves sleep, prevents varicose veins, fluid retention and stretch marks, balances mood swings and encourages a strong bond between mother and baby. However, special care should be taken over the abdomen during the first three months if there is a history of miscarriage.

8. LUMPS

Although lumps are usually innocent, it is always wise to have them checked out by a medically qualified doctor.

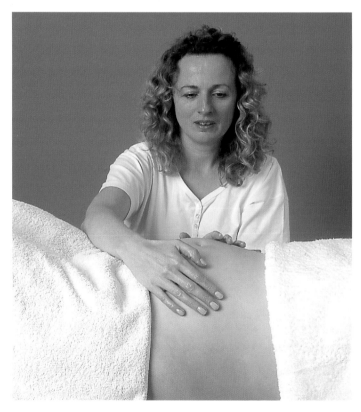

During the first three months of pregnancy take extra special care over the abdomen.

using
Massage Oils

It is essential to use some form of lubricant for your massage to ensure that the hands can glide smoothly over the skin. Massage without any medium is uncomfortable and causes skin irritation, particularly on a hairy body.

Sweet almond oil is the most commonly used carrier oil.

A pure, good quality vegetable, nut or seed oil is recommended. This should be cold pressed (not removed by chemicals), unrefined and additive-free. Such carrier oils contain vitamins, minerals and fatty acids and therefore nourish the skin. Mineral oil, such as commercial baby oil, should never be used since it is not easily absorbed, lacks nutrients and tends to clog the pores. There are a vast number of base oils to choose from and it is a good idea to experiment with several to determine your personal preferences.

The most widely used carrier oil is sweet almond oil, which is easily absorbed by the skin and is not too thick or sticky. It also does not have a strong odour. It is suitable for all skin types and is beneficial for dry, sensitive, inflamed or prematurely aged skin. Apricot kernel and peach kernel oils are also excellent for all skin types and are highly nourishing, although they are more expensive. If you wish you may add thicker, richer oils to make a blend of carrier oils. These oils are usually too heavy and sticky to be used alone, as well as more expensive. However, they do improve absorption and nourish the skin. Suitable carrier oils include calendula, evening primrose and jojoba which are usually added in up to a 10% dilution. Wheatgerm oil is normally added up to 10% as it is an anti-oxidant and helps to preserve the life of a blend.

You can refer to the directory in the Aromatherapy section to find detailed descriptions of the essential oils used here.

The use of oils allows for a smooth and comforting massage.

A typical example of a blend that should allow you to carry out approximately 10 treatments could be:

70mls sweet almond oil
10 mls (two teaspoons) calendula
10 mls (two teaspoons) jojoba
10 mls (two teaspoons) wheatgerm

Pure essential oils can be added to enhance your massage treatment, although they should be respected and used with great care. They are extremely concentrated and should always be blended with a carrier oil in the following dilution: three drops of essential oil to 10 mls (two teaspoons) of carrier oil or six drops of essential oil to 20 mls (four teaspoons) of carrier oil.

APPLYING THE OIL

Make sure that you always keep the oil within easy reach whilst carrying out your therapeutic massage. Once you have made contact with the receiver it is important that you do not break it, as this will destroy the continuity of the massage. Your oil may be kept in a flip top bottle or, if you are using essential oils, a small bowl is ideal. Always warm cold hands before you start. Oils should never be poured directly onto the body. Pour a small amount onto the palm of one hand and then rub your hands together to warm the oil. Then bring your hands down and begin

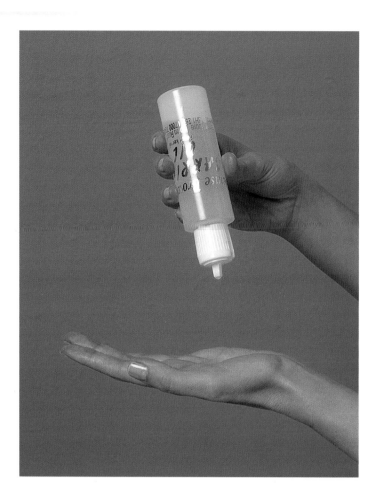

Always pour oils into your hands before applying to the receiver – this enables you to warm the oil before use.

to apply the oil using gentle effleurage movements. When you require more oil, try to keep one hand in contact with the body. It is very common to use too much lubricant when you first start. This is not only uncomfortable and sticky but it makes it impossible for you to make proper contact and perform the basic therapeutic massage movements.

Prue essential oils may be added to your carrier oil to create your own blends.

Massage Techniques

The beauty of massage is that it is so simple and natural that anyone can learn how to perform it. There are four basic techniques used in a therapeutic massage. Other techniques are just a variation on these movements. Once you have mastered these you can begin to create your own strokes and develop your own personal style. Do not concern yourself too much with the 'correct' technique. The most important thing is that the massage should feel good to the receiver. Your movements should be flowing and rhythmical and you must not lose contact with the receiver as your hands flow from one movement to the next.

EFFLEURAGE

Effleurage is a stroking technique that is always performed both at the beginning and at the end of a massage. Stroking is vital as it allows the receiver to become accustomed to your hands and is used to apply oil to each part of the body. It also enables you to flow smoothly from one movement to the next.

Effleurage can be used on any part of the body and is usually performed towards the heart to assist the flow of blood. The palmar surfaces of one or both hands are used as you move slowly along the body, while moulding your hands to the contours of the body. Your hands should be completely relaxed if they are to mould to the curves of the receiver.

Effleurage should feel like one continuous movement to the receiver as you apply firm pressure on the upward stroke and glide back to your starting point with no pressure whatsoever.

Try to maintain a steady rhythm and avoid any jerky or abrupt movements that could make the receiver feel nervous and irritated. Experiment with different amounts of pressure – your movements may be soft and gentle or firm and deep depending on whether you want to work on the superficial or the deeper tissues of the body. Different rhythms can also be used. A slow rhythm will soothe and relax the receiver whereas a fast rhythm will stimulate an area.

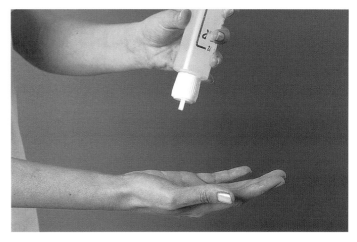

Before beginning effleurage, prepare the oil in your hands before applying

Close your eyes as you effleurage to heighten your sensitivity and intuition.

The back is an excellent area on which to practice your effleurage movements.

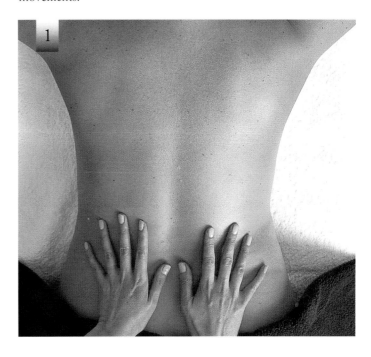

STEP 1. Position yourself to the side of the receiver and place your relaxed hands on the lower back area, one hand either side of the spine.

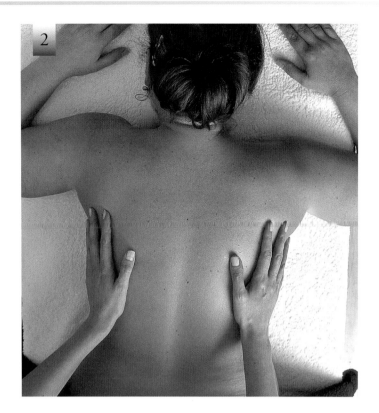

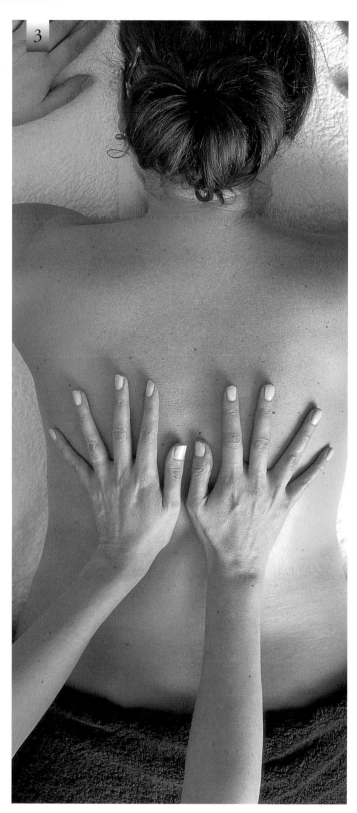

STEP 2. Stroke both hands firmly up the back

STEP 3. As your hands reach the top, spread them outwards across the shoulders.

STEP 4. Allow them to glide back without any pressure. Repeat this movement several times to accustom the receiver to the feel of your hands. Try experimenting with different pressures and rhythms and ask the receiver what he /she prefers.

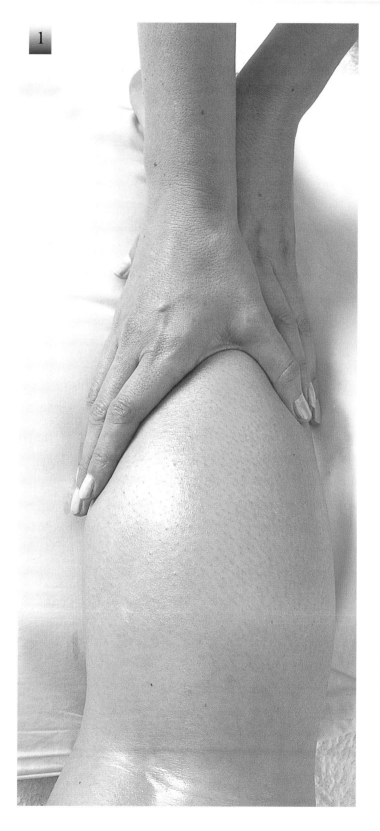

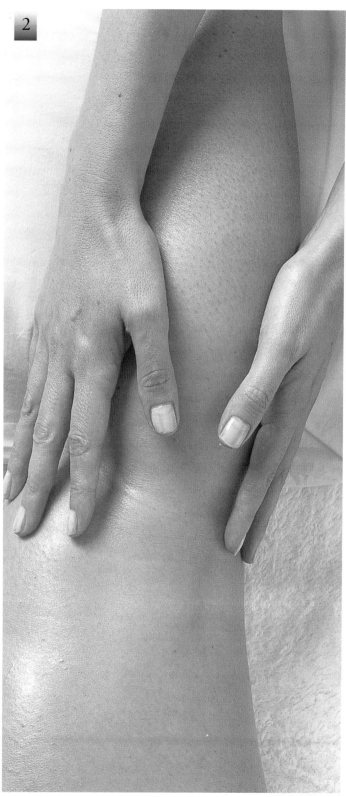

STEP 1. Now you will practice effleurage on the back of the leg. Place both hands palms down just above the ankle in a V-shape. Stroke firmly up the leg applying hardly any pressure to the back of the knee.

STEP 2. As your hands reach the top of the thigh separate them and allow them to glide gently back to your starting position.

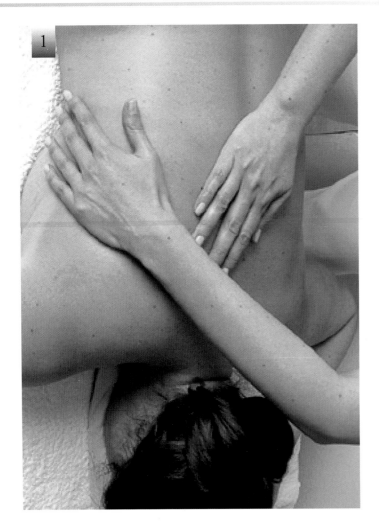

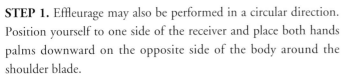

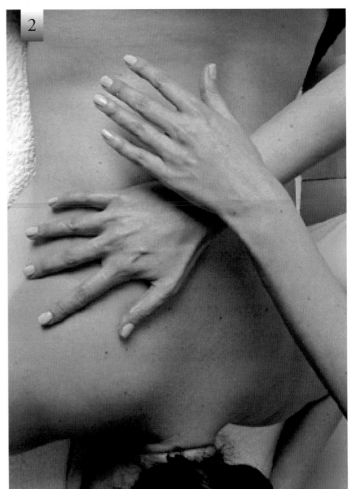

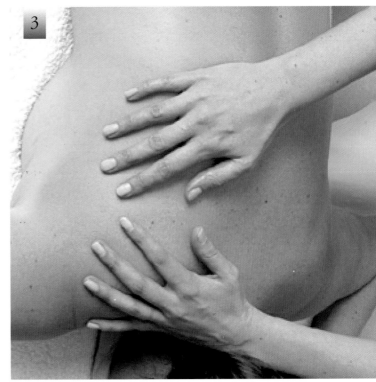

STEP 1. Effleurage may also be performed in a circular direction. Position yourself to one side of the receiver and place both hands palms downward on the opposite side of the body around the shoulder blade.

STEPS 2 - 3. Using the whole of the palms of the hands, make large stroking movements in a circular direction with one hand following the other down towards the buttocks and back up to the shoulders again. Your hands will cross over as you perform your circular movements. Make sure that you always keep contact with the receiver as you will have to lift one hand over the other.

You may perform the circular movements in either a clockwise or an anti-clockwise direction.

THERAPEUTIC EFFECTS OF EFFLEURAGE

● A relationship of trust is established between you and the receiver.

● The receiver experiences a deep sense of relaxation.

● Slow effleurage is excellent for soothing the nerves and is highly beneficial for highly-strung or anxious individuals. Stress can be relieved and headaches and migraines dispelled. Blood pressure can be brought down significantly and patterns of insomnia can be broken. Slow effleurage is excellent after any sporting activity for eliminating waste products such as lactic acid and other deposits from the tissues. Recovery time can be greatly accelerated.

● Brisk effleurage is useful for stimulating the body. It improves the circulation and encourages the flow of lymph so that waste substances can be eliminated. Vigorous effleurage is particularly effective prior to any sporting event. When combined with other massage movements it can increase performance and agility and can prevent muscle strains from occurring.

REMEMBER

Never lose contact with the receiver

❖

Massage towards the heart with no pressure whatsoever on the downward stroke

❖

Ensure that your hands are relaxed and use the palmar surface

❖

Avoid any jerky movements – effleurage is always rhythmic and smooth

❖

Use more oil when treating a hairy person or you could create a rash

If an area needs to be thoroughly warmed up to prepare it for some deeper movements (e.g. the shoulder blade), or firm pressure is required then circular effleurage with one hand reinforcing the other may be performed. Place one hand flat on top of the other on one of the shoulder blades. Using the whole of the hand make large circular movements on and around the scapula. (1)

PETRISSAGE

Petrissage is derived from the word 'pétrir' which means to knead. There are several ways of performing petrissage and here it is divided into picking up, squeezing, rolling and wringing. This technique allows you to work deeply on the muscles and it is particularly effective when performed on fleshy areas such as the calves (shown here), hips, thighs and across the shoulders. This movement is suitable for every area of the body except the face.

PICKING UP

STEP 1. Place the hands palms flat down on the area to be treated. Grasp the muscle (not the skin) with both hands and then pick it up and pull it away as far as possible from the bone. Hold this position for a few seconds and then release the pressure, although your hands should still remain in contact with the receiver. Practice this movement on the back of the legs.

SQUEEZING

STEP 2. To perform this technique pick up the muscle as before and then gently squeeze it between your hands. This allows you to 'squeeze' out any toxins that have accumulated from the deeper tissues.

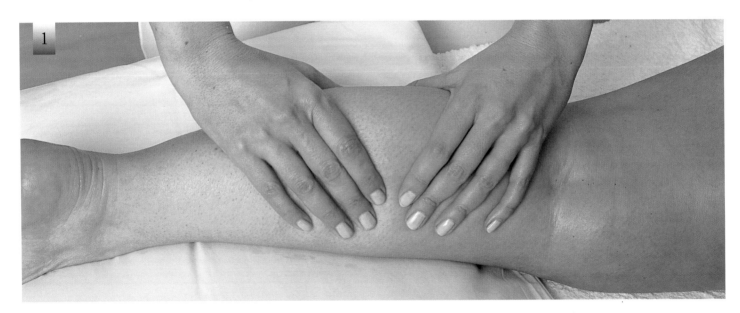

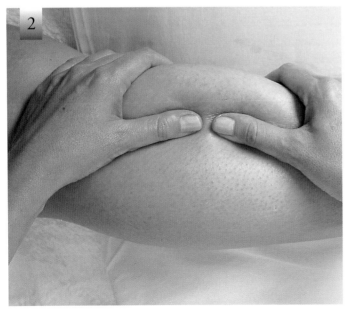

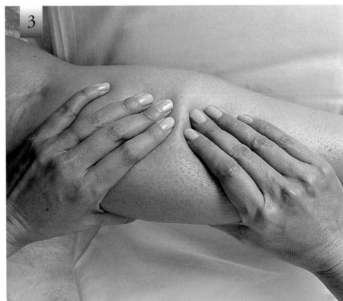

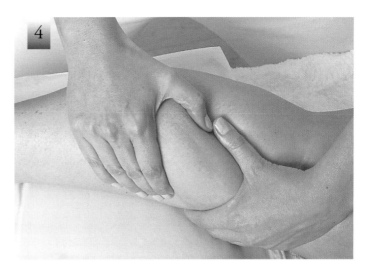

ROLLING

STEP 3. Muscles may be rolled in both directions – the thumbs can roll the muscle towards the fingers or the fingers may roll the muscle towards the thumbs. Place both hands flat onto the area to be treated and lift and roll the muscle in both directions. (2, 3)

WRINGING

STEP 4. For a really deep effect try wringing. Once again this movement is performed on the large muscle groups. The muscle is picked up between the thumb and fingers, each hand working alternately, pulled towards you and 'wrung' out as if you are wringing out a towel or chamois leather.

Wringing may also be done slowly and gently around the shoulder area.

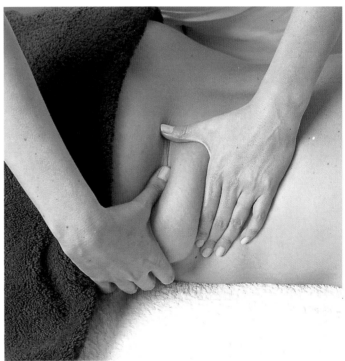

THERAPEUTIC EFFECTS OF PETRISSAGE

● An increased blood supply is brought to the area being treated, bringing fresh nutrients to the muscles.

● The deeper tissues are cleansed of any accumulated toxins.

● Fatty deposits are broken down.

● Muscle tone is improved.

REMEMBER

Make sure that you are grasping the whole of the muscle – not just the skin

❖

Use the whole of your hand and NOT just the fingers and thumbs otherwise you will pinch and cause discomfort to the receiver

Be careful to avoid painful pinching when using petrissage techniques.

F R I C T I O N

To perform friction, the balls of the thumbs are usually employed. However, the fingertips and knuckles can also be used, as well as the elbows. This technique is an excellent way of finding and breaking down knots and nodules which can build up, particularly around the shoulder blades and on either side of the spine. You will perfect this technique on the back.

STEP 1. Place the pads of your thumbs in the dimples at the base of the spine. Keep your arms straight and slowly lean forward so that you are using your body weight to penetrate into the deeper tissues. Press for a few seconds whilst rotating your thumbs then gradually release the pressure and move your thumbs slightly further up the back. Repeat this pressure until you reach the base of the neck.

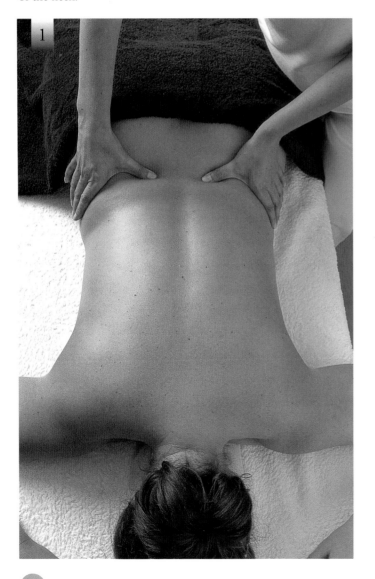

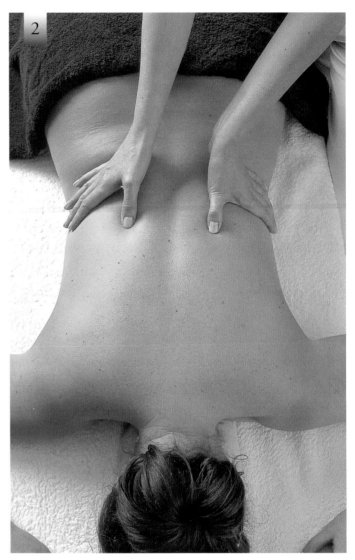

STEP 2. To perform continuous circular friction, assume the same position as before. Perform small deep, outward circular movements with the balls of your thumbs, pulling the muscle away from the spine. Your thumbs should ache by the time you reach the base of the neck. If you find a 'knotty' area then place one thumb on top of the other and perform some circular friction over it.

STEP 3. The knuckles may also be employed for breaking down knots and nodules. Curl your hands into fists and use your knuckles in a circular motion.

3

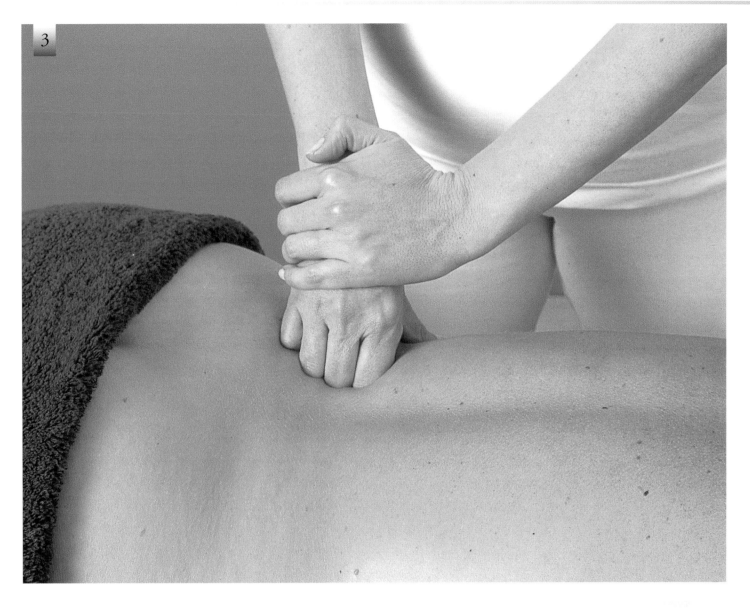

THERAPEUTIC EFFECTS OF FRICTION

● Friction breaks down knots and nodules.

● Waste products are eliminated.

● Fatty deposits are broken down.

● Old scar tissue may be broken down.

● Pain can be relieved.

● Joints can be loosened.

REMEMBER

Make sure that you are working on the deeper muscles and not just the skin

❖

Do not poke and prod. Press slowly into the tissues, gradually working deeper and deeper

❖

Use the pads of the thumbs and not the tips to avoid digging the nails in

P E R C U S S I O N   M O V E M E N T S / T A P O T E M E N T

Tapotement consists of a variety of movements in which the muscles are stimulated using various parts of the hands such as the edge of the hand, the palms or even the fists. Percussion movements are only performed on fleshy, muscular areas – never on bony areas.

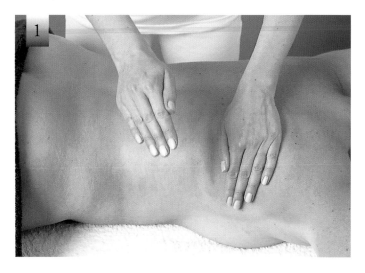

CUPPING

Cupping is also sometimes referred to as a clapping. Form a hollow curve with your fingers and thumbs and bring your cupped hands down on to the body in quick succession. (1)

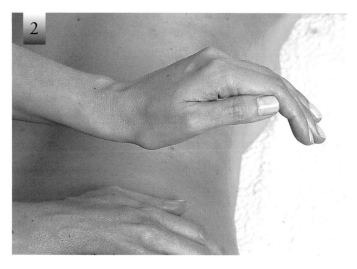

You should hear a hollow sound (NOT a slapping sound) as your cupped hands create a vacuum, trapping air against the skin and then releasing it. When properly applied cupping will not hurt. (2)

THERAPEUTIC EFFECTS OF TAPOTEMENT

● Circulation improves as blood is drawn to the surface.

● Muscle tone is induced.

● Fatty deposits are reduced.

● Cupping can help to loosen mucus in the lungs.

● Percussion movements are stimulating and highly beneficial prior to sporting activities.

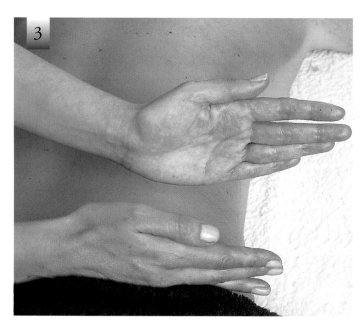

HACKING

This technique is performed with the outer edge of the hands. Make sure that you keep the wrists very loose. Hold your hands over the body, thumbs uppermost with the palms facing each other. Now flick your hands rhythmically up and down in quick succession. Your movements should be light and bouncy and NOT sharp and heavy like a karate chop. (3)

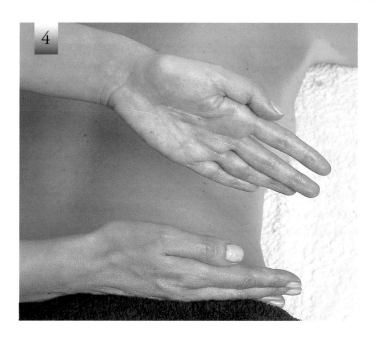

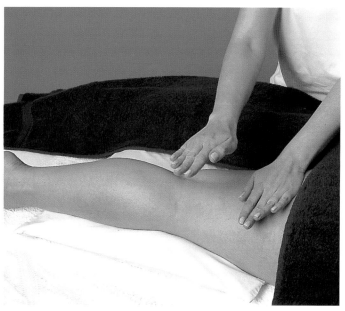

Make sure your hands are cupped rather than flat to avoid 'smacking' the receiver

FLICKING

This is a lighter version of hacking. The difference between these two movements is that in flicking only the sides of the little fingers are used and not the edge of the hand. Flicking has a much softer effect. (4)

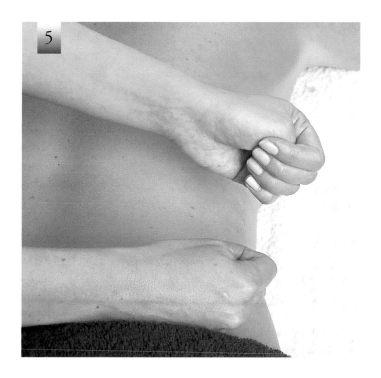

POUNDING

To perform pounding, clench your fists lightly and apply them to the body alternately in quick succession. (5)

REMEMBER

Do not perform over bony areas e.g. shins. Percussion movements should only be used on fleshy muscular areas

❖

Do not perform over sensitive areas e.g. back of the knee, neck, bruises, broken veins etc

❖

When cupping, make sure your hands are cupped and NOT flat to avoid smacking

❖

Keep the wrists loose and your movements light and bouncy to avoid causing discomfort to the receiver

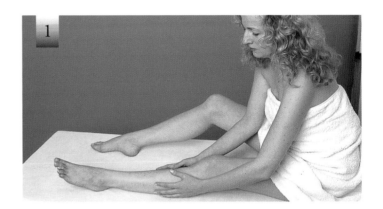

The advantage of self-massage is that you can perform it as often as you wish and whenever you want. It is an invaluable way of discovering which movements feel good, and allows you to experiment with different pressures and rhythms. The more you are able to massage your own body the better you will be at massaging others.

Unfortunately there are several disadvantages to self-massage. There is no exchange of energy from one person to another. It is also impossible to totally relax, since at least one hand will always be massaging and some areas of the body are very difficult to reach without causing discomfort.

However, if you do not have someone to massage you then it is well worth the effort to do it yourself. You may carry out the complete sequence or simply select any area that needs attention.

LEGS

Leg massage is an excellent way to relieve tired and aching muscles. It will also improve your circulation, help to prevent varicose veins and eliminate toxins. It will take you less than five minutes to massage each leg.

STEP 1. EFFLEURAGE THE WHOLE LEG
Sit down on the floor with your legs outstretched in front of you. Effleurage the leg upwards from your ankle to your thigh, moulding your hands to the contours of the leg. If you are not very supple then bend the leg slightly. (1)

STEP 2. EFFLEURAGE THE CALF MUSCLES
Still sitting on the floor, bend one leg up so that the foot is flat on the ground. Using one or both hands, effleurage from the heel to the back of your knee. (2)

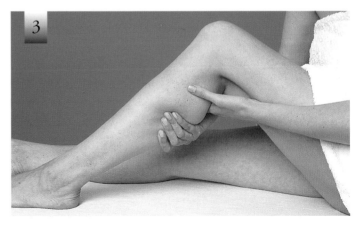

STEP 3. PETRISSAGE THE CALF MUSCLES
Keep your knee bent and petrissage the calf, alternately squeezing and releasing the calf muscles. This will bring the deeper toxins to the surface so that they can be eliminated, and is also an excellent way of preventing and alleviating cramp. (3)

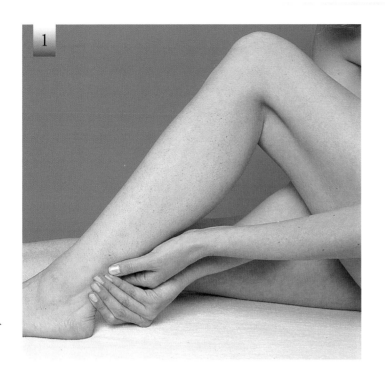

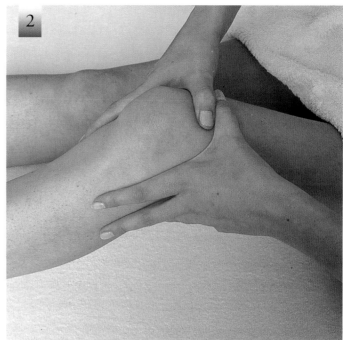

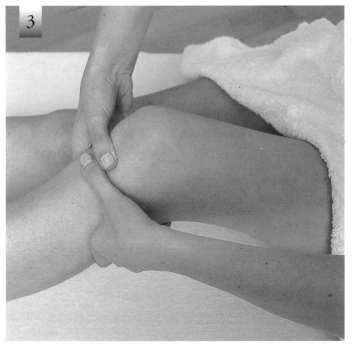

STEP 4. FRICTION THE ACHILLES TENDON
Using your fingers and thumbs, work all around the Achilles tendon. (1)

STEP 5. CIRCLING THE KNEE
Place both thumbs just below the knee and glide them gently around the knee, one thumb either side until they meet at the top. (2)

STEP 6. Then circle the thumbs again until they meet underneath the knee. (3)

STEP 7. LOOSEN THE KNEE
Use the pads of your thumbs or fingertips to work all around the patella using small circular friction movements. This technique is excellent for increasing flexibility of the knee joint. Do this every day if you have arthritis or an old knee injury. (4)

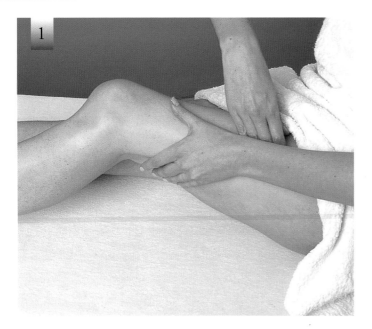

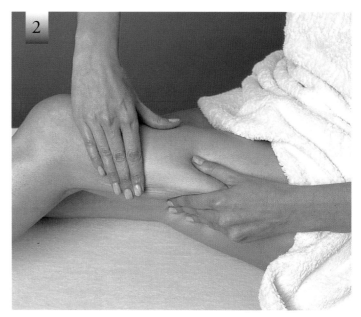

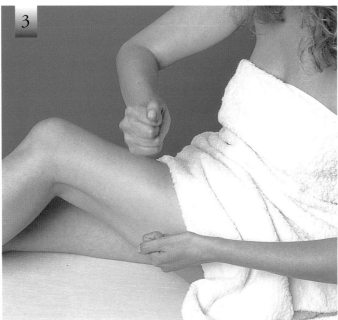

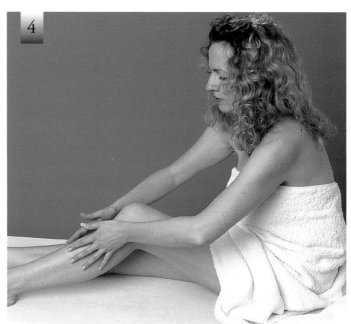

STEP 8. E F F L E U R A G E   T H E   T H I G H

Firmly stroke the muscles of the thigh from the knee to the groin. Make sure that you cover all aspects – the front, the sides and the back. You may effleurage with one hand following the other or, for a firmer pressure, put one hand on top of the other. (1)

STEP 9. P E T R I S S A G E   T H E   T H I G H

Knead the inner, middle and outer thigh to break down fatty deposits and unsightly cellulite. Over a period of time, kneading can really improve the shape of your thighs. If there are areas of cellulite, make your hands into fists and use your knuckles in a circular direction. (2)

STEP 10. P O U N D   T H E   T H I G H

Clench your fists lightly and apply them to the thigh in quick succession. Pounding improves circulation as blood is brought to the surface, reduces fatty deposits and improves muscle tone. (3)

STEP 11. C O M P L E T I O N

To end the sequence, gently stroke the leg from ankle to thigh with a feather light touch. (4)

Repeat on the other leg.

THE FEET

A daily foot massage is excellent not only for de-stressing but also improves your general health since according to foot reflexology the whole of the body can be treated via the feet.

You may either sit on the floor, bed or on a chair and you need to be able to raise one foot on to the opposite knee. If you are working on the floor you may find it comfortable to place a cushion or pillow under your bent knee.

STEP 1. EFFLEURAGE THE FOOT
Place one hand on top of the foot and one under the sole. Using both hands stroke firmly up the foot working from the toes up towards the ankle and back again. (1)

STEP 2. LOOSEN THE SOLE OF THE FOOT
With your thumbs, work into the sole of the foot using small deep circular movements to loosen up the tendons and muscles. (2)

STEP 3. FRICTION THE TOES
Support the foot, with one hand and massage the joints of the toes (top and bottom) between your thumb and index finger to thoroughly loosen them. (3)

STEP 4. MOVE THE TOES
Slowly stretch each toe and then move each one individually both clockwise and anti-clockwise to increase flexibility. (4)

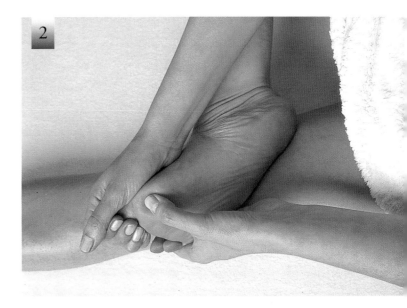
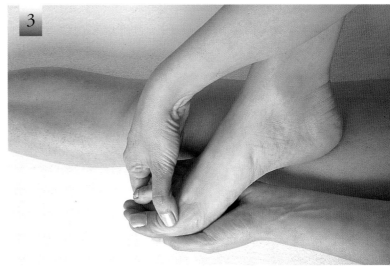
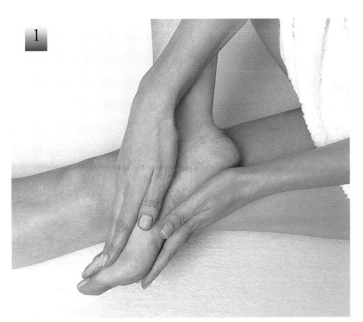
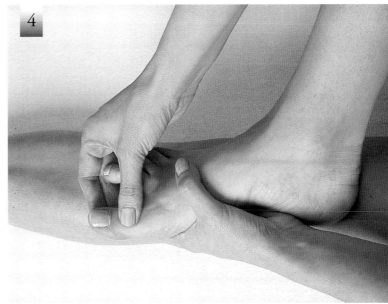

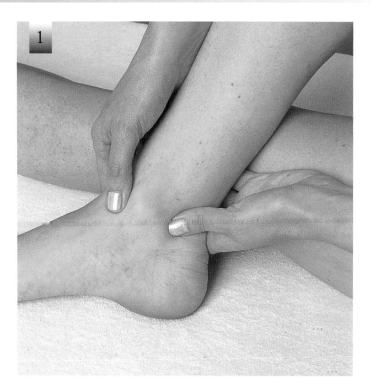

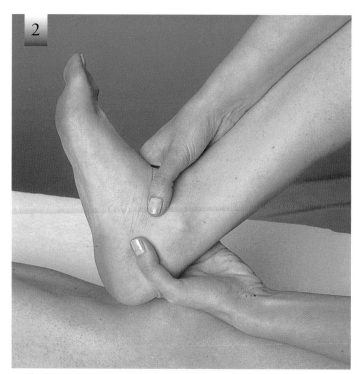

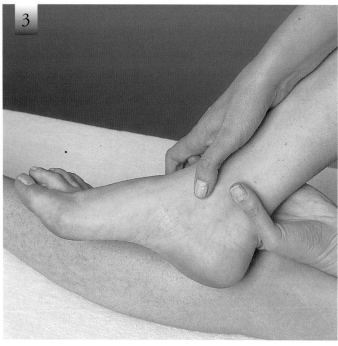

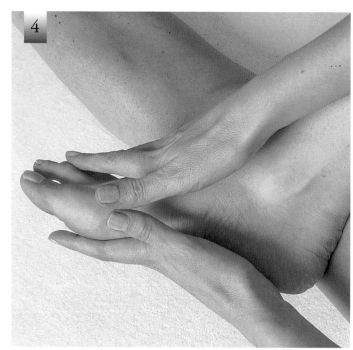

STEP 5. FRICTION THE ANKLE

Using thumbs or fingertips, massage all around the ankle joint with small deep circular movements to break down old scar tissue. (1)

STEP 6. MOVE THE ANKLE

Support the foot with one hand and slowly circle the ankle both clockwise and anti-clockwise. (2,3)

STEP 7. COMPLETION

Using just your fingertips, stroke the foot slowly from the toes to the ankle. Sandwich the foot between the palms of your hands and squeeze gently. (4)

Repeat on the other foot.

N E C K   A N D   S H O U L D E R S

The majority of us suffer occasionally with our neck and shoulders. Tightness in the neck can lead to restrictions and inability to move the head properly and often gives rise to headaches. This massage can be performed sitting on a bed, chair or on the floor. The neck and shoulders are easily accessible and can even be massaged through the clothes. Try working on them when watching television in the evening or travelling to work on the bus or train or whilst sitting in a traffic jam.

STEP 1. FRICTION THE BASE OF THE SKULL

Let your head relax forwards as far as is comfortable and bring your hands behind your head. Use your thumbs and fingertips to make small circular friction movements all around the base of the skull. Firm pressure in this area can get rid of headaches and prevents them from occurring. (1)

STEP 2. EFFLEURAGE THE NECK

Clasp your hands together lightly and stroke the neck outwards from the base of the skull to the shoulders. (2)

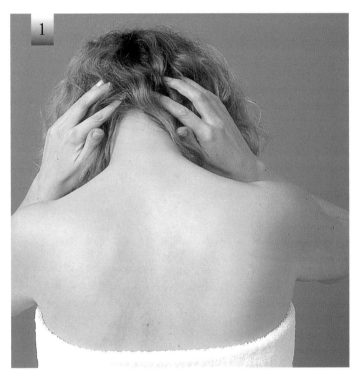

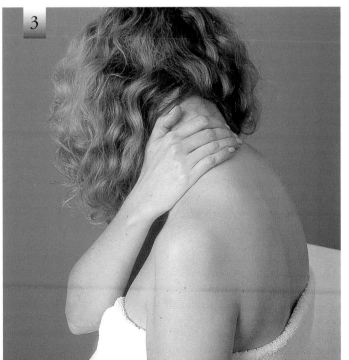

STEP 3. EFFLEURAGE THE SHOULDERS

To massage your left shoulder, place your right hand at the base of the skull and stroke down the side of the neck and over your shoulder. (3)

Then massage your right shoulder using your left hand to thoroughly relax the muscles.

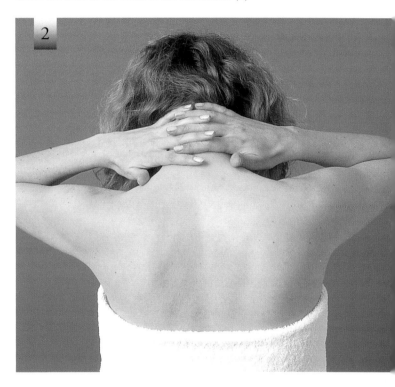

1

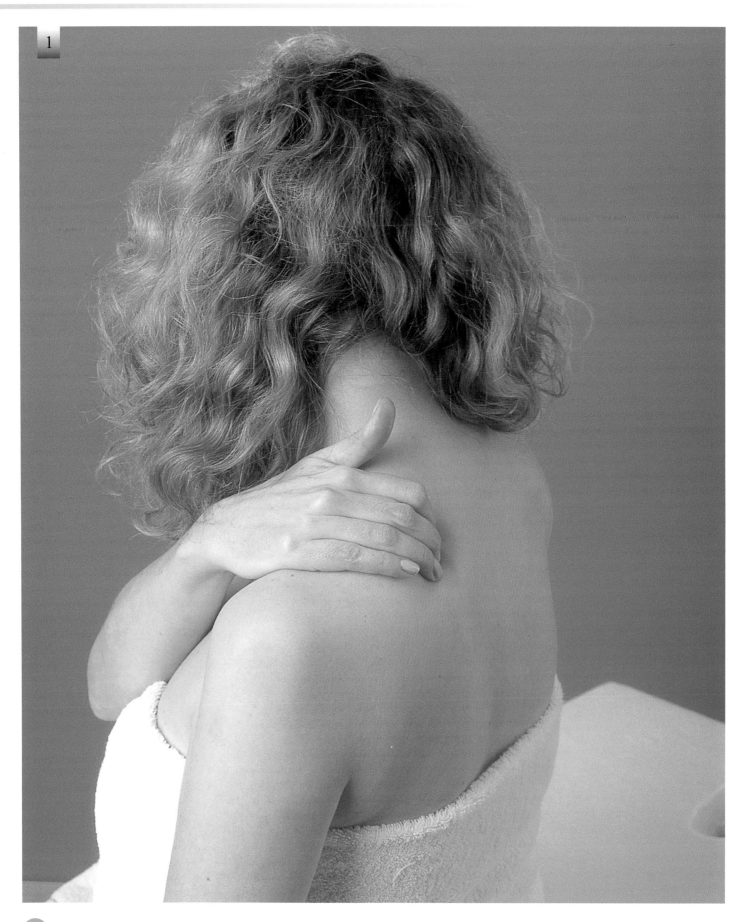

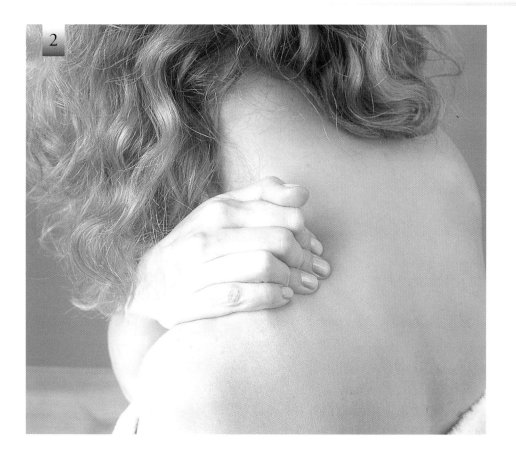

STEP 4. FRICTION THE SHOULDER BLADES

Reach across the front of your body with your right hand to locate your left shoulder blade. Use your fingertips to apply deep circular friction movements into the knots that are so common around the shoulder blade. (1)

Repeat on the other side.

STEP 5. KNEAD THE SHOULDERS

Squeeze and release the left shoulder by reaching across the front of the body with your right hand picking up as much flesh as possible. Now knead the other shoulder. (2)

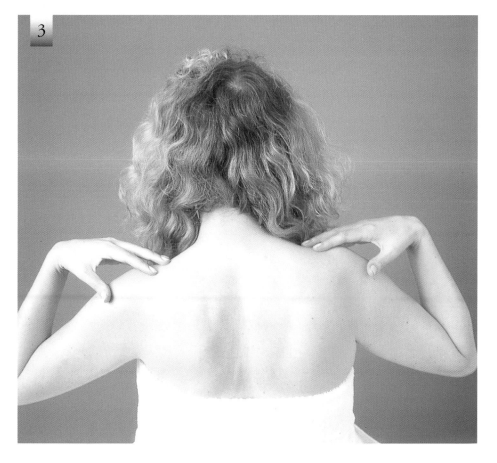

STEP 6. COMPLETION

Place one hand either side of the top of the neck and stroke both hands slowly down the neck and over the shoulders. (3)

ARMS AND HANDS

Massage of the arms and hands is wonderful for people who use them extensively in their work – e.g. hairdressers, gardeners, keyboard operators, writers, etc. Treatment can also prevent sports injuries from occurring.

STEP 1. EFFLEURAGE THE ARM
Rest your hand gently on your lap and effleurage the whole arm from the wrist up to the shoulder. (1)

STEP 2. KNEAD THE UPPER ARM

Pick up and squeeze as much flesh as you can on your upper arm to break down fatty deposits and improve muscle tone. (2)

STEP 3. DEEP STROKING TO THE FOREARM
With your thumb on one side of the arm and your fingers underneath, apply deep stroking movements from the wrist to the elbow. If you find any tight areas then gently loosen them by performing small deep circular friction movements on the troublesome area. (3)

STEP 4. FRICTION AND MOVE THE ELBOW
To loosen the elbow, make small circular friction movements all around the elbow with your fingertips, working deeply into any tight areas. (4)

STEP 5. MOVE THE ELBOW
Cup under the elbow with your hand and gently and slowly bend and stretch the forearm to improve flexibility. (5)

STEP 6. LOOSEN THE WRIST
Use your thumbs or fingertips to perform circular pressures all around the wrist joint to loosen it up. (6)

STEP 7. MOVE THE WRIST Now gently circle your wrist both clockwise and anti-clockwise. (7)

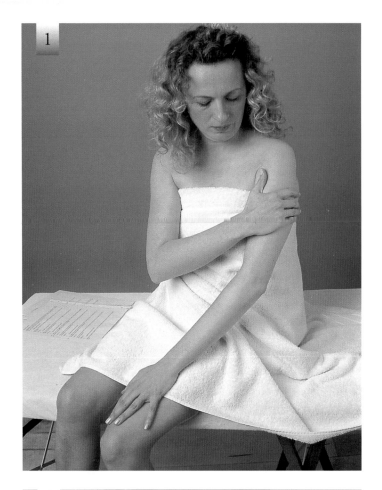

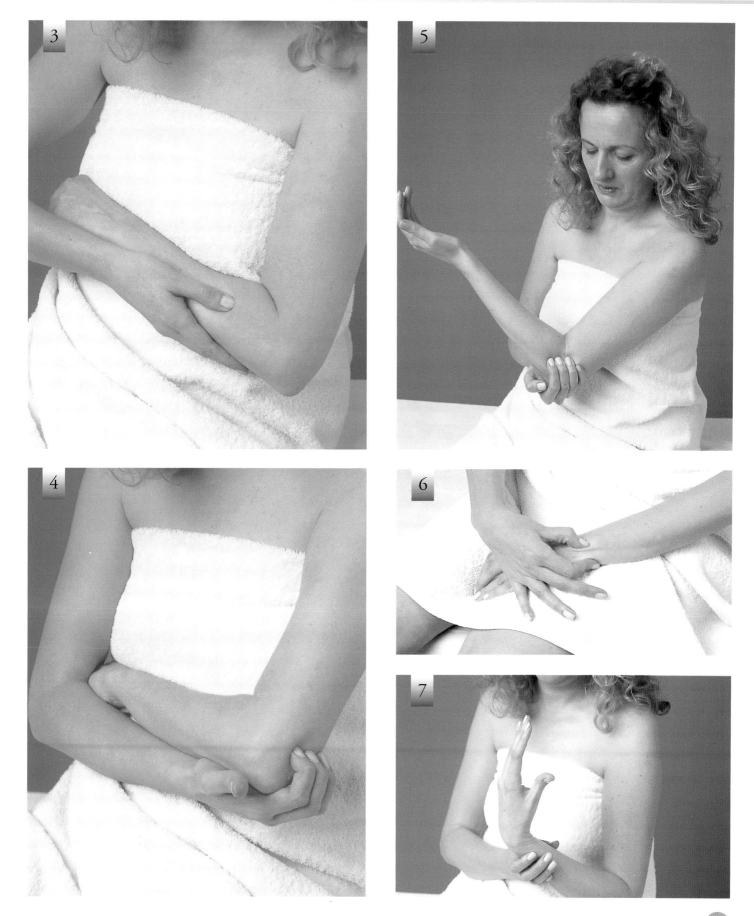

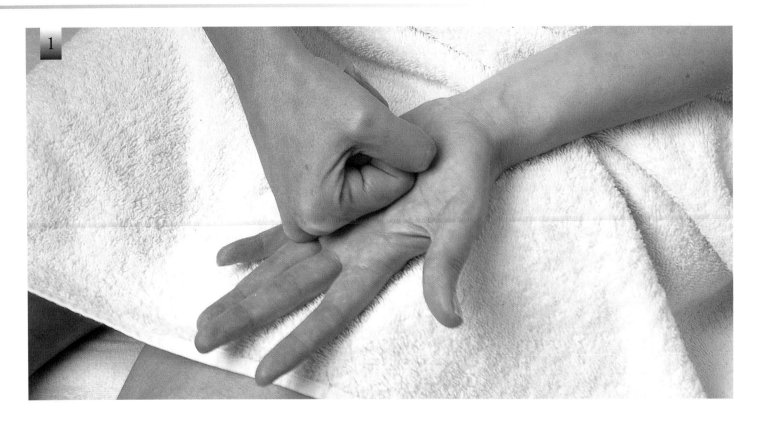

STEP 8. WORK INTO THE PALM OF THE HAND
With a loosely clenched fist, work into the palm of your hand with gentle circular movements. (1)

STEP 9. STROKING BETWEEN THE TENDONS
Turn the hand over and, using your thumb or fingertips, work along each of the furrows between the tendons from the knuckles to the wrist. (2)

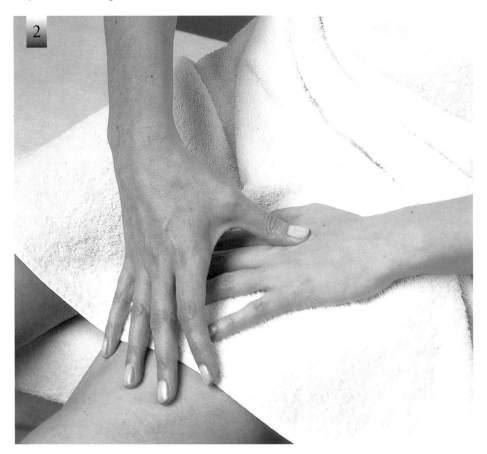

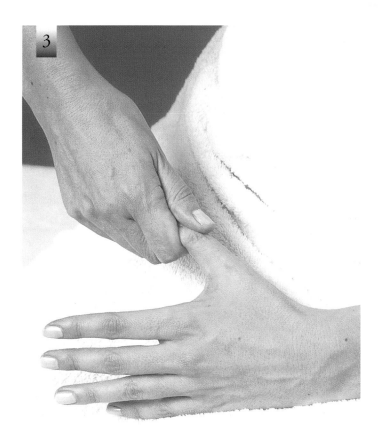

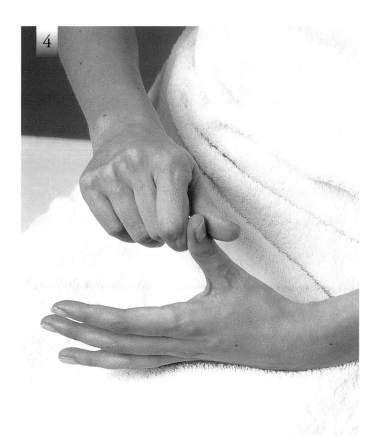

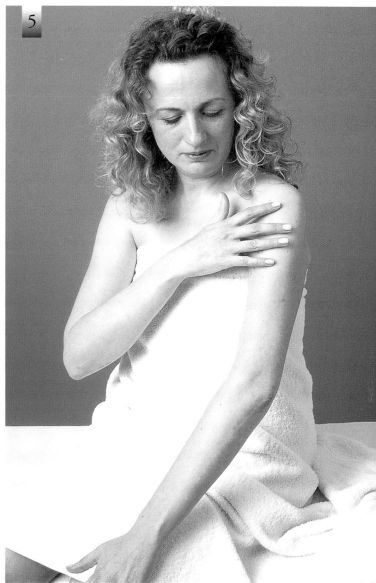

STEP 10. LOOSEN AND MOVE THE FINGERS
AND THUMB
Gently and slowly stretch each finger and thumb individually,
working from the knuckle to the tip, using your thumb and
index finger.(3)Then gently circle them in one direction and then
in the opposite direction. (4) Using just your fingertips, gently
stroke up the arm gently from fingers to the shoulder. Make sure
that you cover all aspects of the arm. (5)

FACE AND SCALP

Place both hands on your forehead, fingertips facing each other and stroke out across the forehead. (1) Then stroke outwards across the cheeks. (2) Finally stroke across the chin. (3)

STEP 2. GENTLE FRICTION

Using your fingertips, perform gentle circular friction movements starting at the hairline and working all the way down the face until you reach the jaw line. (4)

STEP 3. TONE THE EYEBROWS AND CHIN

With your thumbs and index fingers, gently squeeze all along the brow bone. (5) Then repeat the squeezing along your jaw line to help prevent the development of a double chin. (6)

STEP 4. EYES

Using your index or middle fingers, start just below the corner of the eye and stroke gently outwards. This helps to reduce puffiness around the eyes and should be carried out very gently, as this is such a delicate area. (7)

STEP 5. SCALP FRICTION

Rub the scalp vigorously all over in a circular motion with your fingertips. Scalp friction helps to release toxins from the scalp and encourages the hair to grow. (8)

STEP 6. COMPLETION

Place the heel of both hands over your eyes. Hold your hands there for a few seconds allowing your eyes to completely relax. When you take your hands away you will feel remarkably revitalised. (9)

therapeutic massage
for Common Ailments

Therapeutic massage has a wide range of physiological and psychological advantages and can be used to treat a whole host of common diseases. However, where a problem is persistent or serious then a medically qualified doctor should always be consulted. This chapter outlines some of the ailments that can be successfully treated with massage. You will find more details on the essential oils included in this chapter in the Aromatherapy section of this book.

CIRCULATORY PROBLEMS

HIGH BLOOD PRESSURE

High blood pressure is a fairly common disorder with a variety of causes. Stress is a major factor, which causes the muscles to contract and constrict the arteries. Dietary factors such as saturated fats and too much salt can also elevate cholesterol levels and lead to hardening of the arteries. Family history and smoking are also contributory factors.

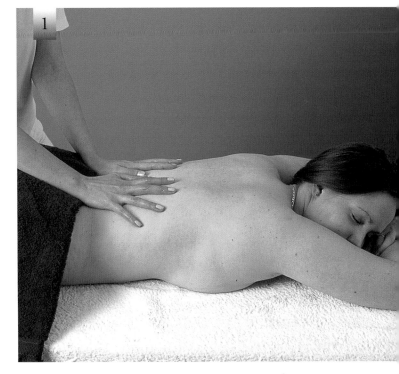

MASSAGE TREATMENT

Massage is a well-accepted therapy for reducing high blood pressure – regular treatment encourages it to reduce – sometimes quite dramatically. When we are anxious or emotional this causes the blood pressure to rise and the deep relaxation afforded by massage will calm even the tensest individuals.

● A full body massage at least once a week should be given. Brisk stimulating movements such as cupping and hacking should be omitted from the sequence.

● A great deal of gentle effleurage should be used particularly over the back during the treatment to calm, soothe and relax the receiver. (1)

● It is highly beneficial to massage either the feet or the hands daily to ensure a calm state of mind. (2)

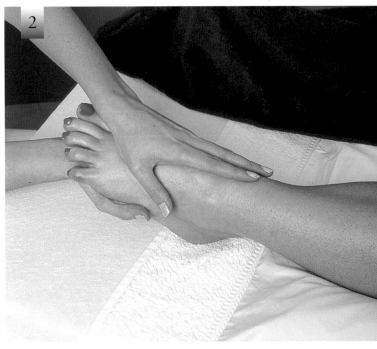

Essential oils of chamomile, geranium or lavender can be added to the massage oil to enhance the relaxation effects either singly or blended together.

To 10 mls (two teaspoons) of carrier oil add:
1 drop chamomile
1 drop geranium
1 drop lavender

OTHER ADVICE
● Eat lots of fruit, vegetables, fibre (especially oats) and garlic. Avoid salt, sugar and saturated fats.
● Try to reduce stress.
● Give up smoking and reduce alcohol and caffeine.
● Take up gentle exercise such as Tai Chi and yoga.

VARICOSE VEINS
Varicose veins occur when the valves in the veins are faulty and are unable to keep the blood from flowing backwards. They affect four times as many women as men with nearly 50% of middle-aged adults affected. Pregnancy, long periods of standing, obesity, genetic weakness and constipation and are all causes of varicose veins.

MASSAGE TREATMENT
You must never carry out the more vigorous movements such as cupping or hacking. Never press directly onto a severe varicose vein or you will cause pain and inflammation.

● Very gentle massage of the legs from the ankle to top of the thigh should be carried out daily, employing lots of effleurage. (1,2)
● Massage your own legs if no one is available. (3)

Lemon and geranium essential oils are invaluable.

To 10 mls (two teaspoons) of carrier oil add:
2 drops of lemon
1 drop of geranium

OTHER ADVICE
● Include lots of garlic (especially raw) to improve the circulation.
● Eat lots of fresh fruit, especially blackberries, blackcurrants, citrus fruits, cherries, pineapples, rose hips and strawberries, to reduce the fragility of the blood vessels.
● Vitamin C, E, ginkgo biloba and garlic capsules are all

excellent.
● Avoid standing for long periods of time.
● Elevate the legs higher than your head for about 15 minutes every day to improve drainage.

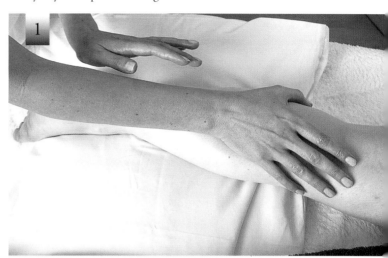
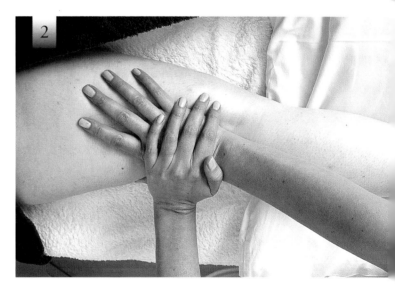
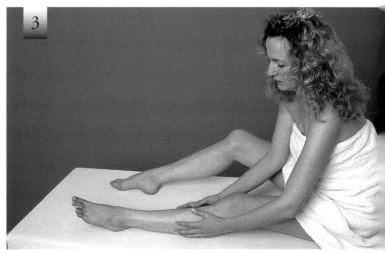

DIGESTIVE PROBLEMS

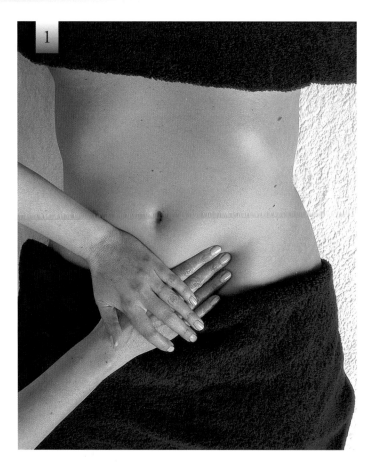

Many people suffer from digestive problems such as constipation, irritable bowel syndrome, indigestion and so on. Such disorders often originate from stress or from eating the wrong foods, inadequate intake of water, lack of exercise or even certain drugs.

MASSAGE TREATMENT
Massage of the abdomen is a highly effective treatment. If the problem is chronic then the abdomen should be treated daily until the bowel moments are regular. Then it should be carried out whenever necessary.

● Place one hand on top of the other on the navel and proceed to massage in a clockwise direction. Then put your three middle fingers at the bottom right hand side of the abdomen. Start to work slowly up the right hand side (ascending colon) with small gentle circular movements. (1)
● Continue working across the abdomen below the rib cage (transverse colon) and then turn and work down the left-hand side of the abdomen (descending colon). Slide lightly back to the lower right hand side and repeat several times. (2) Finish with some effleurage.

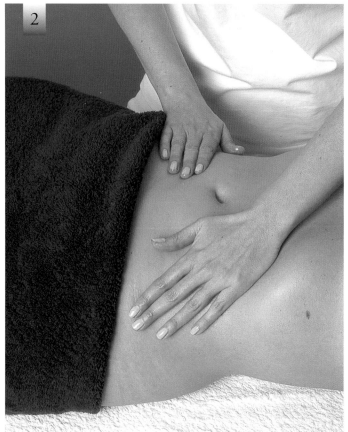

To enhance the massage use essential oils of peppermint and rosemary for constipation or chamomile and mandarin for conditions such as diarrhoea or irritable bowel syndrome to calm and soothe the colon.

OTHER ADVICE
● Eat a healthy high fibre diet to increase the frequency and quality of bowel movements.
● Drink 6-8 glasses of water per day.
● Avoid prolonged use of laxatives, which make the bowel lazy.
● Do not ignore the urge to move your bowels.

GENITO-URINARY PROBLEMS

● Avoid stress.
● Drink peppermint, fennel or chamomile tea.

FLUID RETENTION

Fluid retention is particularly common in the legs, especially around the ankles, although it may also be present around the wrists. Most elderly people will experience some fluid retention. Massage is a highly effective way of helping to drain away accumulated lymphatic fluid.

MASSAGE TREATMENT

● If the swelling is around the ankles, begin with gentle effleurage of the whole leg from ankle to thigh. Perform gentle circular friction movements around the ankle. (1)

● Then gently mobilise the ankle by rotating it clockwise and anti-clockwise. (2)

● For puffiness around the wrists, effleurage up the entire arm from wrist to shoulder. Then perform small pressure circles around the wrists and gently circle them clockwise and anti-clockwise. (3)

To help to reduce the fluid, essential oils of geranium, lemon, mandarin and rosemary are all effective.

To 10 mls (two teaspoons) of carrier oil add:
2 drops of geranium
1 drop of lemon

OR

to 10 mls (two teaspoons) of carrier oil add:
2 drops of mandarin
1 drop of rosemary

OTHER ADVICE

● Drink at least 6-8 glasses of water daily.
● Avoid standing for long periods of time.
● Rotate the ankles/wrists as often as possible.
● Elevate the legs higher than the head twice daily if possible for at least 15 minutes to assist drainage.
● Eat plenty of garlic.
● Reduce salt.

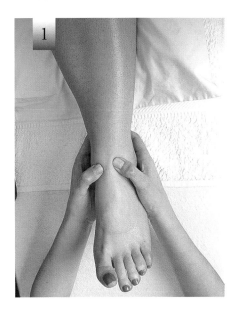
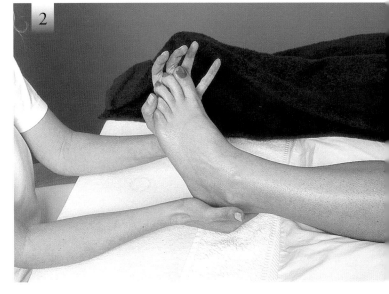
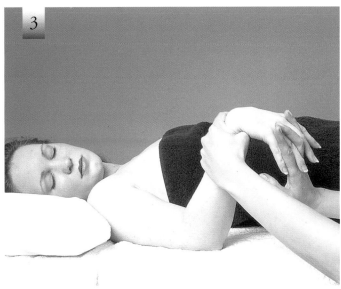

PRE-MENSTRUAL TENSION

Hundreds of symptoms have been attributed to PMT although the main ones include anxiety and mood swings, bloating of the abdomen and general fluid retention.

MASSAGE TREATMENT

Therapeutic massage can help to treat both the physical and emotional symptoms of PMT.

A full body massage should be carried out one or two days prior to the onset of the symptoms to help the woman to relax and balance the emotions. Many women feel as if they are retaining lots of fluid in the abdomen.

Gentle effleurage and stroking in a clockwise direction can be helpful.(1)

Pulling up the sides of the abdomen down towards the bladder can alleviate this problem. (2)

For maximum benefit add essential oils of chamomile, geranium, lavender or mandarin to the carrier oil. These oils are excellent for balancing the hormones as well as for minimising excessive fluid. In addition to therapeutic massage 6 drops of any of the above oils should be added to the bath daily.

OTHER ADVICE

● Reduce salt, sugar, caffeine and alcohol.
● Increase fibre intake.
● Try supplements of B complex and evening Primrose oil.
● Relax with yoga, Tai Chi or meditation.

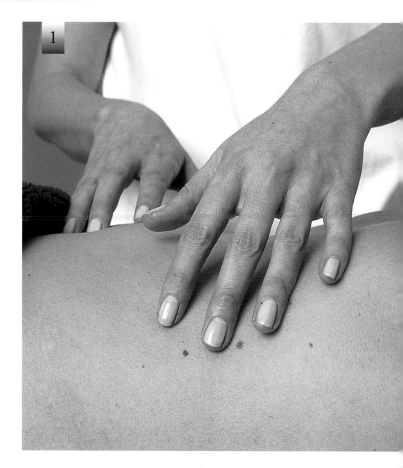

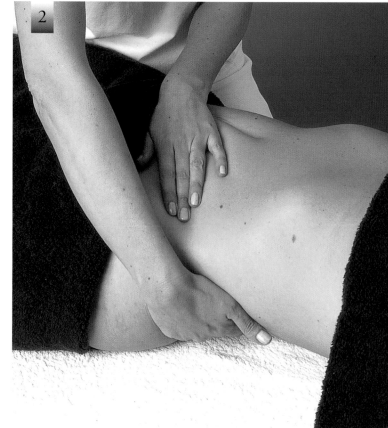

THE HEAD

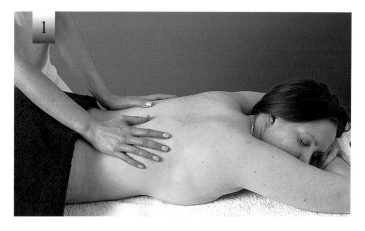

HEADACHES AND MIGRAINE

Headaches are caused by many factors ranging from muscular tension in the neck and shoulders, food allergies, eye strain, sinusitis, hormone imbalances and so forth. Therapeutic massage is very effective in the treatment of headaches since it is the best way of relieving stress and keeping the neck and shoulder muscles relaxed.

MASSAGE TREATMENT

Effleurage the whole back, paying particular attention to the upper back. Then perform small deep circular movements around the shoulder blades breaking down any knots and nodules that you may find. (1)

Knead the shoulders thoroughly squeezing and releasing with alternate hands and gently squeeze the neck muscles.

 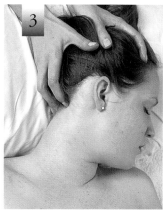

● Ask the receiver to turn over and effleurage both sides of the neck. (2)

● Then friction the base of the skull.(3) Stretch the neck carefully.

● Finally stroke outwards across the forehead to release any remaining tension. (4)

Essential oils of lavender and peppermint are a good combination. Use 2 drops of lavender and 1 drop of peppermint to 10 mls (2 teaspoons) of carrier oil. If the pain is severe then put 3 drops of lavender and 3 drops of peppermint into a small cereal bowl of lukewarm water and place a flannel in it to make a compress. Either place it on the forehead or on the back of the neck for maximum relief.

OTHER ADVICE
● Reduce stress
● Apply self massage to the neck and shoulders daily.
● Avoid foods, which may cause a headache – the main culprits are cheese, chocolate and red wine.
● B complex and zinc and are excellent for stress relief.

M U S C U L O - S K E L E T A L   P R O B L E M S

O S T E O A R T H R I T I S
This is a very common ailment caused by wear and tear, which affects primarily the weight bearing joints –the knees, and hips.

M A S S A G E   T R E A T M E N T
Therapy is aimed at relieving stiffness, reducing pain and improving flexibility of the affected joints. It is a good idea to administer a full treatment every two weeks and to massage the arthritic joints daily. Remember that if a joint is very swollen you should never massage directly on to the inflamed area – work above and below the swelling.

● When treating arthritis of the knee, first effleurage the whole leg from ankle to the top of the thigh. Then effleurage the front of the thigh firmly.

● Gently friction around the knee cap to keep the patella freely movable. (1)

● Finally bend and stretch the knee slowly and carefully to maintain and increase the range of movement. (2,3)

Useful essential oils include chamomile (if there is inflammation), eucalyptus (pain relief), lavender (relaxing, pain relief), lemon (reduces a fluid and helps clear waste products), peppermint (pain relief, cooling) and rosemary (improves circulation, gets rid of toxins, pain relief). Add 3-4 drops of any of the above to 10 mls of carrier oil. If pain is severe then a compress can be made by sprinkling 6 drops of essential oil into a bowl of lukewarm water, soaking it up with a flannel and placing it on the affected area.

O T H E R   A D V I C E
● Keep to your recommended weight.
● Try selenium ACE.
● Take gentle exercise such as yoga and Tai Chi or walking to keep the joints mobile.

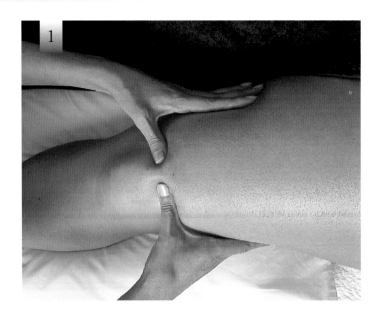

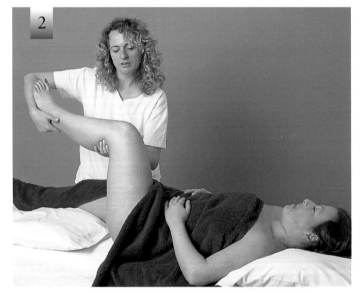

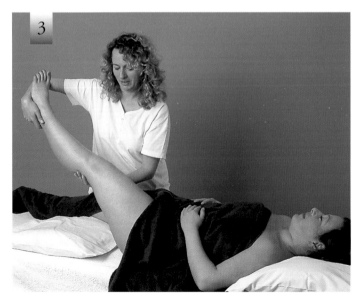

RESPIRATORY PROBLEMS

ASTHMA/COUGHS/NASAL CONGESTION

Asthma is characterised by wheezing caused by inflammation of air passages in the lungs which narrows the airways and reduces airflow in and out of the lungs. Stress and allergies such as pollen, house dust, certain foods etc may induce an attack.

MASSAGE TREATMENT

● Therapeutic massage will be concentrated upon the chest and upper back. Place the hands in the centre of the chest and effleurage outwards to open up the chest and encourage deeper breathing. (1)

To further release the chest place the heels of your hands so that they are cupped over the shoulders. Press down and hold for five seconds and repeat several times to open out the chest. Encourage the receiver to take a few deep breaths to encourage full inhalation and exhalation. (2)

Congestion in the chest may be relieved with percussion movements. Cup and hack over the back of the rib cage to stimulate the respiratory system and to loosen mucus and phlegm from the bronchial tubes.

Essential oils of eucalyptus and rosemary are particularly effective for bronchial congestion. Lavender helps to promote sleep and boosts the immune system, encouraging healing to take place. Lemon can break down mucus and fights off infections in the respiratory tract. A good chest rub would be:

To 10 mls (two teaspoons) of carrier oil:
1 drop of cucalyptus
1 drop of rosemary
OR
2 drops of lavender
1 drop of lemon

If someone is having an asthma attack and is very tense and panicky then put a couple of drops of lavender onto their palms and encourage them to breathe deeply.

● For nasal congestion therapeutic massage is excellent. Pay particular attention to the forehead, cheeks and nose area. (3)

Add 2 drops of lavender and 1 drop of rosemary to 10 mls of carrier oil for a de-congestive facial blend. Also sprinkle a few drops of eucalyptus or rosemary onto a handkerchief and place it in your pocket so that you can inhale the aroma all day long.

OTHER ADVICE

● Avoid stress which can precipitate an asthma attack and depletes the immune system, making you more susceptible to coughs and colds.
● Eliminate or at least cut down on dairy foods which encourage the production of mucus. Eat lots of fruit, vegetables and salad.
● Eat garlic, preferably raw daily as it is 'nature's antibiotic'. Ginger helps to break down phlegm.
● Take vitamin C to prevent coughs and colds.
● Practice gentle exercise such as yoga, which includes lots of breathing exercises.
● Open a window at night whilst you are sleeping to ensure a good supply of fresh air.

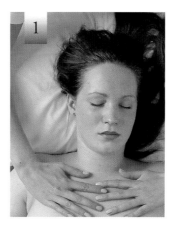
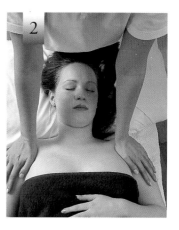
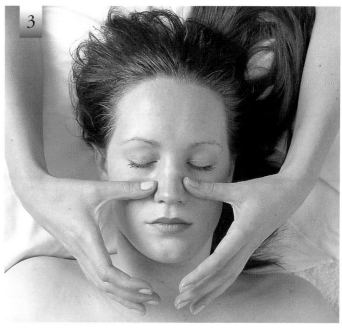

introduction to
Sensual Massage

BENEFITS OF SENSUAL MASSAGE

For thousands of years, lovers have delighted in the pleasures of sensual massage, and the joy of both giving and receiving pleasure from gentle touching and caressing has been recorded in cultures the world over. In today's climate of instant gratification, the art of sensual massage is equally important, giving lovers the chance to express their love in a tender and spiritual way.

Sensual massage has been enjoyed by lovers all over the world for thousands of years.

The pleasures of sensual massage are described in the Indian Kama Sutra (meaning 'Scripture of Love'). Known primarily as an adventurous sex manual, the Kama Sutra also refers to the less explicit, but equally erotic, use of seductive oils and perfumes to heighten sensual pleasure.

In Egypt, sensual massage was common. Priests were skilled at making love potions and Egyptian women were well aware of how perfumes could be used for sexual attraction. In Greece we think of the goddess Aphrodite who was worshipped as the Goddess of Love, beauty and sexuality. It is of course from her name that the word 'aphrodisiac' is derived. From her son's name Eros comes the word 'erotic'. From Rome comes Venus the goddess of love and her son Cupid. The word 'venery' meaning sexual desire is derived from the word Venus. Public baths, which were visited by the Romans each day, were perfumed with rosewater, and fragrant oils were commonly rubbed into the body for sensual pleasure.

Josephine adored oils and employed them lavishly to tempt and seduce her lover Napoleon. A wide range of aromatic potions was used during their nights of passion.

All over the world since the dawn of civilisation the use of massage coupled with sensual aromas to arouse sexual desire has been, and still is, widespread.

Massage using essential oils can provide a deeply pleasurable experience.

IMPORTANT NOTICE

This book must not be used as a substitute for treatment of medical conditions when it is important that the help of a doctor is sought. The information is not intended to diagnose or treat and any safety guidelines covered throughout the book must be adhered to.

It is of particular importance that essential oils are not to be taken internally and all other contra-indications regarding the oils are closely observed.

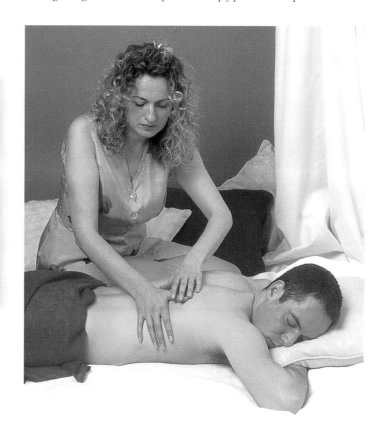

As well as being enjoyable, sensual massage can also promote physical health and a general sense of wellbeing.

As well as being an exciting prelude to lovemaking, sensual massage can be equally enjoyable in itself. It is an excellent way of getting closer to your lover.

BENEFITS OF SENSUAL MASSAGE

The benefits of sensual massage have been known for a long time. It is not only one of the most pleasurable experiences imaginable, but will also strengthen the immune system thus improving your health and preventing disease from occurring.

Massage also stimulates our lymphatic system allowing the body to effectively eliminate toxins. It is also aids digestion, improving conditions such as constipation and irritable bowel syndrome, speeds up the circulation and improves breathing and bronchial disorders. Muscles are relaxed, alleviating neck, shoulder and back pain. Nerves are soothed and the stresses and strains of everyday life melt away.

Even when the act of sexual intercourse is not performed, the physical pleasure of touch in the form of sensual massage is extremely enjoyable. To both give and receive massage can be a highly sensual experience and can add a new dimension to your sex life.

In this section you will learn new and exciting techniques to bring more fun into your relationship with your lover. You will discover how to attract your lover and create your own exclusive love potions. As you enhance and harmonise your sexual relationships be assured that you are also helping to create and maintain a healthy and happy body.

Enjoy the sensual pleasures that lie before you!

CREATING A SENSUAL AMBIENCE

It is essential to create a romantic and sensual environment for your massage, so try to prepare well in advance. Choose a time when you will not be disturbed. Take all telephones off the hook and do not allow children or pets to wander in and out of the room. Select some music, which you will both enjoy whether it be soothing and relaxing, or your own special piece.

A warm and inviting environment will enhance your enjoyment of sensual massage.

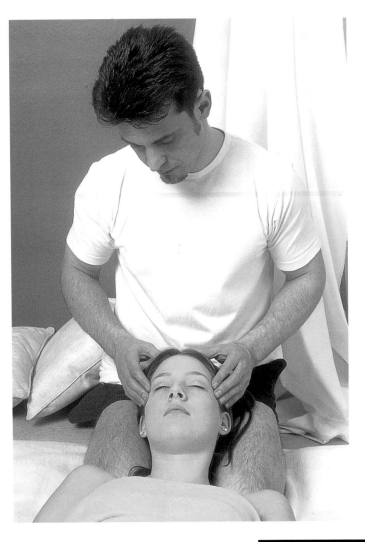

Make sure your lover is warm and relaxed. Provide plenty of throws and cushions, and remember not to break contact during the massage.

WARMTH

Heat the room beforehand to make it warm and inviting. If you are lucky enough to have an open fireplace, log fires are ideal. Your lover will find it is impossible to relax if he/she feels chilly, and the body temperature drops once the skin is exposed. Have plenty of throws, towels or blankets at your disposal to cover up any parts of the body that you are not working on. You will also need cushions or pillows, a small bowl and your massage oil on hand so that once you have started the massage you do not have to break contact with your lover.

LIGHTING

Lighting should be soft and romantic. Dim or turn off the lights and light a few candles around the room for the perfect setting. You may wish to use coloured candles — pink candles will encourage romance and gentleness, red candles can induce passion and violet candles are deep and mysterious.

Softly flickering candles can heighten the sensual ambience of your room.

SCENTING

Scent the room by burning incense or even better use essential oils. A clay burner is perfect. Put a few teaspoons of water into the loose bowl on top and sprinkle a few drops of essential oil into it. Light the night-light and allow the wonderful aromas to diffuse into the atmosphere. You can achieve the same effect by putting a saucer or small bowl of warm water on top of a hot radiator and adding a few drops of essential oil to the water. Choose from any of the erotic oils outlined later in this book according to your aroma preference, or try one of the recipes below in your burner.

2 drops rose
2 drops sandalwood
OR
2 drops bergamot
2 drops neroli
OR
2 drops jasmine
2 drops geranium
OR
2 drops ylang ylang
2 drops rosewood
You may also decide to scent your towels,

pillows or bed linen. There are several ways of doing this:

- Fill a small plant spray with spring water, add 10 drops of your chosen essential oil(s) and then spray your towels and pillows lightly.
- Put a few drops of essential oil on to cotton-wool balls and place them inside your pillowcases or under your towels or sheets.
- Add some drops of essential oil to the final rinse when washing your towels and pillowcases.

Particularly suitable oils would be frankincense, jasmine, neroli, patchouli, rose, sandalwood and ylang ylang as all these aromas have aphrodisiac properties and will last for a long time.

A few drops of your favourite oil in a burner or diffuser will give off a sensuous aroma.

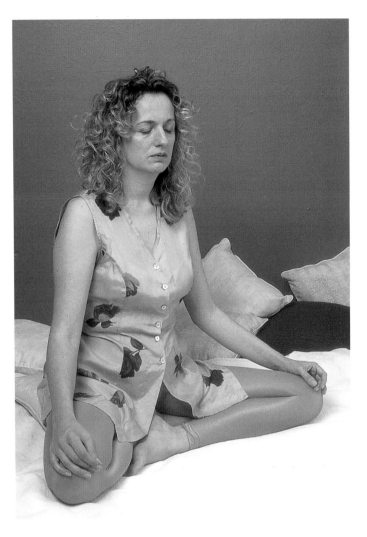

Before beginning your massage, it is important to centre yourself, to make sure you are completely relaxed.

CLOTHES

It is vital to wear comfortable and loose-fitting clothes preferably something short-sleeved or you will get too hot. You need to be able to move around your lover's body freely as you will often be changing your position. A loose T-shirt is ideal but any garments that are not constricting would be suitable. Go barefoot for maximum comfort and take off watches, bracelets, rings and necklaces which can scratch your lover's skin. Your lover should undress down to whatever level you both feel comfortable with. They should undress down to at least their underwear.

CENTERING YOURSELF

If you are to give a sensual massage a calm state of mind is essential. If you are feeling irritable, tired or depressed then your negative feelings will be transmitted to your lover. Therefore, prior to the massage you must try to completely empty your mind of your problems and spend time consciously relaxing yourself.
Lie down or sit comfortably with your back straight and take a few deep breaths from your abdomen allowing all your tension, mental and physical, to flow out of your body. If any thoughts pop into your head just let them go.

Stay in this relaxed position concentrating on your deep breathing for a few minutes until you feel completely relaxed. Breathe in peace and relaxation and as you breathe out let go of the tension from your mind and body.

MASSAGE SURFACE

Sensual massage can take place on a bed or on a firm well-padded surface. Spread out on the floor a thick duvet, two or three blankets, a sleeping bag or a futon. Use plenty of cushions or pillows to make your lover comfortable and relaxed during the massage.

When your lover is lying on his/her back place a cushion or pillow under the head and another one under the knees to take the pressure off the lower back. When your lover is lying on his/her front place a pillow or cushion under the shoulders one under the ankles and one under the abdomen if desired.

For your own comfort, and to avoid sore knees, make sure that you have something to kneel on too. You need to be just as relaxed as your lover.

Make sure your lover has plenty of cushions for comfort, otherwise the sensual atmosphere will be spoilt.

Essential Oils

using erotic

Essential oils can greatly enhance a sensual massage and increase sexual arousal. The combination of touch and aroma is very potent. However it is vital to remember that pure essential oils are highly concentrated and should NEVER be applied undiluted. They should be blended with a suitable carrier oil in the appropriate dilution. Please follow these guidelines:

- •3 drops of essential oil to 10 mls of carrier oil
- •4-5 drops to 15 mls of carrier oil
- •6 drops to 20 mls of carrier oil

A teaspoon holds approximately 5 mls and a complete sensual massage should never require more than 4 teaspoons of carrier oil (i.e. 20 mls). Do not be tempted to use more essential oil. This will not make the formulation more effective and it could create an unpleasant side effect such as a skin reaction.

To begin with, referring to the directory in the Aromatherapy section, choose just ONE of these essential oils: frankincense, ylang ylang, cedarwood, neroli, bergamot, jasmine, geranium, black pepper, patchouli, rose, clary sage, sandalwood or ginger. After you have mixed up your love potion, rub a small amount onto your lover's hand and smell it. If the aroma is pleasurable to BOTH of you then use it — if you both like the aroma it will have the desired effect. No one particular essential oil will appeal to everyone — aroma preference is a matter of personal taste. After you have acquired several essential oils try blending two or three together to create your own special recipes.

OTHER WAYS OF USING EROTIC OILS

There are numerous ways of using essential oils. Some of the simplest and most effective techniques for you and your lover are outlined here.

BATH — fill the bath and sprinkle in SIX drops of your chosen undiluted oil. Disperse the oil thoroughly and close the door so that the precious vapours cannot escape. Soak in the bath and allow the aromas to envelop you. Why not surround the bath with flickering candles and ask your lover to join you?

SITZ baths and BIDETS —Sitz baths are highly beneficial in cases of cystitis, vaginal discharges, thrush etc. They are also invaluable for protecting against infections and viruses. Simply add six drops of essential oil to a bidet or a bowl of hand-hot water. Agitate thoroughly and sit in it for about ten minutes.

SCENTING — scenting the room with essential oils helps to create the perfect sensual environment.

The combination of touch and aroma is irresistible, and enhances your sensual pleasure.

sensual massage
Techniques

STROKING

Stroking forms the basis of a sensual massage. In fact by varying your stroking movements you could carry out a complete sensual massage as it can be performed on any area of the body and can be varied enormously by changing the speed or pressure of the strokes.

Your movements can be long or short, firm or gentle, slow or brisk. These variations will help to keep your lover's interest and he/she will wonder what is coming next.

Stroking signals the beginning and the end of a sensual massage and allows you to flow from one technique to the next. It is a deeply relaxing movement, which establishes a sense of trust and allows your lover to feel loving and yielding as you gently caress the body. Stress and tension is relieved as muscles relax, circulation improves and toxins are eliminated from the body.

To perform this technique, the palms of both hands are used as you glide over the surface of the skin moulding your hands to the contours of the body part on which you are working. A steady, even pressure is applied through the palms of your hands as you glide over the body. On the return stroke use a feather light touch to return to your starting point. There are many different stroking techniques. Once you have mastered these it is a natural next step to create your own special strokes. Always use your intuition and be spontaneous.

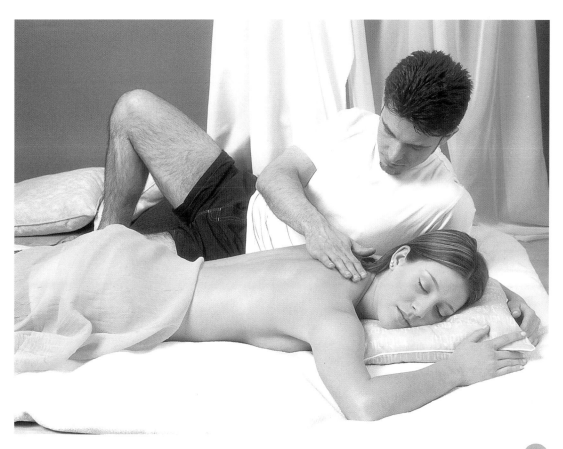

Stroking is one of the most important elements of a sensual massage. You will feel your lover relax as tension melts away.

LONG STROKING

To perform this movement, position yourself in a comfortable kneeling position at your lover's head. Place the palms of your relaxed hands side by side on their shoulders.

1. Stroke the entire back, using the palms of both hands, gliding down the sides of the spine.

2. When you reach the base of the spine, separate your hands and glide over the buttocks.

Allow your hands to glide back to your starting point without any pressure. Notice your lover's breathing as you perform this movement as well as your own. You will find that your breathing starts to follow the same pattern. You and your lover start to breath in and out at the same pace. A strong, deeply intimate connection is established.

CIRCLE STROKING
(ONE HAND FOLLOWING THE OTHER)

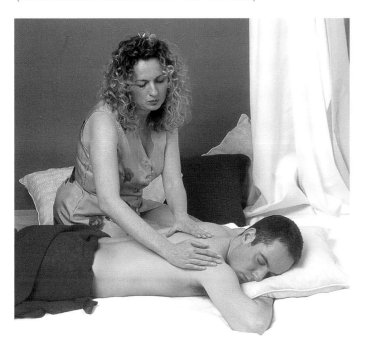

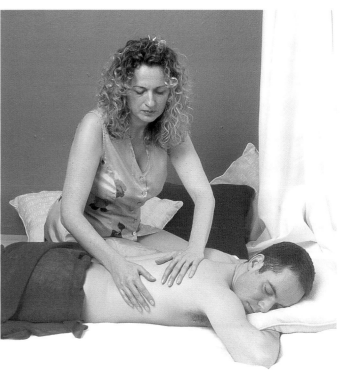

Position yourself to one side of your lover and place both hands on one side of the body around the shoulder blade. Using the whole of the palms of your hands, make large stroking movements in a circular motion.

Your hands will cross over as you perform your circles. Although you will have to lift one hand over the other, always keep contact with one hand. You may work right the way down your lover's body towards the buttocks and back up towards the shoulders again.

CIRCLE STROKING
(ONE HAND ON TOP OF THE OTHER)

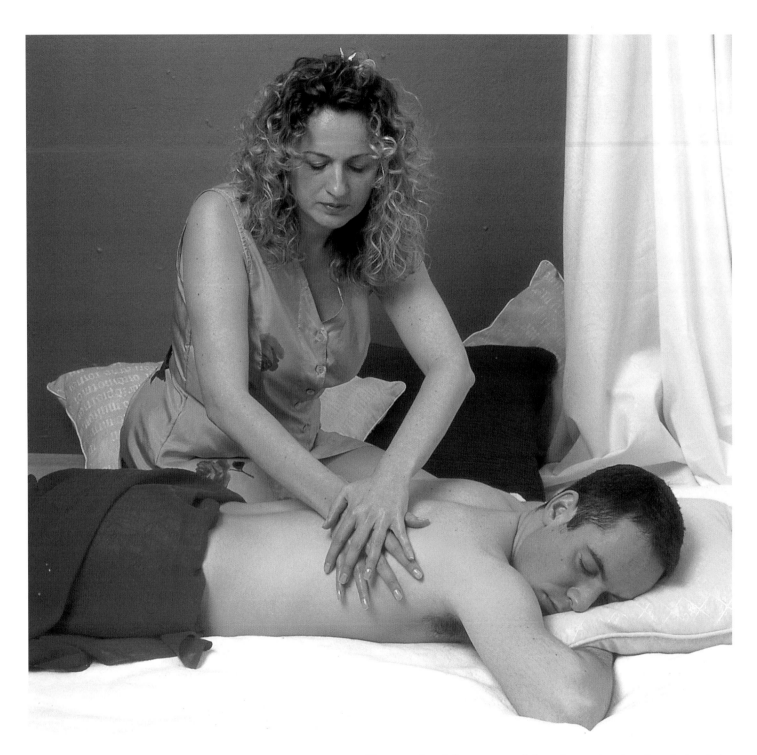

Place one hand flat on top of the other and, using the whole of the hand, make large circular movements working from the top of the shoulder blade down towards the buttocks. Then work from the buttocks up towards the shoulder blade. Repeat on the other side of the spine.

FINGERTIP STROKING
(ALTERNATE FINGERTIPS)

Position yourself at the side of your lover close to the buttocks — or you may even sit astride your lover. Starting at the top of the body, stroke down the back slowly using just the fingertips of one hand so that you are barely touching the skin. One hand follows the other. As your first hand reaches your lover's buttocks, lift it gently off as your other hand commences the movement.

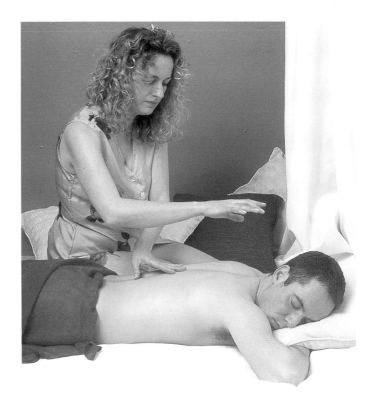

For some of the techniques, you may find sitting astride your lover is more comfortable — as well as making you feel closer.

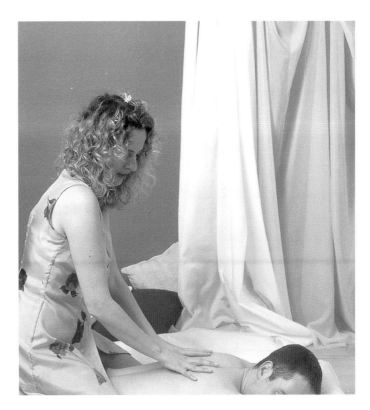

FINGERTIP STROKING – BOTH FINGERTIPS

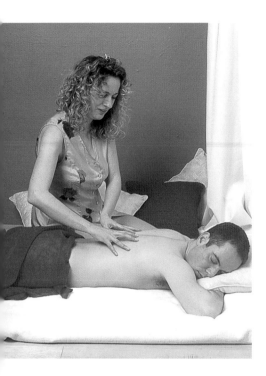

Sitting in the same position gently place both hands, fingertips down, at the top of your lover's shoulders. With both hands, stroke down the body on either side of the spine using just your fingertips. Most people find this movement very erotic.

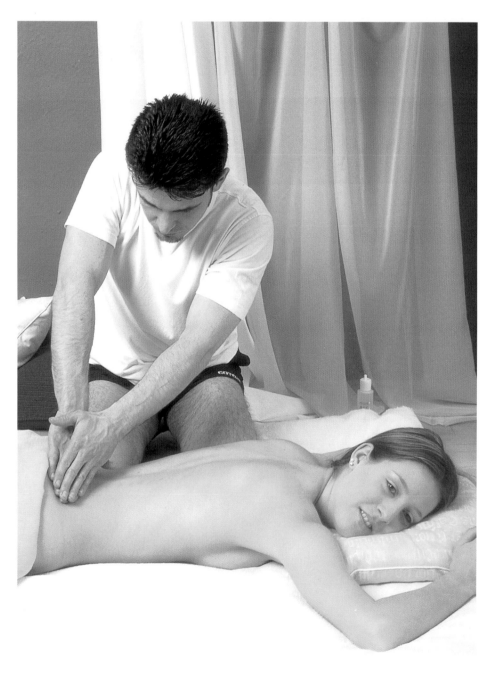

Gentle stroking with both hands is one of the most erotic massage movements.

CAT STROKING

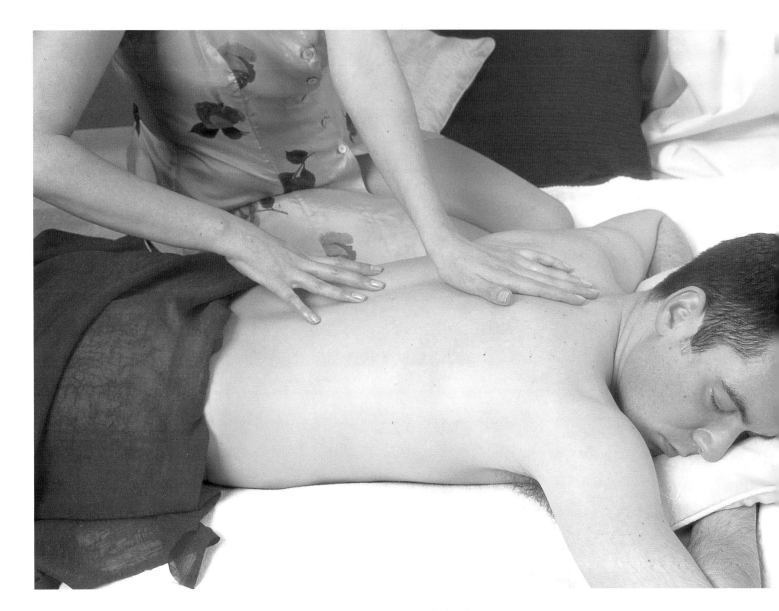

Position yourself to the side of your lover near the buttocks, and place the whole of your right hand palm downward at the base of the neck on the spine. Stroke your hand smoothly down the body using virtually no pressure. As your right hand reaches the buttocks, lift it off and repeat the movement with your left hand. Repeat these movements several times, one hand following the other. It should feel like one continuous movement.

DIAGONAL STROKING

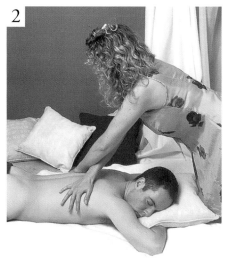

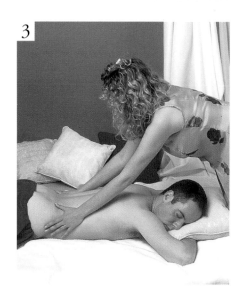

1. Kneel at your lover's head. Allow your hands to float down to rest, one hand crossed on top of the other at the base of the neck.

2. Move them slowly away from each other in opposite directions so that by the time they reach the sides of the body your hands and palms are making a 'V'.

3. Then slowly glide them back together again. Repeat this movement until you reach the buttocks and then work from the buttocks up to the neck.

STROKING WITH THE BACK OF THE HANDS

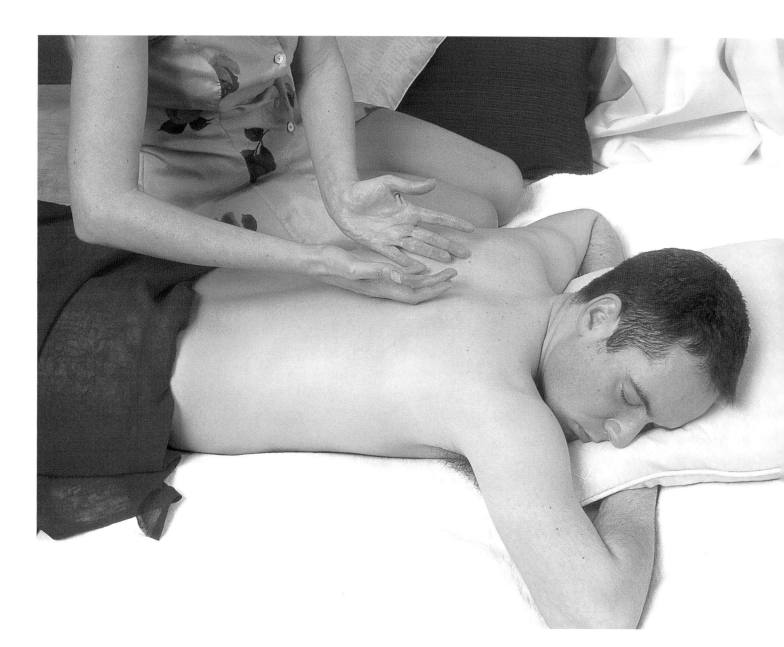

Position yourself to one side of your lover or sit astride him/her. Place the backs of both hands at the top of the body with each hand either side of the spine. Stroke them gently down towards the buttocks. As your hands reach the buttocks, glide back upward to the starting position travelling along the sides of the body.

DEEPER TECHNIQUES

Now that you have relaxed your lover and mastered the flowing movements of stroking you are going to work more deeply into the body with the following techniques.

KNEADING/WRINGING

Kneading is a very beneficial movement. It helps to relax tight muscles, increases the blood supply to the muscles being worked on and helps to get rid of toxins. It is used on fleshy areas such as the thighs, buttocks and hips. Here the shoulder is illustrated. Place your hands flat on the part to be treated and with one hand grasp and squeeze the muscle (not the skin) between your fingers and thumb and bring it towards your other hand. As you release, use the other hand to grasp a new handful of flesh.

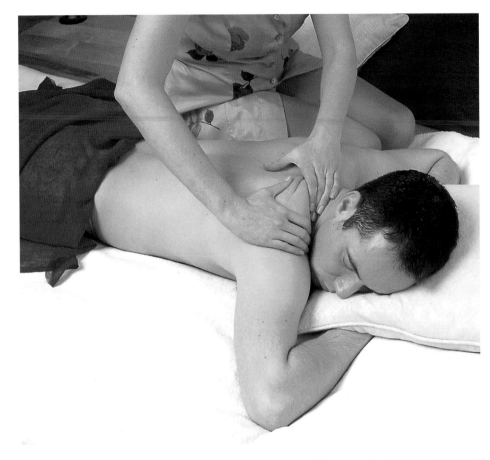

Alternately squeeze and release with both hands as if you are kneading dough. This technique is illustrated on the waist.

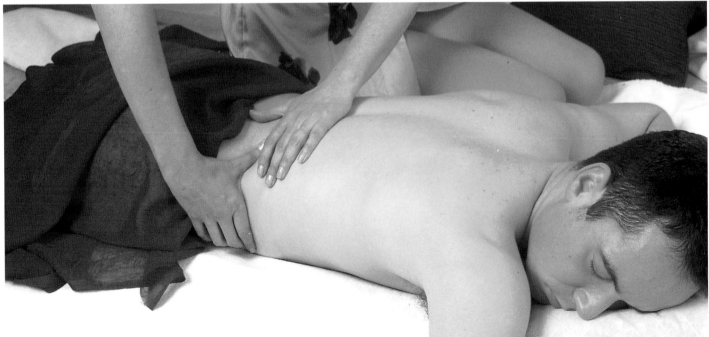

PULLING

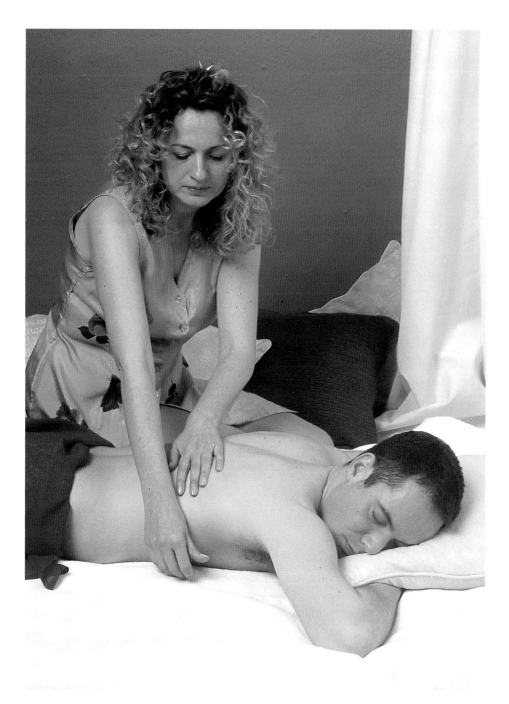

Now pull up the muscle with your other hand. As you pull up with alternate hands, gradually work your way up the side of the back. You may also work down the back. Repeat on the other side of the back.

Kneel comfortably by the side of your lover facing the buttock area. Place both hands on your lover's far side with your fingertips touching the massage surface. Lean over the body and pull up the muscle with your hand.

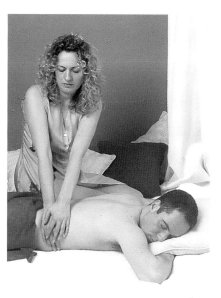

Pulling may also be performed using both hands at the same time.

PUSHING

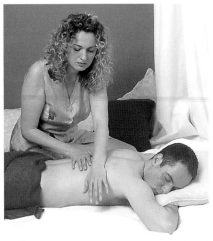

Work your way up your lover's back with pushing movements using alternate hands, one closely following the other. Perform this movement up and down the back. Now try it on the other side.

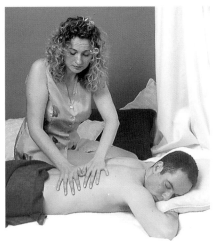

Position yourself as for the pulling technique. Place both hands on the opposite side of the back close to, but NOT touching, the spine itself.

Now try pushing using both hands at the same time.

PRESSURES/FRICTION STROKES

These movements allow you to penetrate deeper into the layers of muscles and to work around joints. Deeper pressure is particularly useful for dispelling tension, which builds up either side of the spine, and around the shoulder blades. Very gentle pressures are also used for the sexual arousal points mentioned in the Quick Reference Treatments chapter. The balls of the thumbs are usually used to perform pressure techniques although fingertips, heels of the hands, knuckles or even the elbows may be used.

Remember to always apply pressure gradually and slowly–

never prod sharply into the tissues or dig in with long nails. You will find it easier if you apply just a small amount of oil otherwise your thumbs will slide around and you will only be able to move the skin instead of the deeper tissues underneath.

Use your body weight to add greater depth to your pressure movements-the body is far less delicate than you might think. However, always ask for feedback, as you don't want to inflict any pain and discomfort on your lover.

THUMB PRESSURES

To perform pressure circles on the spinal muscles, position yourself at the side of your lover. Place both hands either side of the spine with the heels of your hands almost touching. Place the balls of your thumbs in the two dimples at the base of the spine. Make small outward circular movements with your thumbs.

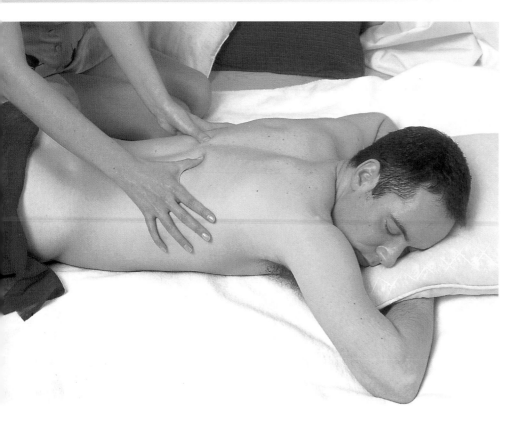

Gradually work up the back until you reach the base of the neck. When you first start it is likely that your thumbs will ache until they become accustomed to the pressure. Make sure that you don't hunch up or you will create knots in your own back and shoulders.

Now try this technique around the shoulder blade. Position yourself close to the shoulder, which you wish to treat. To make it easier you can ask your lover to put their arm behind their back, but if they find it at all uncomfortable or they are asleep leave the arm by their side.

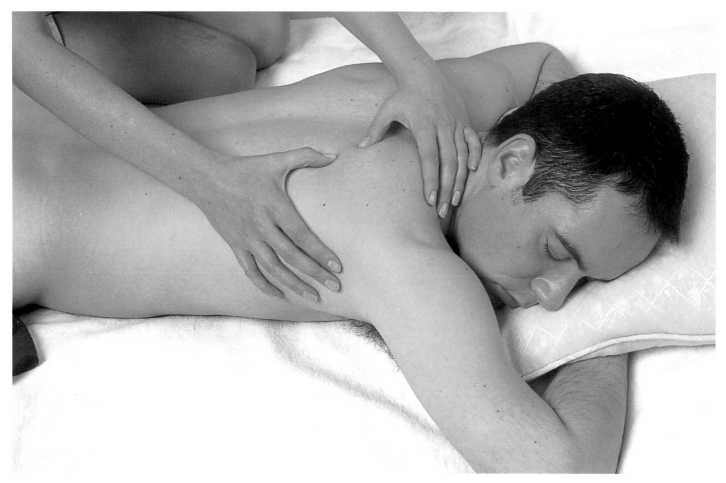

HEEL OF HAND PRESSURE

Instead of using the balls of the thumbs you are now going to use the heels of your hands to apply deep pressure. You will practice this technique on the back of the thigh. This is a wonderful movement for fleshy areas such as the buttocks and thighs.

Sit or kneel comfortably at the side of your lover and place the heels of your hands just above the back of the knee. Do NOT press into the back of the knee, which is a very delicate area. Push one hand gently but firmly into the flesh, working up the leg and then push with your other hand. Allow the heels of your hands to move alternately up the back of the thigh.

KNUCKLING

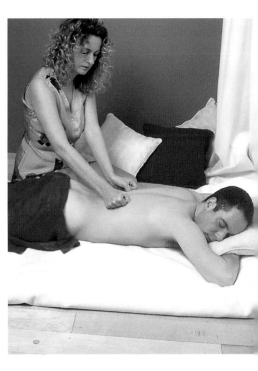

Knuckling feels wonderful when used on the shoulders, back, upper chest, palms of the hands and soles of the feet. Make your hands into loose fists and place them palms down onto the body. Rotate the middle section of your fingers around in a circular direction without taking your hands off the body.

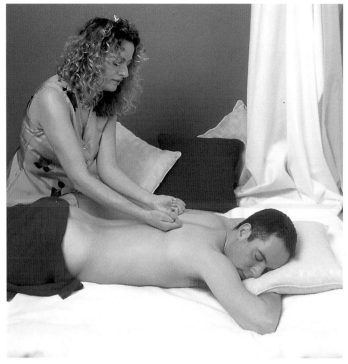

You can also perform this technique using a forward or backward motion instead of a circular motion. Again curl your hands into loose fists, place them on the area to be massaged and slide them forward into the skin. The back is an ideal place to use this technique.

This movement can also be done on the chest area.

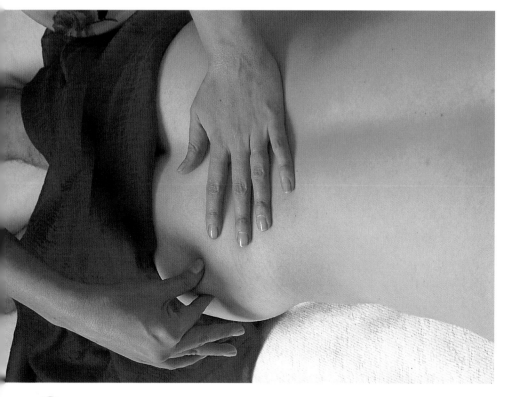

PLUCKING

This technique can be employed over fleshy, muscular areas such as the buttocks and thighs. As well as improving the circulation and toning the skin, plucking is very sensual. Place both hands, palms down, onto the buttocks. Gently pick up small areas of flesh between your thumbs and fingers and let them slip through your hands.

THE BACK

1. Tune in
2. Spreading the oil/long stroking
3. Alternate hands long stroking
4. Circle stroking
5. Stretching the back (hands)
6. Stretching the back (forearms)
7. Pulling up the sides of the back
8. Kneading the sides of the back
9. Circular thumb pressures on the spinal muscles
10. Pushing down the sides of the back
11. Circular stroking of the buttocks
12. Kneading the buttocks
13. Pressures on the sexual arousal points
14. Knuckling the buttocks
15. Plucking the buttocks
16. Circling both shoulder blades
17. Circular stroking of one shoulder
18. Thumb pressure around the shoulder blade

Repeat steps 17 — 18 on the other shoulder

19. Kneading the shoulders
20. Kneading the neck
21. Long stroking the whole back
22. Diagonal stroking
23. Cat stroking
24. Stroking with the back of the hands
25. The final touch — fingertip stroking

BACK OF THE LEG

1. Tune in
2. Long stroking (both legs)
3. Kneading the leg
4. Knuckling the thigh
5. Alternate heel of hand stroking up the back of the thigh
6. Plucking the thigh
7. The final touch — alternate fingertip stroking

Repeat steps 3 — 7 on the other leg

FRONT OF THE BODY

FOOT AND FRONT OF THE LEG

1. Greeting and stroking the foot
2. Kneading the foot
3. Spreading the foot
4. Push and pull the foot
5. Toe loosening
6. Freeing the ankle
7. Long stroking of the front of the leg
8. Kneading the thigh
9. Circular thumb pressures on the thigh
10. The final touch — fingertip stroking

Repeat all steps on the other foot and front of the leg

ARM AND HAND

1. Tuning in
2. Stroking the arm
3. Kneading the upper arm
4. Kneading the forearm
5. Loosening the wrist
6. Moving the wrist
7. Stroking the hands
8. Opening the hands
9. Stretch and squeeze the fingers and thumb
10. Circling
11. Fingertip stroking of the hand
12. The final touch — stroking of the arm

Repeat all steps on the other arm and hand

CHEST AND NECK

1. Tuning in
2. Opening up the chest
3. Circular pressures
4. Knuckling
5. Releasing neck tension
6. Side stroking the neck
7. The final touch — back of the hand stroking of the chest and neck

FACE

1. Tuning in
2. Stroking the forehead
3. Stroking the cheeks
4. Stroking the chin
5. Pressure circles on the face
6. Massaging the ears
7. The final touch — stroking the hair

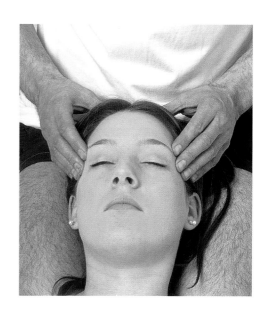

ABDOMEN

1. Tuning in
2. Circling the navel
3. Circle stroking
4. Pull
5. Kneading
6. The final touch — fingertip circular stroking

sensual massage for
Common Problems

Making love should be a beautiful experience. However, problems can arise which interfere with our sexual enjoyment. This chapter explores how sensual massage and flower essences can help you to overcome any difficulties so that you can enjoy your sex life to the full.

WOMEN

BREAST TONING

Women are never totally happy with the size of their breasts and it is unfortunate that to some it becomes an obsession. Usually women desire larger breasts and the following formulae may not increase size, but they will certainly help to tone the breasts and give them a more attractive appearance.

To 10 mls (two teaspoons) of carrier oil add:
1 drop of geranium
1 drop of fennel
1 drop of clary sage

OR

To 10 mls (two teaspoons) of carrier oil add:
1 drop of geranium
1 drop of lemongrass
1 drop of rose

Massage each breast outwards towards the underarms in a circular direction every day, and you should notice an improvement after a couple of months.

Geranium is an excellent oil for helping to tone the breasts.

INFERTILITY

Massage is very successful for treating women's infertility. Obviously if there is a serious physiological problem then it is unlikely that essential oils can succeed. However, there are many women who are unable to conceive for no reason at all.

Sensual massage is the perfect solution for relieving all the stress and anxiety which surrounds the longing for a baby.

The essential oil that seems to enjoy the most success is rose otto. Any of the formulae below can aid conception.
Massage them into the lower back (shown here) and abdomen daily. They should also be used as a prelude to making love when ovulation is due.

To 10 mls (two teaspoons) of carrier oil add:
1 drop of rose otto
2 drops of geranium

OR

To 10 mls (two teaspoons) of carrier oil add:
2 drops of clary sage
1 drop of melissa

Gentle massage of the lower back is an effective way to aid fertility in women.

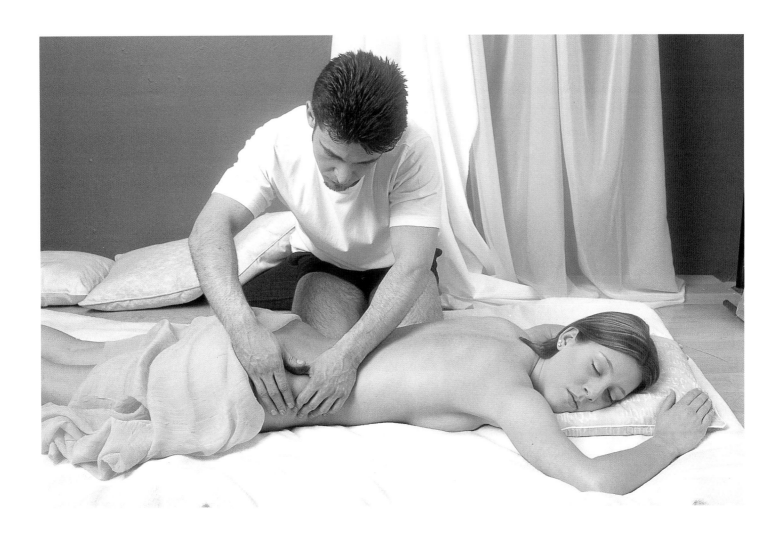

LOW SEX DRIVE

Whether you wish to increase your libido or you have an aversion to sexual intercourse, sensual massage is beneficial. Tiredness and anxiety due to work pressures and family or money worries will deplete any woman's sex drive. Women who are bored or left unsatisfied will also have a poor sexual appetite.

Sensual massage used alone will boost libido but when combined with one or several of the erotic oils, is more powerful. Remember that the aromas you like best will be particularly effective. Some of the most effective oils for increasing desire in women are bergamot, clary sage, frankincense, jasmine, myrtle, neroli, patchouli, rose, sandalwood and ylang ylang.

Any of the erotic oils can be used daily in your bath. One of the following blends should be applied for at least two weeks paying particular attention to the thighs, abdomen, lower back and buttocks to ensure that all the sexual arousal points are stimulated.

To 10 mls (two teaspoons) of carrier oil add:
2 drops of bergamot
1 drop of neroli

OR

To 10 mls (two teaspoons) of carrier oil add:
2 drops of myrtle
1 drop of rose

Myrtle and ylang ylang are just two of the essential oils used to boost libido.

To raise a low sex drive, massage of the sexual pressure points, such as those situated on the lower back and buttocks, can be very effective.

VAGINAL DRYNESS

Lack of vaginal secretion makes intercourse uncomfortable or even impossible. It is not usually caused by a woman finding her lover unattractive. Anxiety, the menopause or the contraceptive pill are far more likely to be the culprits.

Prior to intercourse, a small amount of jojoba carrier oil applied to the vagina is a temporary solution. However, daily baths or regular massage with one of the formulae will have a longer lasting effect.

Baths
3 drops of clary sage
2 drops of geranium
1 drop of rose

OR

1 drop of melissa
2 drops of neroli
3 drops of sandalwood

Massage
To 10 mls (two teaspoons) of carrier oil add:
1 drop of geranium
1 drop of neroli
1 drop of sandalwood

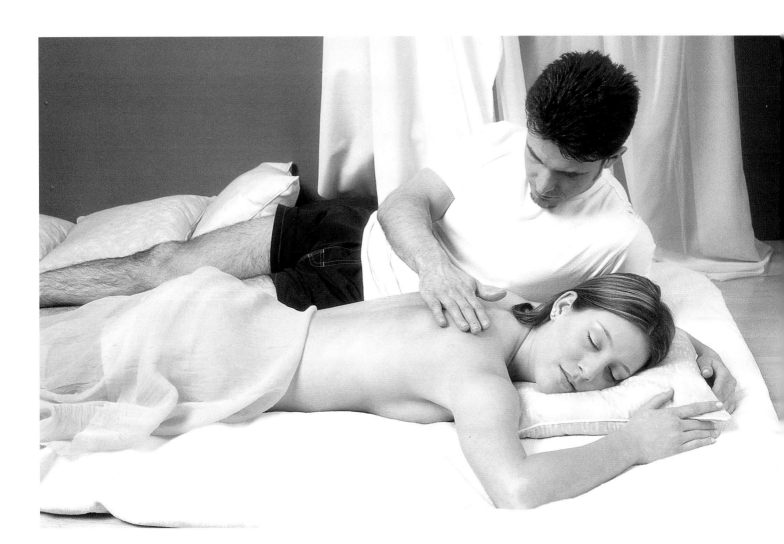

Regular massage with one of the suggested oil blends can ease feminine discomfort.

MEN

IMPOTENCE

Although drugs such as Viagra can improve your sex life, there will obviously be unwanted side effects. Sensual massage offers a natural alternative for boosting a man's sex drive.

Impotence is the most common male sexual disorder and it affects most men, often temporarily, at some point in their lives. Psychological factors such as stress, lack of confidence, guilt or depression can all lead to impotence. Physical illnesses such as diabetes can also be the cause, as can various drugs such as antidepressants, diuretics and blood pressure tablets.

A daily bath with one of the erotic essential oils is recommended. Suitable oils include black pepper, cedarwood, clary sage, frankincense, ginger, jasmine, neroli, rose, sandalwood and ylang ylang.

Sensual massage of the abdomen, thighs and back will also help with particular attention to the sexy stimulation points. Do not expect immediate results it may take two weeks or it may take two months.

To 10 mls (two teaspoons) of carrier oil add:
1 drop of black pepper
1 drop of cedarwood
1 drop of ginger

OR

To 10 mls (two teaspoons) of carrier oil add:
1 drop of neroli
1 drop of ginger
1 drop of sandalwood

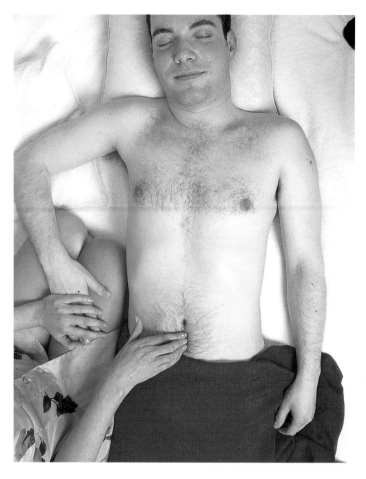

Massage of the sexual massage points, such as those on the abdomen can aid impotence.

Another way to boost the male sex drive is sensual massage of the thighs.

LOW SPERM COUNT

Both the quality and quantity of sperm is rapidly falling, and because of this male infertility is becoming more common. At the present time sperm defects are responsible for a quarter of all cases of infertility. However, fertility can be increased in the following ways.

1. There are several essential oils that may increase the sperm count. The most effective of these appear to be jasmine and rose. Make up a massage oil using two drops of jasmine and one drop of rose to 10 mls (two teaspoons) of carrier oil. Pay particular attention to the lower back area and the lower muscles of the abdomen to stimulate the production of sperm.

2. The optimum temperature for sperm production is 35ºC, and if the testicles are too warm then the production of sperm is affected. Therefore men should avoid tight underwear, hot baths and saunas. Immersing the scrotum in cold water for at least ten minutes twice a day is also said to increase sperm production.

3. Smoking lowers both the quality and quantity of the sperm so stopping is vital.

4. Heavy drinkers have a low sperm count. Therefore men should not exceed more than 21 units per week.

5. Diets also have an important part to play. More fruit and vegetables (especially organic) are excellent, as are vitamins C and E, selenium and especially zinc.

6. Stress is also a contributory factor as it adversely affects the quality of semen. Regular sensual massage at least twice a week can significantly reduce it.

Jasmine and rose seem to be the most effective oils for increasing sperm count.

The lower abdomen contains sexual pressure points that can be stimulated to increase sperm count.

Diet also plays an important role in maintaining male fertility. Ensure that plenty of fresh fruit is eaten regularly.

flower Remedies

Flower essences can help us to unlock our full potential and resolve our sexual difficulties. These remedies come from all corners of the globe and provide an excellent way to balance mind, body and spirit. Those remedies, which can help you overcome sexual difficulties are described here.

As well as the essential oils described in this book, there are a wide variety of Flower remedies from around the world that can be used to treat and ease problems and ailments.

Mixing a Remedy

You will need a 30ml tinted dropper bottle, some spring water and a little brandy. Fill the dropper bottle almost to the top with spring water and add a teaspoon of brandy to preserve your remedy. You may use apple cider vinegar as a substitute for the brandy if you prefer. Put 2 drops of each of your chosen essences into the bottle.

How Often to Take the Remedy

Take seven drops three times a day either straight onto the tongue or in a glass of water, juice or herbal tea. The remedy should be administered for ten to fourteen days. In chronic cases they may need to be taken for a longer period.

Essences from the Australian Bush

Australian aborigines have used flowers for thousands of years to heal the emotional and physical problems. Australia has the world's oldest and largest number of flowering plants. It is also one of the most unpolluted countries.

Billy Goat Plum
Useful for sexual revulsion or disgust of oneself. This remedy will enable you to relax and enjoy sex.

Flannel Flower
For those who have a dislike of being touched, particularly males. Flannel flower encourages sensitivity and sensuality.

She Oak
For infertility, particularly if there appears to be no reason.

Wisteria
For women who have a fear of intimacy, frigidity. Their fear may have arisen from sexual abuse. This remedy encourages a fulfilling sexual relationship.

Essences from Europe — Bach Flower Remedies

Crab Apple

For self-disgust. This is a remedy that helps to cleanse away traumas from the past, e.g. sexual abuse.

Larch

For boosting confidence and dispelling feelings of inadequacy. Excellent for problems such as premature ejaculation, impotence and frigidity.

Olive

For tiredness and exhaustion. This remedy helps to boost libido.

Mimulus

For fear of failure, e.g. fear of premature ejaculation, fear of sex, fear of intimacy, etc

White Chestnut

For any sexual worries which circulate in the mind.

ESSENCES FROM INDIA

Cannon Ball Tree

For frigidity in women who are very fearful of sex.

Ixora

For couples who have lost sexual interest in each other. This remedy will enhance sexual activity.

Meenalih

For people who try to repress their sexuality as they have been brought up to believe it is sinful.

Rippy Hillox

For those who are fearful about sex due to a traumatic experience in the past e.g. rape.

Water Lily

For anyone who is inhibited about sex.

NORTH AMERICAN FLOWER ESSENCES

Black-Eyed Susan

For those who have repressed traumatic sexual experiences such as rape or incest.

Easter Lily

For those who feel that sex is impure and unclean.

Hibiscus

For women who are unresponsive to sex — often due to prior sexual abuse.

Sticky Monkeyflower

For those who have a fear of sexual intimacy.

HAWAIIAN FLOWER ESSENCES

Amazon Swordplant

For those who need to break down their emotional blocks.

Avocado

For those who have a fear of being touched. This remedy promotes relaxation and sexual pleasure.

Day-Blooming Waterlily

For those who have a negative mental attitude towards sex due to feelings of fear, guilt and inadequacy. This remedy encourages sexual fulfilment.

Lehua

For increasing sensuality in both men and women

Night Blooming Waterlily

For developing and enriching a close sexual relationship.

Spider Lily

For men who are afraid of relation-ships with women.

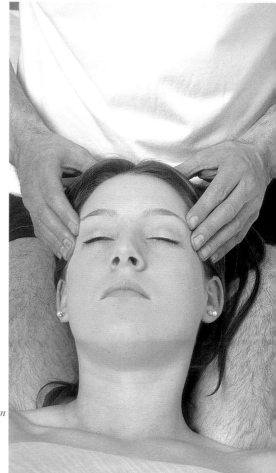

One drop of your chosen flower essence may be added to your massage blend to help to ease sexual problems.

introduction to
Reflexology

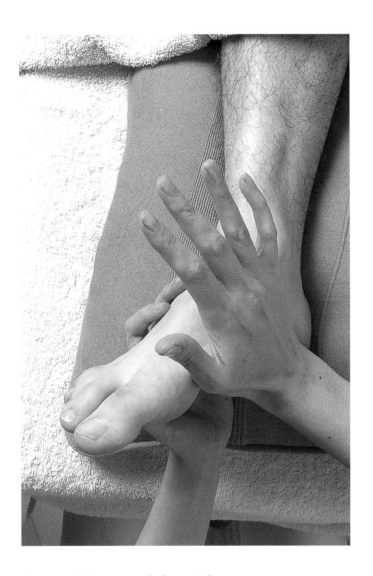

Pressure applied to areas on the feet can influence corresponding regions of the body. This simple movement encourages the spine to relax.

Reflexology is a simple, non-invasive, harmless and natural way to optimum health. It is easy to perform, and no special equipment is required in order to practise it. All you need are your hands and a willing partner. Firm pressure is applied through the thumbs and fingers to reflex points which are located on all parts of the feet. By applying pressure on these points, all the organs, glands and structures of the body can be stimulated and encouraged to heal.

This section will enable the complete beginner to soothe away the stresses and strains of everyday life and promote well-being. It will also allow you to alleviate a whole host of common conditions such as headaches, backache, digestive problems, menstrual problems, arthritis, coughs and colds, insomnia and much more. It is important to realise, however, that reflexology should not be used instead of orthodox medical treatment – if problems persist then medical advice should be sought. Reflexology must also never be used to diagnose illness. Diagnosis is the prerogative of the doctor.

Reflexology has enormous physiological and psychological benefits on all the systems of the body.

THE BENEFITS OF REFLEXOLOGY

1.   Reflexology induces relaxation

Stress is a part of our everyday life, and if we do not manage stress properly then the body's defences break down, making us more susceptible to illness. It is generally conceded that 75% to 80% of ailments are attributed to stress and reflexology is capable of inducing a state of deep relaxation and tranquillity. The alpha state of relaxation is generated during a treatment which leads to a level of consciousness at which healing can take place. During a reflexology session most people will fall asleep and awake refreshed and restored with a wonderful sense of well-being and inner harmony.

Calming accessories can aid relaxation.

2.   Reflexology is preventative health care

Reflexology boosts the immune system and thus prevents illnesses and diseases from occurring. As the reflex zones on the feet are treated, the natural healing forces within the body are released and mobilised, restoring the body to harmony. Since the time of Hippocrates, health has been defined as a balanced state and disease as an unbalanced state or dis-ease. Instead of passively waiting for the harmony to fall into disorder, which allows health problems to develop, reflexology aims to achieve this homeostasis. Patients who receive regular reflexology treatments report that they are far less susceptible to catching colds and flu even though everyone around them may be coughing and sneezing. Reflexology has effectively strengthened their immunological defences and thus enhanced their health.

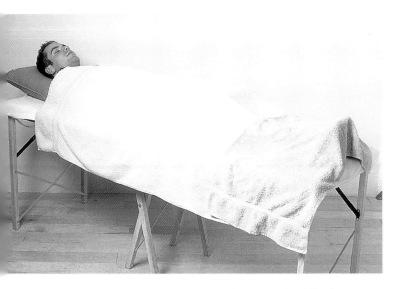

A reflexology treatment is so relaxing that the patient often falls asleep.

3.   Reflexology improves the circulation

It is vital for blood to flow freely throughout the body as it carries essential oxygen and nutrients to the cells. Circulation can become sluggish and the blood flow can be restricted and impeded. Reflexology can improve the blood flow to every part of the body.

4.   Reflexology detoxifies the body

The lymphatic system and the systems of elimination such as the colon, kidneys and skin are responsible for the detoxification of the body. If they are not functioning properly then toxins will build up. These waste deposits can be palpated by sensitive fingers on the reflex zones of the feet like small grains of sugar and can be broken down by reflexology massage and eliminated.

5   Reflexology revitalises energy

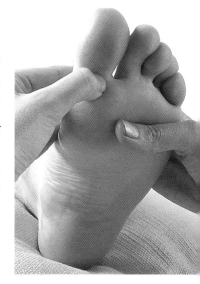

Reflexology regenerates and opens up energy pathways, revitalising the body and supplying it with renewed and invigorating energy. We are all very much aware of when our 'batteries' are low, and many individuals feel tired and lethargic all the time. It is vital that we recharge our batteries with reflexology as often as we are able.

6   Reflexology improves mental function

Toxins can be identified as small grains, and broken down during a reflexology treatment.

Reflexology calms the mind and relieves it of all unnecessary 'clutter'. Thus mental alertness is restored, thoughts can be clarified and new ideas can be stimulated.

7   Reflexology stimulates emotional release

Reflexology can adjust emotional imbalances in the body. During treatments, unresolved emotional problems are encouraged to rise to the surface and can then be dealt with. Many physical ailments stem from an emotional source. Negative states of mind will block the free flow of the life force and cause disease. As the old, unwanted emotions are released, changes in attitude and personality often take place and balanced health is restored.

origins and principles of
Reflexology

Reflexology is an ancient therapeutic treatment for activating the innate healing powers of the body. Ancient techniques of pressure have been practised for thousands of years by many different cultures. It is widely thought, although never proven, that reflexology has its origins in China over 5,000 years ago. However, the first evidence depicting the practice of reflexology comes from Egypt. In Saqqara, in the tomb of Ankmahor, an Egyptian physician, an ancient painting which dates back to around 2330 BC depicts treatments of the hands and feet actually taking place. The hieroglyphics are as follows:

"Do not let it be painful." (patient)
"I shall act so you praise me." (practitioner)

Illustration from Ankmahor's tomb in Saqqara, Egypt. Dated around 2330 BC.

Our modern concepts of reflexology originated with the zone therapy of the American physician Dr. William Fitzgerald (1872-1942). Born in Connecticut, he graduated from the University of Vermont in 1895 and practised at Boston City Hospital, the Central London Ear Nose and Throat (E.N.T.) Hospital and also in Vienna. Dr. Fitzgerald became the head physician in the ear, nose and throat department at St. Francis's Hospital, Connecticut and it was from here that he made the medical profession aware of his 'zone therapy'. Dr. Fitzgerald discovered that if pressure was applied to specific areas or points on the body, an anaesthetic effect could be induced. Not only could pain be relieved but also the conditions producing the pain.

In 1917 Dr. Fitzgerald, together with his colleague Dr.Edwin Bowers, published a book entitled 'Zone Therapy, Relieving Pain at Home', and devised a dramatic demonstration for convincing sceptics of the theory's validity. First they applied pressure to a volunteer's hand, then stuck a pin into the anaesthetised area of the person's face – with no apparent pain.

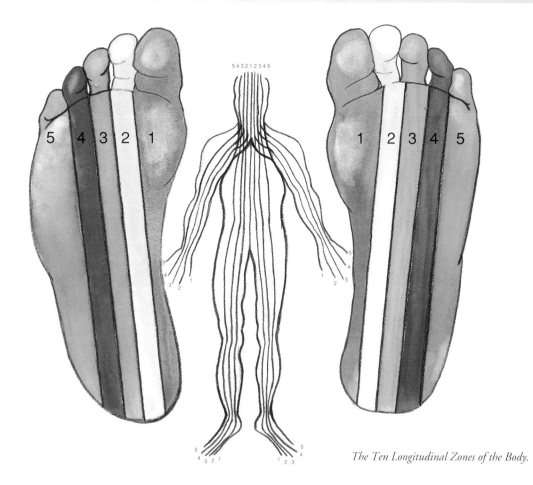

The Ten Longitudinal Zones of the Body.

In this book, Fitzgerald divided the body into ten longitudinal zones of equal width running the length of the body from the tips of the toes to the head and out to the fingertips and vice versa. He claimed that if a line is drawn through the centre of the body there are five zones to the right of this mid-line and five zones to the left of it. Zone one runs from the big toe, up the leg and centre of the body to the head and then down to the thumb. Zone two runs from the second toe, up to the head and down to the index finger. Zone three extends from the third toe, up to the head, down to the third finger and so on. All organs and parts of the body lie along one or more of these zones. Stimulating any part of a zone in the foot by applying direct pressure affects the entire zone throughout the body.

Dr. Fitzgerald's theories began to spread across America. Although many in the medical profession were sceptical about his work, Dr. Joseph Shelby-Riley, a chiropractor, was a true believer. Fitzgerald taught zone therapy to Shelby-Riley and his wife Elizabeth who were both keen practitioners. Dr.Shelby-Riley wrote several books including 'Zone Therapy Simplified', (1919). He is renowned for introducing Eunice Ingham, a physiotherapist, to zone therapy.

Eunice Ingham (1879-1974) is considered to be the founder and mother of modern reflexology. It was through her work that foot reflexology was born in the early 1930s. In 1938 she published 'Stories the Feet Can Tell', followed by the sequel 'Stories the Feet Have Told'. These classic texts are still used by reflexologists today.

She mapped out the entire body on the feet which she viewed as being a mirror or a mini-map of the body. When Eunice retired in the 1970s after dedicating her life to reflexology, her work was continued by her nephew Dwight Byers.

Reflexology was introduced into Britain in the 1960s by Doreen Bayley (1900 - 1979) who had trained with Eunice Ingham.

Apart from the longitudinal zones, the feet can also be divided into transverse or horizontal sections. Transverse zones were first described by the German reflexologist, Hanne Marquart, who also trained with Eunice Ingham. The four transverse lines are as follows:

A. The shoulder girdle line located just below the base of the toes.

B. The diaphragm line located just below the ball of the foot.

C. The waist line in the middle of the foot in the centre of the arch of the foot.

D. The pelvic line just above the heel.

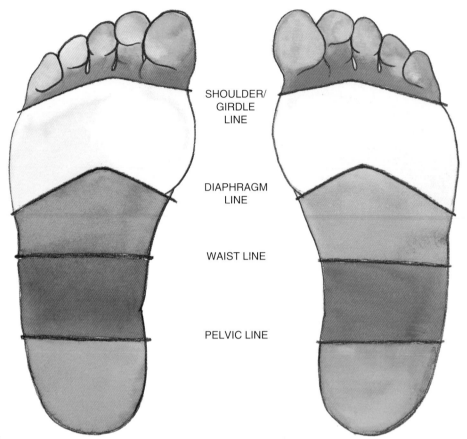

The Four Transverse Zones.

These imaginary lines help us to map out the body on the feet. All the organs and structures of the head and neck lie above the first transverse zone – the shoulder girdle line.

All organs above the diaphragm on the body will be represented above the diaphragm line on the foot.

All organs below the diaphragm are found below the diaphragm line on the foot.

The feet precisely mirror the body. The right foot corresponds to the right hand side of the body, while the left foot reflects the left hand side. Paired organs such as the lungs, kidneys or ovaries are found one in each foot. Single organs such as the liver or spleen are found either in the right or the left foot according to where they are located in the body.

The spine, which is in the centre of the body, is found in both feet along the inside (medial aspect) of the foot. Outer parts of the body such as the shoulders, knees and hips are found on the outside (lateral aspect) of the foot.

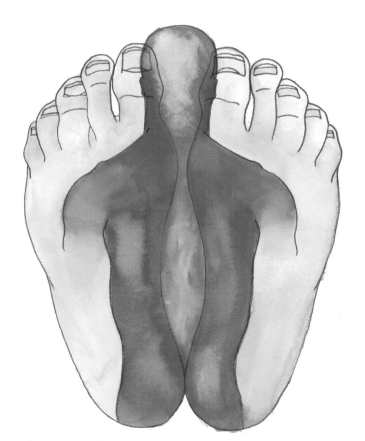

The Feet Mirror the Body.

Getting started

CREATING THE RIGHT AMBIENCE

Reflexology does not require any complicated or expensive equipment. All you need are your hands, your intuition and the desire to help others. Although reflexology can be performed almost anywhere it is well-worth creating the right environment to allow the recipient to derive maximum benefit from a treatment.

The surroundings should be as peaceful as possible. As the aim of your treatment is to induce relaxation, the noise of telephones, children or traffic will not help create a healing atmosphere. Take the telephone off the hook and make sure that your family know that you are carrying out a treatment. Some people will enjoy listening to relaxation music in the background during their reflexology. Others will prefer silence to help them relax. It is entirely up to individual preference.

SETTING OUT YOUR ROOM

The room should be very warm and inviting. Although only shoes and socks are removed, some loss of body heat is inevitable as the treatment progresses. Warmth will encourage feelings of security and relaxation. Lighting should be soft and subdued. Bright lights should be dimmed or even switched off and replaced with candles. Tinted bulbs can also provide the perfect setting. You may wish to burn some essential oils or some incense prior to your treatment or have a vase of fresh flowers in the room to enhance the environment.

Small clay burners for diffusing essential oils are readily available and reasonably priced. Put a few teaspoons of water into the loose bowl on the top and sprinkle a few drops of your chosen essential oil into it. Light the night light and allow the wonderful aromas to diffuse into the atmosphere. Suitable essential oils for creating an atmosphere of relaxation include lavender, clary sage, geranium, jasmine, neroli, ylang-ylang or rose.

Candles can enhance the ambient atmosphere needed for reflexology.

A few drops of soothing aromatic oil in a burner provide an added effect.

Fresh flowers help create a relaxing environment.

Place a pillow under the receiver's knees for added comfort.

It is important to sit with a correct posture in order to perform reflexology effectively.

POSITIONS FOR WORKING

A professional reflexologist will use a massage couch but it is not essential to buy one. You may decide to invest in one later on but for home use, a bed is all that you require. The receiver should lie down with his/her feet at the foot of the bed. Pillows should be placed under the head to support the neck and to allow you to observe any facial expressions. You may also wish to place a pillow under the receiver's knees to take any pressure off the lower back. A pillow or cushion placed under the foot that you are working on may be useful for your own comfort. It is important that you are just as relaxed as the receiver.

Position yourself on a swivel chair or a stool within easy reach of the receiver's feet in a relaxed upright manner. Your legs and knees should be slightly apart, your feet on the ground and your shoulders should be down and relaxed. If there is any tension in your body then the receiver will almost certainly be aware of it. Tense hands cannot move smoothly, and they will be unable to feel any abnormal reflex areas in the feet.

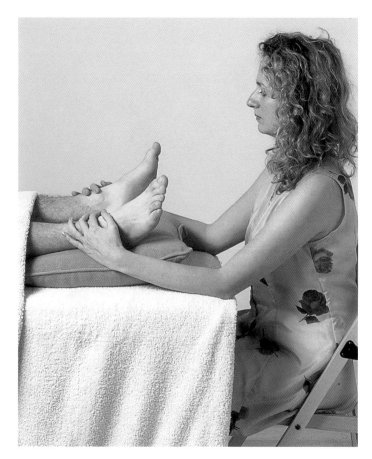

If a couch or bed is unavailable, reflexology can be easily practised on the floor.

You may prefer to work on the floor using a well-padded surface. Place a thick duvet or two or three blankets on the floor. Either kneel or sit cross-legged and rest the receiver's foot on your lap or on a pillow. You will still need pillows or cushions under the receiver's head and the knees.

Some people like to work with the receiver sitting on a chair but this will not suit everyone. It is not as comfortable for either the giver or the receiver. It also seems to encourage conversation and it is important to keep talking to a minimum for best results. Relaxation is essential to allow both of your energies to flow freely throughout the treatment.

A light blanket or towel should be used to cover up the receiver even though the clothes are not removed. As the treatment progresses there will be some loss of body heat.

Any restrictive clothing such as ties and belts should be removed to allow the energies to flow freely. You should also remove any jewellery from your hands to avoid scratching. Ensure that your fingernails are closely clipped to avoid any discomfort. Always remember to wash your hands both before and after a treatment.

Ensure hands are clean and nails are clipped before beginning a treatment. Remove jewellery.

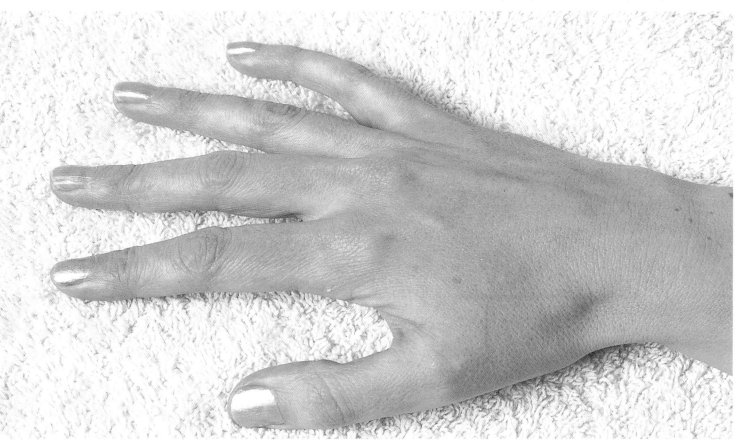

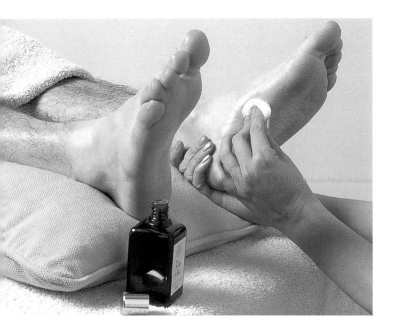

Rosewater is ideal for cleansing the feet.

REFRESHING THE FEET

You may wish to cleanse the feet prior to a reflexology session. Sweaty, unpleasant smelling feet can cause embarrassment to the receiver and are not pleasant to work on either. You may want to soak the feet for a few minutes in a bowl of warm water, or simply wipe feet gently with moist cotton wool. Add a few drops of essential oil of lavender, tea tree, lemon or peppermint to the water to relax and cleanse feet. If you do not have any essential oils you may add a sprig of fresh lavender or peppermint from your garden or squeeze some fresh lemon juice into your bowl. Rosewater is excellent for cleansing the feet. However you decide to refresh the feet always dry them thoroughly. Avoid using oils or creams during your treatment. Too much lubricant will make it difficult for you to hold the foot properly and will cause your walking thumb or finger to slip. A barrier will also be created, decreasing your sensitivity and making it difficult for you to detect any abnormalities. Some people use talcum powder on the feet, but this can be messy, and may block up the pores.

Essential oils should never be applied undiluted to the skin. To make up a massage blend just three drops of essential oil are added to two teaspoons of cold-pressed, unrefined, additive-free carrier oil such as sweet almond or apricot kernel. You may prefer to add your essential oils to a pure organic skin cream in the same dilution. To a 30gm amber coloured glass jar add up to 9 drops of essential oil to create an excellent foot cream.

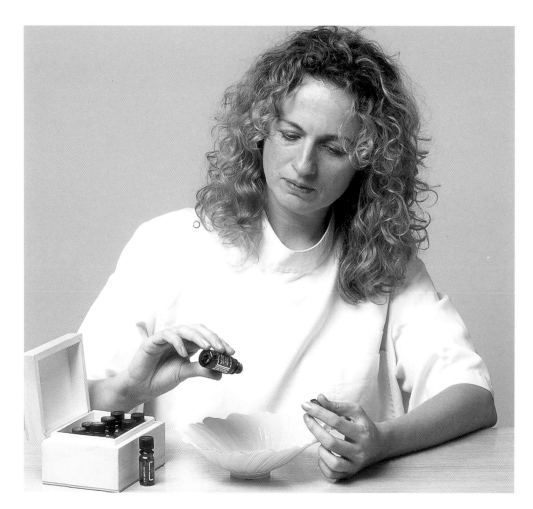

Oils can be mixed to create an individual massage blend to be used at the end of the treatment.

REACTIONS FROM REFLEXOLOGY

Both during and after a reflexology treatment, physical and psychological changes may occur. All responses should be seen as positive and highly desirable as reactions show that the body's self healing mechanism is being activated. The body is trying to expel unwanted toxins. Reactions have been divided into those which may occur during a treatment and those which may appear between treatments.

Possible reactions during a treatment

- Changes in expression
- Visible contraction of the muscles e.g. shoulders
- A feeling of deep relaxation and the desire to sleep
- A warm glow as energy blockages are released
- Feelings of euphoria
- Sensations of the body expanding and spreading as it relaxes
- Shooting sensations as blockages release
- Running nose if the head zones are being treated and are blocked
- Twitching or tingling
- Warmth in the area of the body being worked on

Possible reactions between treatments

- A state of deep relaxation
- An alteration in sleep patterns eventually leading to deep sleep
- More frequent and noticeable dreams
- Emotional changes with a greater awareness of feelings
- Increased skin activity – pimples, rashes, increased perspiration. Eventually skin tone and texture improves
- Increase in urination
- Cloudy or unpleasant smelling urine
- Bowels move more frequently
- Increase in bulk and volume of the stools
- Nasal discharges
- Coughing and secretions from the bronchi
- Colds
- Sneezing
- Watery eyes
- Sore throat
- Fever
- Vaginal discharges
- Toothache
- A need to drink more water to flush away the toxins
- Previous illnesses which have been suppressed may flare up temporarily and then disappear.

IMPORTANT – these reactions NEVER occur simultaneously.

After a treatment one or two reactions MAY occur.

141

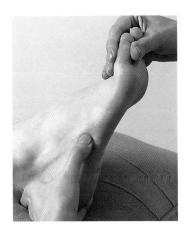

Contra-indications to Reflexology

NEVER USE REFLEXOLOGY IN THESE CIRCUMSTANCES:

- Immediately after surgery until the doctor has pronounced complete recovery
- When the receiver is suffering from a fever – the body is already fighting off toxins and a reflexology treatment would release more toxins into the system
- If the receiver has an infectious skin conditions such as scabies, as you do not want to spread the condition or infect yourself. NB: Conditions such as eczema and psoriasis are NOT infectious and should improve with treatment.
- If the receiver suffers from thrombosis – reflexology could move a clot
- During pregnancy where there is an element of risk especially during the first 12-14 weeks or if the pregnancy is complicated

Be careful of:

- Corns and calluses – use gently pressure if they are painful
- The pancreas reflexes when treating a diabetic
- Pressure when treating a diabetic. Use less pressure, as the skin can be thinner, bruises easily and diabetics may heal more slowly
- The heart area if there are cardiac problems or if the receiver has a pacemaker
- Over treating any one particular area
- After a heavy meal – wait a couple of hours before treatment

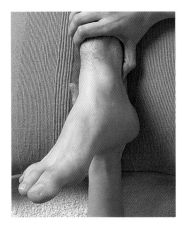

Never:

- Diagnose or promise to cure a condition
- Apply strong pressure. A treatment should NEVER be painful
- Press directly over a cut, bruise, recent scar, painful area or severe varicose vein

basic reflexology
Techniques

In this chapter you are going to learn the basic techniques which you will be using in your reflexology routine. Please ensure that your nails are trimmed before you start so that they do not scratch or dig into the receiver's foot. Reflexology should NEVER be painful. Your pressure should be firm yet not uncomfortable. If the receiver flinches or tries to withdraw his or her feet then you are pressing too hard. Every individual's feet will be different – some are much more sensitive than others. As you work, use your intuition and watch the facial expressions of the person receiving treatment. Adjust your pressure accordingly.

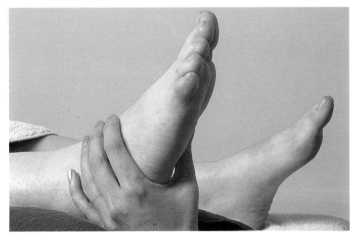

HOLDING TECHNIQUE

To be a good reflexologist it is important to hold the foot correctly so that the reflex zones can be easily reached, accurately pinpointed and stimulated. You need to develop good teamwork between your hands as you will always be holding and working the foot with your two hands. One hand is used to support and hold whilst the other hand will work the reflexes.

To work on the right foot place the heel of your left hand against the outer aspect of the foot. Wrap the fingers of your left hand lightly over the front of the toes and the thumb under the back of the toes.

This position allows you to support and control the movement of the foot very effectively. The foot can be pushed backwards away from you brought towards you or even twisted slightly.

Practice this holding technique on the left foot too. This time your right hand will act as the holding hand leaving your left hand free to work on the reflexes.

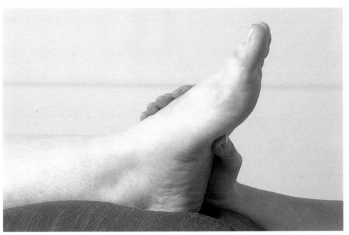

REMEMBER
Do not grip the foot too tightly

Thumb/Caterpillar Walking Technique

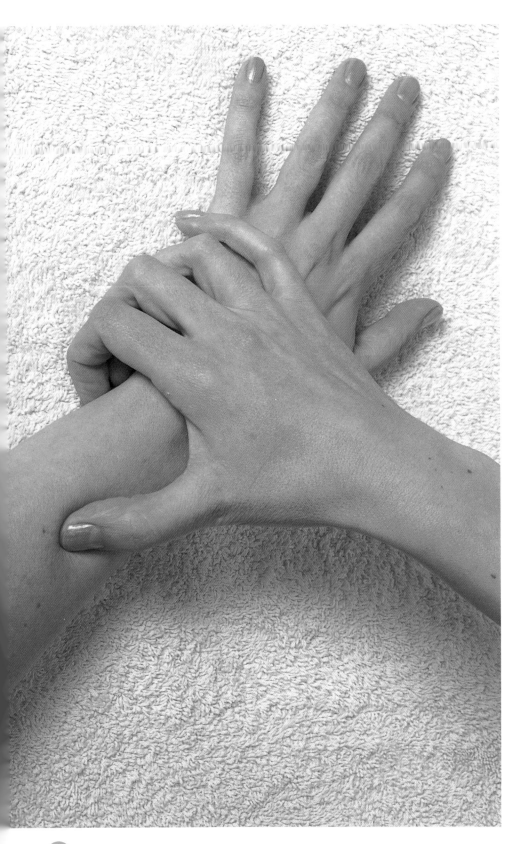

This movement is performed with the outer edge of the thumb.

To find this point place your hand palm downwards onto a table and notice the tip of the thumb that touches the surface of the table – this outside tip is to be the working area of your thumb.

Strength in reflexology is made possible by the appropriate use of leverage, and leverage is achieved by the use of the four fingers in opposition to the thumb. First of all practice the caterpillar walking on the palm of your hand or on your forearm.

To walk the thumb bend ONLY the first joint of the thumb slightly and then unbend the joint slightly. Only allow the thumb to take very SMALL steps as it walks along the hand/forearm. The walking movement is always performed forwards never backwards nor sideways. You should aim to maintain a constant, steady and even pressure. An on-off-on-off pressure should not be felt at each bend of the thumb. Do not worry if your thumbs start to ache or feel sore at first. With practice your thumbs will increase in tolerance and build up strength. Do not be discouraged – be patient and keep trying. As the thumb is walking, the four fingers should be moulded to the contours of the hand/forearm. The four fingers should be kept together comfortably to ensure maximum leverage. If they are spread out then some of the leverage will be lost.

Then practice thumb walking up each of the five zones along the entire length of the foot. Ensure that you are holding the foot correctly with your supporting hand wrapped around the toes. Work from the base of the heel in zone five up towards the base of the little toe – see sequence 1–3.

Now work from the base of the heel in zone four up towards toe four and repeat this thumb walking up each of the other zones. Then walk up each of the five zones on the other foot – see sequence 4–6.

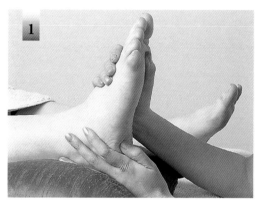

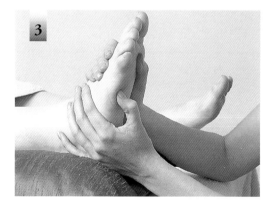

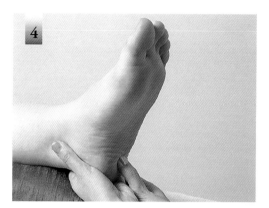

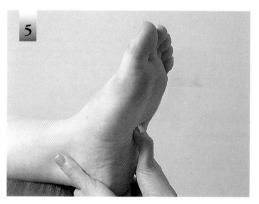

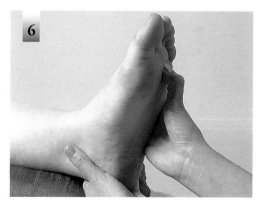

REMEMBER

- Ensure that you are holding the foot properly
- Use the outer edge of the thumb
- Do not dig your nail into the skin
- Bend only the first joint of the thumb slightly

- Employ a constant, steady pressure NOT on-off-on-off pressure
- The thumb always moves FORWARDS, never backwards or sideways

FINGER WALKING

The finger walking technique is basically the same as the thumb walking technique. The first joint of the index finger is used.

Excellent places to practice your finger walking are on the back of your hand or on your forearm. Use the corner edge of your index finger as you walk forwards taking the smallest bites possible while exerting a constant, steady pressure. Leverage is obtained by the use of the thumb in opposition to the fingers.

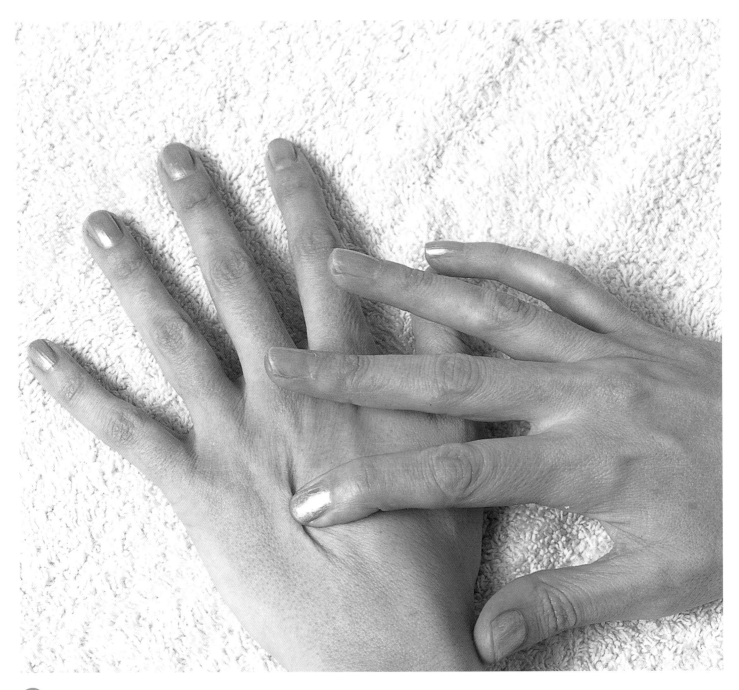

Once you have mastered finger walking with the index finger, try using your other fingers. (1) Any finger may perform this technique.

Now try the technique on the receiver's foot. Usually only one finger is used at any one time (2).

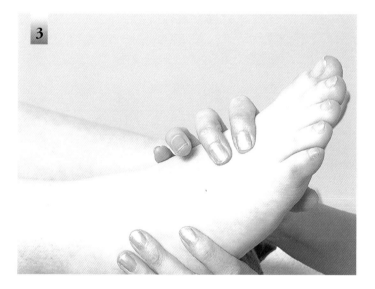

However, two or more fingers may sometimes be used, for example when working across the top of the foot (3).

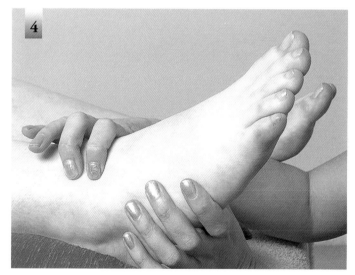

Finger walking is the most appropriate technique when working on bony and sensitive areas such as the top of the foot and around the ankle (4).

REMEMBER

- Take only very small steps to cover the area
- Do not dig in your nails or press too hard
- Always move your index finger **forwards**, not backwards or sideways

HOOK IN AND BACK-UP/PINPOINTING TECHNIQUE

This technique is used to apply pressure to specific points, and requires great accuracy. Certain points on the feet are either too small or too deep for the walking techniques to be used effectively. However, this very precise technique should never be employed when covering a large area. It is ideal for contacting the tiny reflex points such as the pituitary gland which is found on the big toe.

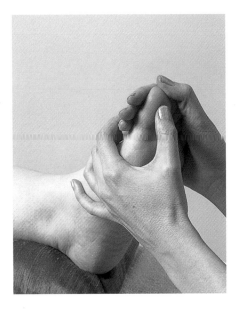

Once again the outside edge of your thumb will be your contact point.

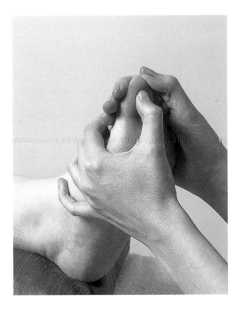

Place the thumb of your working hand onto your chosen reflex point. Apply pressure with your thumb to this point. (In this case the pituitary gland).

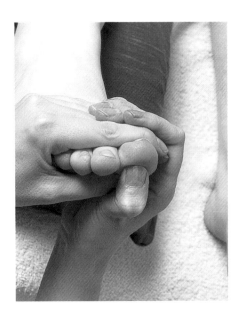

Now pull back across the point with the thumb. Push in, then back up. You may repeat this technique several times.

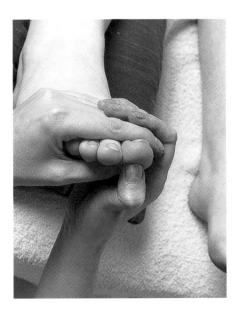

This technique has been likened to a bee inserting a sting. A bee lands on a spot and backs the stinger into your flesh. Your thumb lands on a small point and hooks in and backs up.

REMEMBER

- Never use the very tip of your thumb otherwise your nail will dig in
- Use the flat pad part of the outside edge of your thumb

PRESSURE CIRCLES ON A POINT

This technique is particularly recommended for working on tender reflexes or sensitive areas on the foot.

Hold the foot comfortably with one hand and place the flat pad part of the thumb of the other hand onto the tender area. Here the solar plexus area is illustrated. Press slowly into the area and circle your thumb gently over the area several times. After a few pressure circles any tenderness should have diminished.

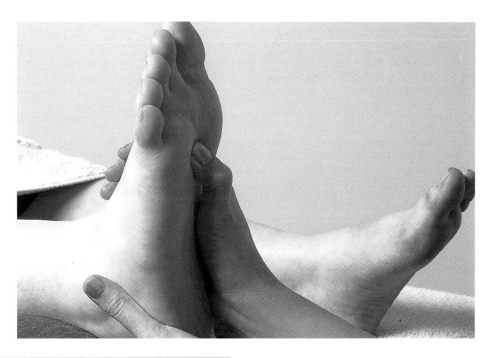

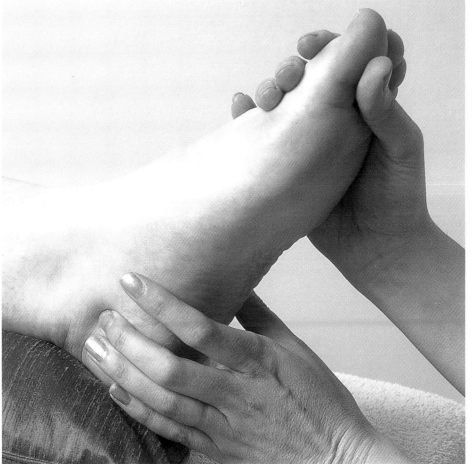

The thumb is always used for this technique apart from the uterus/prostate and ovary/testicle points where the index or the third finger is used. Here the uterus area is illustrated.

REMEMBER
- Do not dig in with your fingernails
- If the tenderness does not diminish, leave the area and return to it later

---

ROTATION ON A POINT

This technique may also be used on any tender reflexes.

Support the foot comfortably with one hand and place the pad of the thumb of your other hand onto the relevant reflex point. With your holding hand, flex the foot slowly into the thumb.

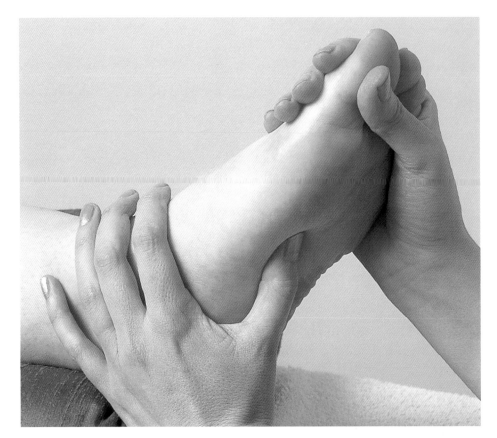

Rotate the foot in a circular motion around the thumb. In this illustration the technique is performed on the kidney reflex.

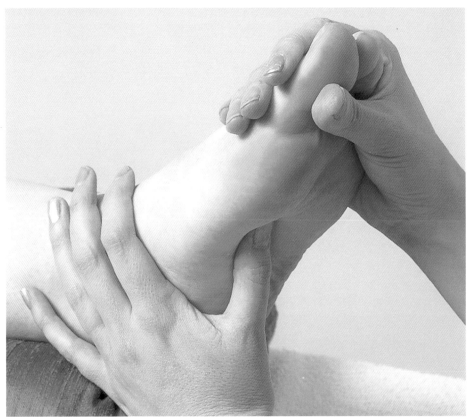

REMEMBER
- Rotate the foot slowly with your holding hand for maximum relaxation
- Ensure that you are not digging in with your thumbnail
- Do not allow your thumb to slip off the reflex point

reflexology relaxation
Techniques

Relaxation techniques are always used prior to a reflexology treatment. They are designed to put the receiver at ease and to help to establish a relationship of trust. Someone having their feet worked on for the first time is bound to feel a little nervous and often worries that the treatment will feel ticklish. These techniques will help to dispel any initial nervousness. They will also loosen any muscular tension in the feet and make them soft, supple and easy to work on.

Use these techniques in any order, and repeat some of them throughout your reflexology treatment. It is not necessary to master all of them so choose your favourites. As your confidence grows it is quite acceptable to create your own.

Use a few relaxation techniques at the end of a complete treatment as a 'dessert' to enable the receiver to gain maximum benefit and pleasure.

TUNING INTO THE FEET

To begin the relaxation sequence, hold both feet. Take a few deep breaths allowing all the tension to flow out of your body. You should be able to and feel the receiver completely relax.

As you tune into the person you are treating, imagine the healing energy flowing freely through your hands and body.

REMEMBER

- Use no oils or creams for your preliminary relaxation sequence (although they may be used at the end of the treatment)
- Make sure that you remove rings, bracelets and watches before you work
- Check that fingernails are short and even

EFFLEURAGE/STROKING

Using both hands, stroke the whole foot firmly covering both the top, the sides and the sole of the foot.

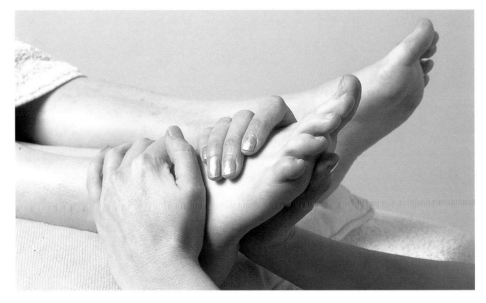

Work up from the toes, gliding around the ankle bones and back again.

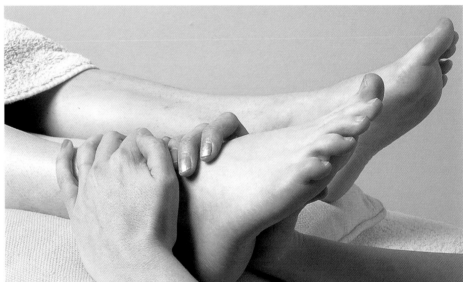

Repeat this movement several times. Stroking relaxes, increases blood flow and helps to disperse any excess fluid especially around the ankles.

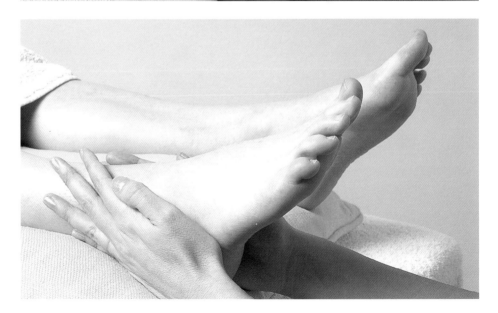

METATARSAL KNEADING

If working on the left foot, hold the top of the left foot with your right hand just below the base of the toes. Your hand should 'wrap' around the foot, with your thumb on the sole of the foot and fingers on the top of the foot. Make a fist with the left hand and place it on the fleshy area on the ball of the foot.

Work from the ball of the foot to the heel using a gentle circular motion.

This technique helps to soften the tissues on the sole of the foot.

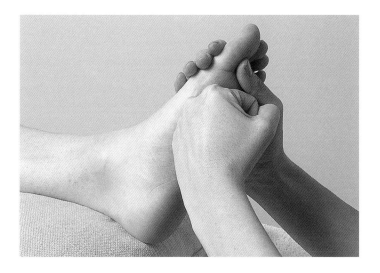 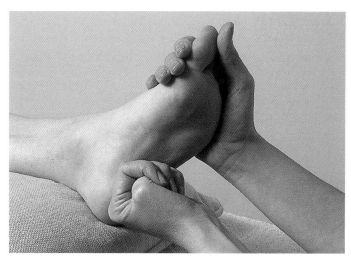

ALTERNATE THUMB ROTATIONS

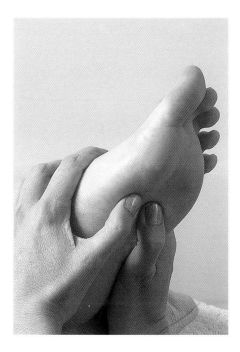 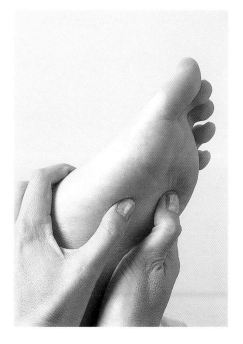 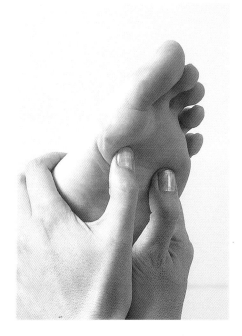

Grasp one foot with both hands so that your thumbs are on the bottom of the sole of the foot and your fingers are on the top.

Rotate one thumb at a time using small circular movements – alternate right thumb clockwise, left thumb anti-clockwise.

Work up from the heel towards the toes.

ZIG-ZAG/SPREADING THE FOOT

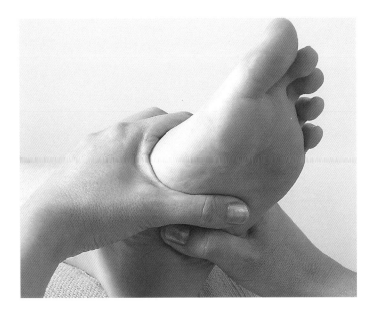

Hold the foot with both hands so that the balls of the thumbs are placed flat against the sole and the fingers are flat on top – one hand will be slightly higher than the other.

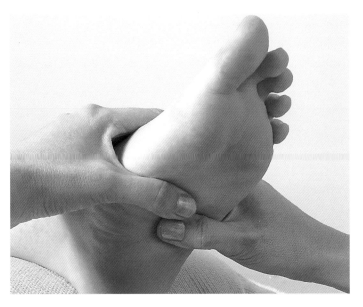

Pull the thumbs away and past each other towards the edges of the foot and then allow them to slide back towards each other.

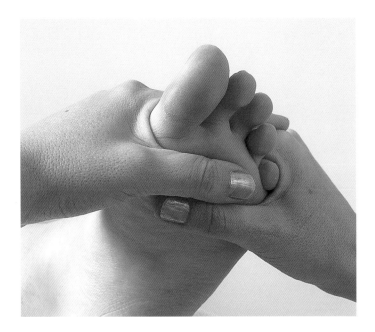

Work the thumbs in this zig-zag movement from the base of the toes to the base of the heels and back again.

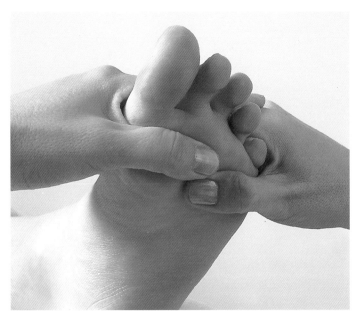

Feel that you are opening out the foot.

FANNING THE SPINE (SPINAL STROKING)

Cup the heel of one foot so that it is resting in the palm of your hand. This holding technique is first illustrated on the left foot to show hand position clearly.

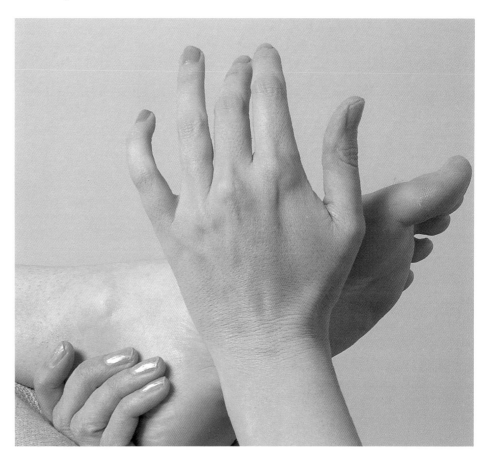

With the heel of the other hand stroke firmly down the inside (medial aspect) of the foot working from the big toe towards the heel. This movement is illustrated on the right foot.

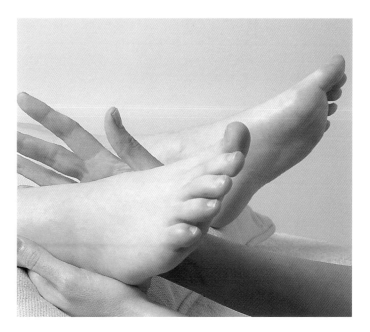

As the inside edge of the foot corresponds to the spine, this technique will encourage the spine to relax and is excellent for neck and back pain sufferers.

SPINAL TWIST/PUSH AND PULL

 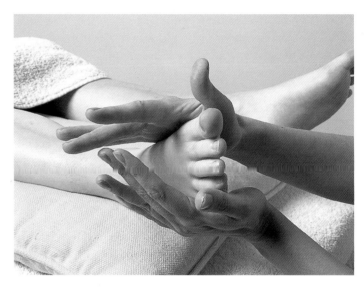

Place one hand on the inside of the foot and your other hand on the outside of the foot. Using the heels of the hands pull the outside of the foot towards you with one hand as you push the inside of the foot away from you, and vice versa.

Work along the edges of the foot from the heel to the toes and back down again. Perform these movements slowly to further relax and improve mobility in the spine.

Twisting the bottom of the foot loosens the lower back and working either side of the ball of the foot loosens the upper back and alleviates stiffness in the shoulders.

TOE LOOSENING

Support the foot gently with one hand, thumb on the sole of the foot, fingers wrapped around the top of the foot. Using your thumb and index finger close to the base of each joint, gently stretch each toe and then rotate each toe both clockwise and anti-clockwise (sequence 1–3) This technique will increase the flexibility of the toes and will also loosen the muscles around the neck and shoulders.

ANKLE ROTATIONS

Support the heel in one hand, thumb on the outside of the ankle, fingers on the inside.

Grasp the top of the foot in your other hand and slowly and gently rotate the ankle several times in one direction (1) and then in the other direction (2). This movement helps relaxation, and increases mobility in the lower back and pelvis.

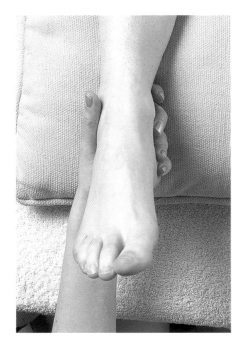

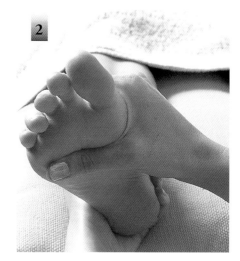

FOOT ROCKING

Place the palms of your hands one either side of the foot. Move them alternately and rapidly from side to side so that the foot vibrates.

This movement stimulates circulation and relaxes the muscles in the foot, ankle and calf.

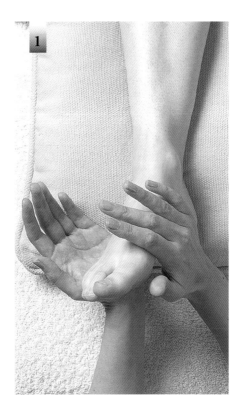

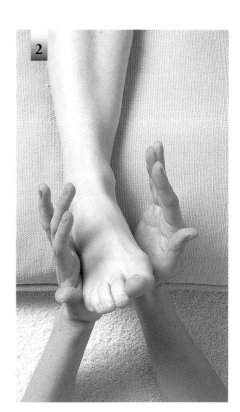

LOWER BACK RELEASE

Grasp under the heels of both feet.

Lean backwards, and slowly and gently pull the feet towards you. Release the stretch just as slowly.

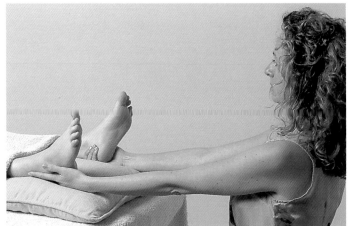

SOLAR PLEXUS/DIAPHRAGM RELEASE

The solar plexus is the main area which stores our stress and tension. Applying pressure to this area encourages a state of relaxation and also helps the breathing to deepen and slow down. This is the ultimate in relaxation techniques. It should always be used to complete a treatment. The solar plexus release may be performed on one or both feet.

To locate the solar plexus, place one hand over the top of the upper part of the foot and squeeze gently. A hollow will appear on the sole of the foot at the diaphragm line this is the solar plexus (1).

Release the foot, remembering where this point is. Now find the solar plexus on the other foot.

Take the left foot in your right hand and the right foot in your left hand, fingers on top, thumbs on the bottom. Place your thumbs onto the solar plexus reflex. Press the solar plexus reflex very gently and slowly (2). Hold for a few seconds. Release your pressure gradually but do not lose contact with the feet. Do this several times.

You can synchronise this technique with the receiver's breathing. Ask them to take a deep breath and, as they do, press into the solar plexus. As they slowly breathe out you should release your pressure on the points.

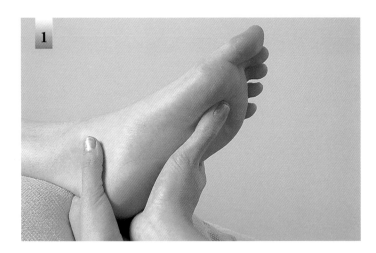

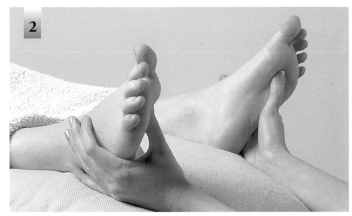

beginning a reflexology Treatment

A complete treatment should be around 45 minutes, but individual's needs may vary.

INTRODUCTION

Now that you have familiarised yourself with the basic techniques and have mastered some of the reflexology relaxation techniques you are ready to work on the reflex points.

Remember that you should never diagnose conditions – this is the prerogative of the medically qualified only. Reflexology is not a substitute for orthodox medical treatment. If the receiver has a problem which does not resolve then always seek the advice of a medically qualified doctor.

LENGTH OF TREATMENTS

The timing of treatments and the amount of pressure used varies from individual to individual depending upon their needs. A complete treatment with practice will probably take you about 45 minutes. For your initial treatment allow at least an hour. When working on a child, the younger the child the shorter the treatment. A baby would only need a five minute treatment consisting of stroking movements whereas an older child of 12 would be able to receive about 30 minutes. A treatment would also be shorter if you are working on elderly or very sick people. Reflexology is suitable for all ages and it is rare to find someone who will not benefit from treatment.

Do not be tempted to spend too long on a treatment. If the session is too lengthy then there is the possibility of overstimulating the body. This could cause excessive elimination resulting in diarrhoea or some other uncomfortable condition.

HOW MUCH PRESSURE TO USE

Applying excessive pressure can cause pain or discomfort.

It is important to work very gently during the first treatment session in order to see how the person reacts. The amount of pressure required will vary from one individual to another. If your partner feels as if he/she is being tickled then more pressure is needed. If the feet are jerked backwards away from you, then obviously you need to reduce the intensity of your treatment. Once you have established the right pressure you should sustain it evenly throughout the session.

It is interesting that a person will not necessarily always require the same amount of pressure. Factors such as emotional trauma or hormonal changes could well result in the feet becoming more sensitive. If the person is highly stressed or very debilitated then again light pressure should be used. Drugs such as painkillers or any medication that de-sensitises feeling will make the feet less sensitive.

As conditions improve you will probably find that you can use firmer pressure. However this does not mean that sensitive reflexes indicate an unhealthy person and insensitive reflexes mean a healthy person. Some unhealthy people can have very insensitive reflexes, whereas some healthy people have very tender feet.

Always stroke the foot at frequent intervals throughout the treatment. This is not only very pleasant and relaxing but also will help to disperse any toxins which have been released

WHAT TO DO IF AN AREA IS PAINFUL

If you discover any tender reflexes on the feet you should only use GENTLE pressure over these areas for a short time. Treatment should NEVER be applied continuously over the same reflex point. It is far more effective (and more comfortable) to return to any painful areas at frequent intervals and to return to them at the end of the treatment. Any uncomfortable areas should eventually disappear as health and balance are restored.

NUMBER OF TREATMENTS

After the first treatment it is highly likely that an effect will be experienced. Most reactions are very pleasant but some minor irritations may be felt as the body rids itself of any toxins. Any adverse reaction should pass within 24 hours. For optimum results and especially where there are minor ailments you should try to treat the receiver once a week for approximately seven treatments. Carrying out a complete treatment more than once a week is not recommended as this could result in an area being overstimulated. After the initial sessions, depending on how much time you have, once every 2 – 4 weeks is quite adequate.

If you want to pamper the receiver with more sessions it is quite acceptable to use the relaxation techniques as often as you like.

WHAT A TREATMENT FEELS LIKE

On the whole a treatment is extremely pleasurable and very addictive. Most people will fall asleep during a treatment which is excellent for healing. However, they may experience some strange sensations. Several people report feeling needle-like sensations, while others can experience a dull ache in certain areas of the foot. Tingling sensations may also be felt as blockages are released. Overall, however, your receiver will feel incredibly relaxed yet light and revitalised by the end of the session.

Stroking feet regularly will relax the receiver, as well as dispersing toxins.

THE TREATMENT

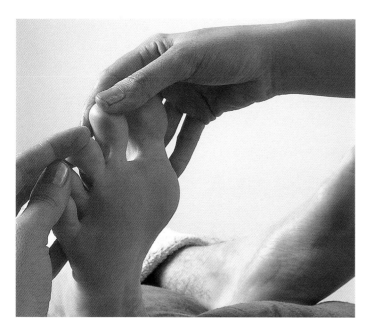

Check feet for tender areas before beginning treatment.

You are now ready to begin. Ask the receiver to lie on the bed or couch, make them warm and comfortable and if necessary cleanse the feet. Check for any cuts, bruises, corns, verrucae, ingrowing toenails etc. which could be tender or contagious. You will need to work gently on these areas or even avoid them altogether. Remember to always cover the foot you are not working on.

When working on one foot, always keep the other warmly wrapped.

PERSONAL PREPARATION

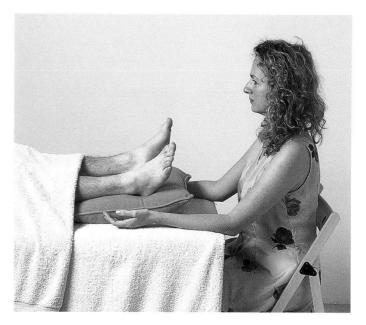

Ensure that you are calm and relaxed before beginning a treatment.

Before commencing your reflexology massage it is important to prepare not only the environment and the receiver but also yourself. You need to centre yourself, and clear your mind of all thoughts. Consciously release all tense areas of your body particularly your neck, back and shoulders. To do this take a few deep breaths and as you exhale feel the tension melting away leaving you relaxed and calm. As you breathe in draw in healing energy.

The order of the sequence can be simplified as follows:
1. Relaxation techniques
2. All toes – the head and neck area
3. Inside of the foot – the spine
4. Ball of the foot – the chest, breast, lungs, thyroid etc.
5. Arch/instep of the foot – the abdominal area containing organs such as the stomach, pancreas, intestines, kidneys etc.
6. Outside of the foot – joints such as the knee, hip, elbow etc.
7. Heel – the pelvic and leg reflexes
8. Ankles – the reproductive area and lymphatics
9. Relaxation techniques

Thus, you are going to work each foot in a logical manner from the toes down to the heels.

Treatments

BOTH FEET

- tuning into the feet.

RIGHT FOOT

RELAXATION TECHNIQUES

- effleurage/stroking
- metatarsal kneading
- alternate thumb rotations
- zig/zag spreading the foot
- spinal stroking
- spinal twist
- toe loosening
- ankle rotations
- foot rocking

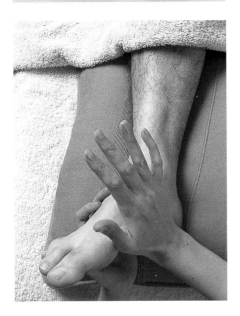

STEP BY STEP SEQUENCE

- solar plexus/diaphragm
- head and brain – thumb walk back and sides of the big toe
- pituitary gland – hook in and back-up technique on centre of big toe
- face – finger walk front of big toe
- neck
  - rotate big toe
  - thumb walk across back of base of big toe
  - thumb walk across front base of big toe
- sinuses – walk down the centre and two sides of the small toes
- teeth – finger walk down the fronts of the toes
- upper lymphatics – gently squeeze the webbing between each of the toes
- spine – caterpillar walk down the inside of the foot. Repeat walking up the foot
- eyes and ears – thumb walk along the ridge at the base of toes. Press into eye point – between toes 2 & 3, ear points between toes 4 & 5

SHOULDER GIRDLE TO DIAPHRAGM LINES

- thyroid, parathyroid, thymus – thumb walk ball of foot beneath big toe. Press thyroid point – centre of pad, parathyroid – over to the left slightly, thymus right of thyroid gland
- right lung/chest – thumb walk chest area from diaphragm line to shoulder girdle line on sole of foot
- right breast/lung/mammary glands – finger walk front of foot from base of the toes to diaphragm line

DIAPHRAGM LINE TO WAISTLINE

- liver/gallbladder – thumb walk triangular liver area between diaphragm line and waistline. Rotate onto gallbladder
- stomach/pancreas/duodenum – thumb walk from inside of foot to approximately the centre of the foot
- right adrenal gland – rotate onto adrenal gland

LEFT FOOT

BELOW THE WAISTLINE

- right kidney/ureter tube/bladder – circle over kidney point, turn thumb and caterpillar walk down towards inside of foot to bladder reflex
- small intestines – thumb walk from waistline to pelvic floor line.
- ileocaecal valve/ascending/ transverse colons – hook in and back-up on ileocaecal reflex, thumb walk up ascending colon, rotate on hepatic flexure, thumb walk across transverse colon
- right shoulder/arm/elbow/hand/ hip/ knee/leg – caterpillar walk up and down outer edge of the foot
- sciatic nerve line/pelvic area thumb walk down Achilles tendon area on inside of foot across hard heel pad and up Achilles tendon on outside of foot. Knuckle heel pad on sole of the foot
- uterus/prostate – pressure circles with index finger on reflex points between inner ankle bone and tip of heel
- fallopian tube/vasdeferens/lymph/ groin thumb walk from inside of ankle, across the top of foot to outside of ankle and back again.
- right ovary/testicle – pressure circles with index finger reflex located midway between outer ankle bone and tip of heel
- effleurage/stroke right foot

RELAXATION TECHNIQUES

- effleurage/stroking
- metatarsal kneading
- alternate thumb rotation
- zig/zag spreading the foot
- spinal stroking
- spinal twist
- toe loosening
- ankle rotations
- foot rocking

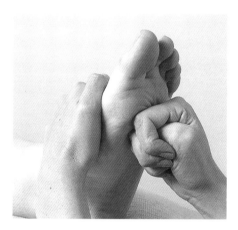

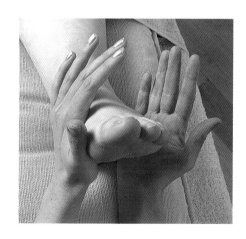

STEP BY STEP SEQUENCE

- solar plexus/diaphragm
- head and brain – thumb walk back and sides of big toe.
- pituitary gland – hook in and back-up on centre of big toe
- face – finger walk front of big toe
- neck
  - rotate big toe
  - thumb walk across back of base of big toe
  - thumb walk across front of base of big toe
- sinuses – walk down the centre and both sides of the small toes.
- teeth – finger walk down the fronts of the toes
- upper lymphatics – gently squeeze webbing between each of the toes.
- spine – caterpillar walk down the inside of the foot. Repeat walking up the foot
- eyes and ears – thumb walk across ridge at base of toes. Press into eye point between toe 2 & 3, ear point between toes 4 & 5

SHOULDER GIRDLE TO DIAPHRAGM LINES

- thyroid/parathyroid, thymus – thumb walk pad between big toe. Press thyroid point – centre of big toe, parathyroid over to the right slightly, thymus – left of thyroid gland
- left lung/chest – thumb walk chest area on sole of foot from diaphragm line to shoulder girdle line
- left lung/breast/mammary glands – finger walk front of foot from base of toes to diaphragm line
- heart area – thumb circles on upper third of sole of foot, index finger circles on top of foot

DIAPHRAGM LINE TO WAISTLINE

- stomach/pancreas/duodenum – thumb walk from the zone one to four from diaphragm line to waistline in horizontal rows
- spleen – thumb walk from a zone five to zone four in horizontal rows
- left adrenal gland – rotate onto adrenal gland

BELOW THE WAISTLINE

- left kidney/ureter tube/bladder – circle over kidney area, turn thumb and caterpillar walk to bladder area.
- small intestines – thumb walk in horizontal rows from waistline to pelvic floor line
- transverse colon/descending colon/sigmoid colon – thumb walk across transverse colon, walk down descending colon (zone five), just before pelvic floor line turn thumb to the left until you reach sciatic line, circle over sigmoid colon, caterpillar walk towards bladder area
- left shoulder/arm/elbow/hand/hip and/knee/leg – caterpillar walk up and down outer edge of foot
- sciatic nerve line/pelvic area – thumb walk down Achilles tendon on inside of foot, across hard heel pad and up Achilles tendon on outside of foot. Knuckle heel pad on the sole of foot
- uterus/prostate – pressure circles with index finger on reflex found midway between inner ankle bone and tip of heel
- fallopian tube/vas deferens/lymph/ groin – thumb walk from inside of ankle, across the top of foot to outside of ankle and back again
- left ovary/testicle – pressure circles with index finger on reflex located midway between outer ankle bone and tip of heel
- effleurage – stroke left foot

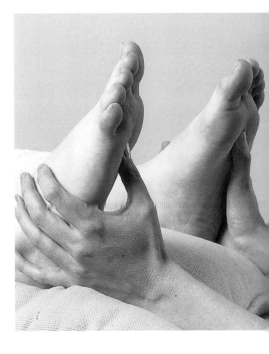

FINALE

- return to any reflex points which were tender
- perform any favourite relaxation techniques
- run fingertips lightly over both feet
- solar plexus release
- cover up feet and allow recipient to relax
- offer a glass of water and encourage recipient to drink plenty of water over next 24 hours

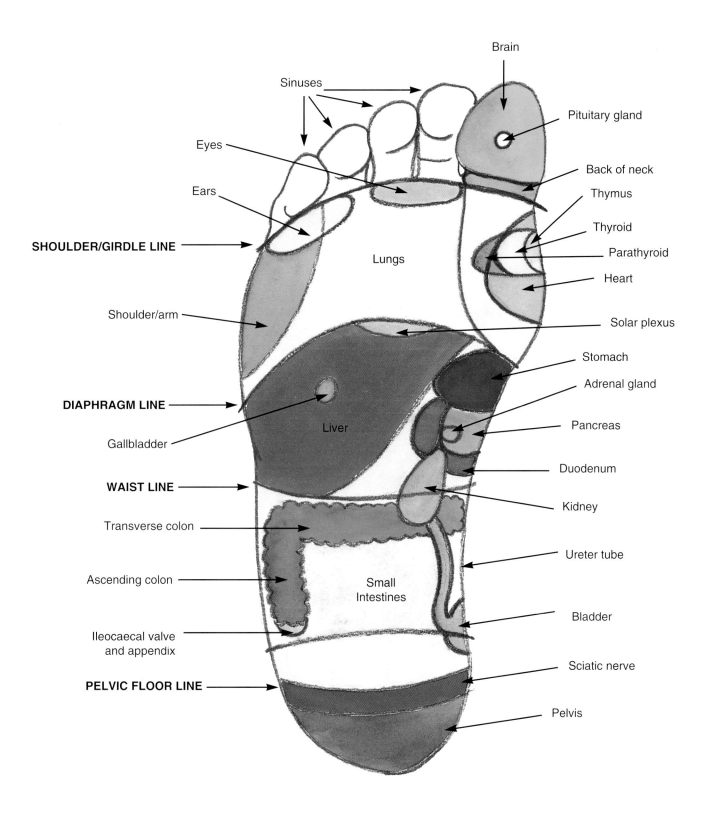

Brain

Sinuses

Eyes

Ears

SHOULDER/GIRDLE LINE

Lungs

Pituitary gland

Back of neck

Thymus

Thyroid

Parathyroid

Heart

Shoulder/arm

Solar plexus

DIAPHRAGM LINE

Gallbladder

Liver

Stomach

Adrenal gland

Pancreas

Duodenum

WAIST LINE

Kidney

Transverse colon

Ascending colon

Small
Intestines

Ureter tube

Ileocaecal valve
and appendix

Bladder

PELVIC FLOOR LINE

Sciatic nerve

Pelvis

RIGHT SOLE

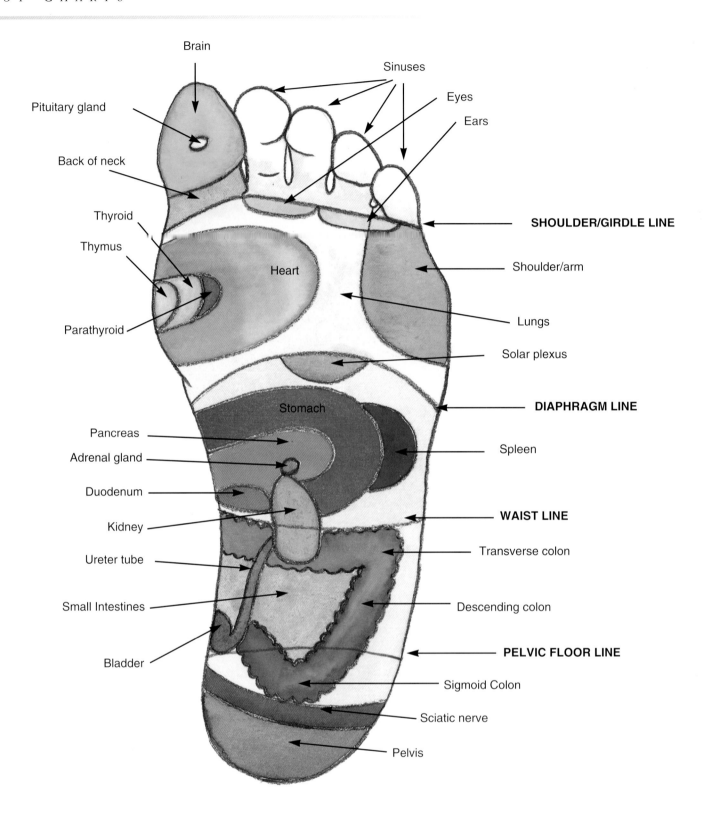

Brain

Sinuses

Pituitary gland

Eyes

Ears

Back of neck

SHOULDER/GIRDLE LINE

Thyroid

Thymus

Heart

Shoulder/arm

Parathyroid

Lungs

Solar plexus

DIAPHRAGM LINE

Stomach

Pancreas

Spleen

Adrenal gland

Duodenum

WAIST LINE

Kidney

Transverse colon

Ureter tube

Small Intestines

Descending colon

PELVIC FLOOR LINE

Bladder

Sigmoid Colon

Sciatic nerve

Pelvis

LEFT SOLE

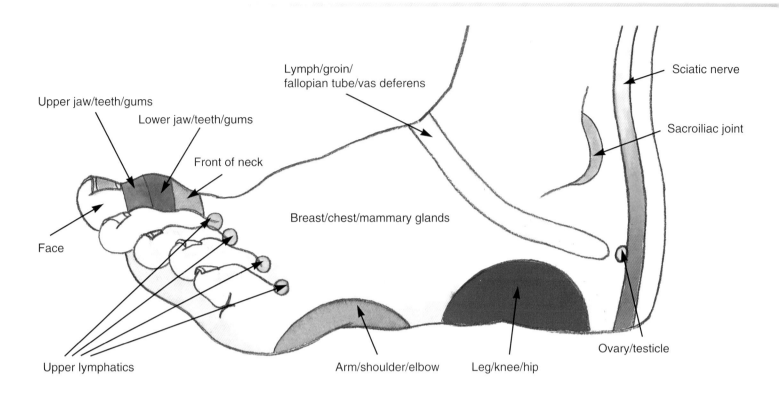

Lymph/groin/
fallopian tube/vas deferens

Sciatic nerve

Upper jaw/teeth/gums

Lower jaw/teeth/gums

Sacroiliac joint

Front of neck

Breast/chest/mammary glands

Face

Upper lymphatics

Arm/shoulder/elbow

Leg/knee/hip

Ovary/testicle

OUTSIDE VIEW – LEFT FOOT

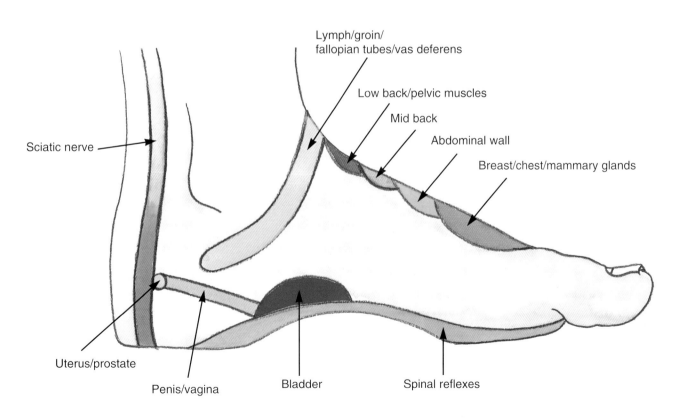

Lymph/groin/
fallopian tubes/vas deferens

Low back/pelvic muscles

Mid back

Abdominal wall

Breast/chest/mammary glands

Sciatic nerve

Uterus/prostate

Penis/vagina

Bladder

Spinal reflexes

INSIDE VIEW – LEFT FOOT

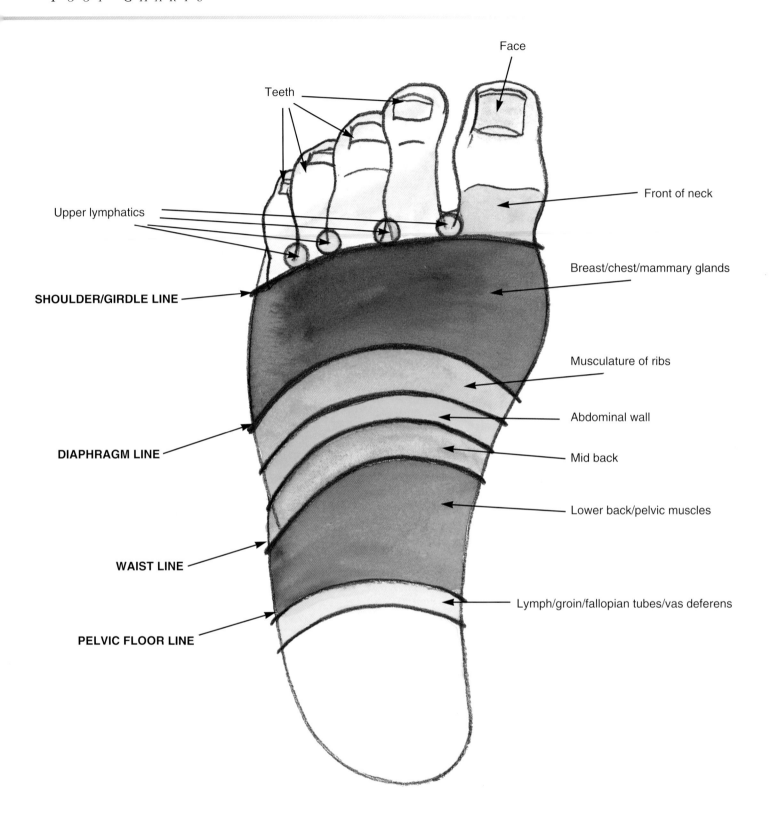

Face

Teeth

Front of neck

Upper lymphatics

Breast/chest/mammary glands

SHOULDER/GIRDLE LINE

Musculature of ribs

Abdominal wall

DIAPHRAGM LINE

Mid back

Lower back/pelvic muscles

WAIST LINE

Lymph/groin/fallopian tubes/vas deferens

PELVIC FLOOR LINE

DORSUM - LEFT FOOT

Common Ailments

MAIN TREATMENTS

During a reflexology session, tender areas may indicate certain imbalances. After a treatment you can come back to these tender areas to give them more attention.

This section looks at some common ailments, and suggests areas to concentrate on. Many of these areas feature in all or most of the recommended treatments. These are illustrated here. Other, specific areas are illustrated throughout the section. If you are uncertain of any point, please refer back to these pages.

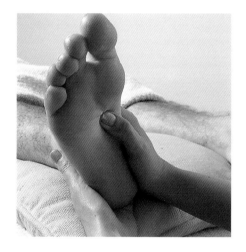

Adrenals

Diaphragm

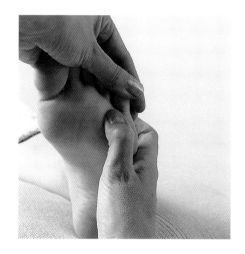

Ears

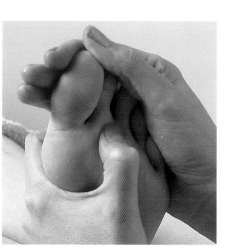

Eyes

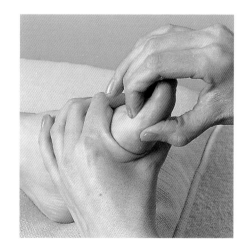

Face

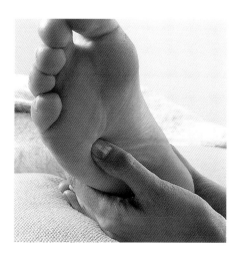

Gallbladder

Head and brain

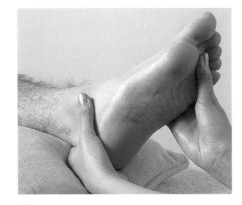

Heart area

Kidneys

Liver

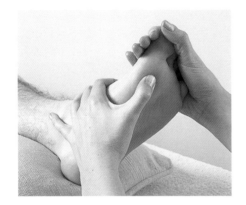

Lung/chest area

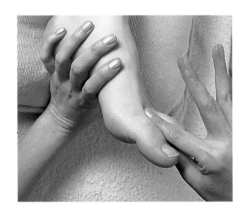

Upper Lymphatics

Pituitary gland

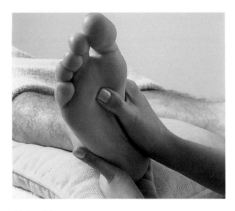

Solar Plexus

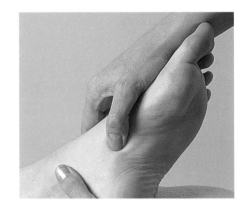

Spine

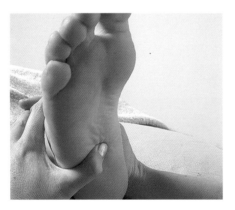

Transverse colon

CIRCULATORY PROBLEMS

Heart disease is one of the main causes of premature death in the developed countries. Contributory factors include poor diet, obesity, high stress levels, lack of exercise, genetic predisposition and smoking. Reflexology is excellent for improving the circulation, balancing the blood pressure and reducing stress on the heart.

ANGINA

Angina is caused by a lack of oxygen reaching the heart muscle usually as a result of hardening of the arteries. Chest pain is experienced due to the decreased blood and oxygen supply to the heart tissue.

Causes
- high fat diet
- stress
- lack of exercise
- hereditary factors
- smoking

Other advice
- eat a healthy diet — avoid junk food, sugar and salt, fried foods and saturated animal fats. Instead eat plenty of fresh fruit and vegetables, fibre and virgin olive oil
- give up smoking
- take regular, gentle physical exercise – e.g. a 20 minutes walk daily, Tai Chi or yoga

Reflexology Treatment

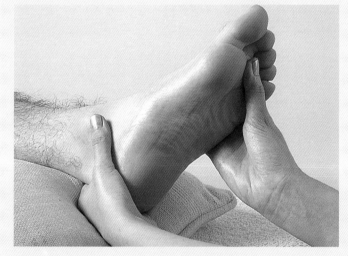

Heart area

Solar Plexus

- Heart area
- Liver – to help normalise cholesterol
- Adrenals – to relieve stress
- Solar plexus
- Diaphragm — to deepen breathing
- Lungs and chest – to relax and open up chest area

HYPERTENSION (HIGH BLOOD PRESSURE)

High blood pressure is a fairly common disorder which increases with age. Hypertension, if left untreated, can result in heart and kidney failure or strokes.

Causes

- stress
- obesity
- smoking
- family history

Other advice

- avoid salt, sugar and saturated fats
- eat lots of fruit, vegetables, fibre (especially oats) and garlic
- give up smoking and reduce alcohol and caffeine intake
- reduce stress
- take gentle, regular exercise

Reflexology Treatment

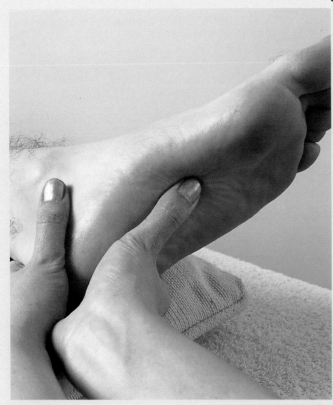

Kidneys

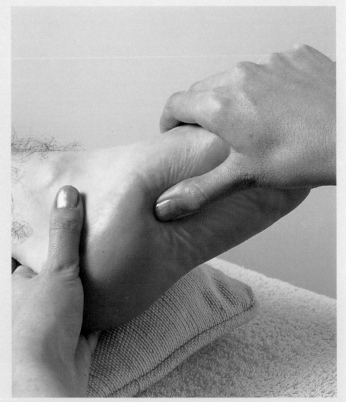

Working from the kidney towards the bladder

- Heart area
- Kidneys
- Adrenal glands – to reduce stress
- Solar plexus
- Diaphragm – to deepen breathing
- Lungs and chest – to relax the chest area

DIGESTIVE PROBLEMS

The majority of people suffer at some time from a digestive disorder. The digestive system is very prone to upset particularly by stress. Imbalance can be caused by emotions such as anger, tension and fear or by eating food too quickly. Many of us snack on junk foods and refined foods with little nutritional value which also may contain harmful colourings and preservatives.

We also drink far too much tea, coffee and soft carbonated drinks with caffeine in them. Our bodies would prefer 6-8 glasses of water a day!

Reflexology is an excellent tool for releasing tension and aiding the process of digestion and elimination.

A doctor should of course always be consulted for any digestive problem if it is persistent or accompanied by weight loss, blood in the faeces or a general sense of being unwell.

INDIGESTION/HEARTBURN (DYSPEPSIA)

Causes
- excessive eating and drinking, rushing or not chewing food properly
- eating the wrong foods e.g. dairy foods, refined foods such as cakes and biscuits, fatty foods, hot and spicy or rich foods
- stress which increases stomach acid

Other advice
- avoid stressful situations
- reduce foods that cause heartburn

Reflexology Treatment

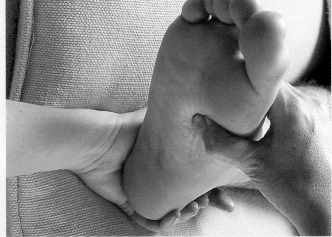

Stomach/pancreas/duodenum

Liver/gallbladder

- Stomach/pancreas/duodenum
- Liver/gallbladder – if there is nausea
- Solar plexus – to reduce tension
- Adrenal gland – to reduce inflammation

CONSTIPATION

Causes

- poor diet and inadequate intake of water
- lack of exercise
- tension
- certain drugs such as too many laxatives which make the bowel lazy, antibiotics, pain killers, steroids and diuretics

IRRITABLE BOWEL SYNDROME

This disorder is becoming increasingly prevalent and is characterised by pain in the abdominal area which can be very intense and a combination of constipation and diarrhoea.

Causes

- stress is a major trigger of irritable bowel syndrome
- certain types of foods which can cause an attack vary enormously but common culprits include dairy foods, wheat, chocolate, coffee and alcohol

Reflexology Treatment

- Small intestines
- Ileocaecal valve, which controls movement between the small and large intestines
- Large intestines:
  - ascending colon
  - transverse (right foot) colon
  - transverse (left foot) colon
  - descending colon
- Chronic rectum
- Solar plexus – to reduce tension

For irritable bowel syndrome only:
- Adrenals – to reduce inflammation and irritation within the digestive tract

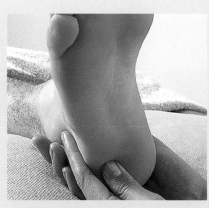

Ileocaecal valve

Ascending colon

Adrenals

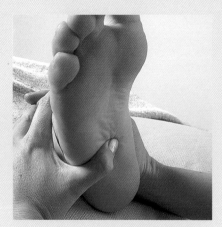

Transverse colon

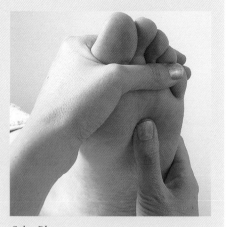

Solar Plexus

Other advice

- avoid stress
- eat a healthy high fibre diet to increase the frequency and quantity of bowel movements
- drink 6 – 8 glasses of water per day
- do not ignore the urge to move your bowels
- avoid prolonged use of laxatives which can make the bowel lazy

LIVER/GALLBLADDER PROBLEMS

NB. The gallbladder should always be treated with care. Never massage the gallbladder vigorously where there are gallstones. Gentle reflexology on this area however is often very successful: certain patients awaiting operations have had their gallstones eliminated with the aid of reflexology. Gallstones are formed from cholesterol, bile pigments and calcium compounds. They can cause colicky pain when found in the gallbladder (although only about 20% of gallstones cause symptoms). If they are found in the bile ducts (which connect the gallbladder and liver to the duodenum) then the pain can be excruciating.

Causes
* fatty diet
* obesity

Other advice
* eat a low fat, low sugar diet
* increase fibre in the diet
* drink fresh lemon squeezed into warm water
* eat celery

Reflexology Treatment

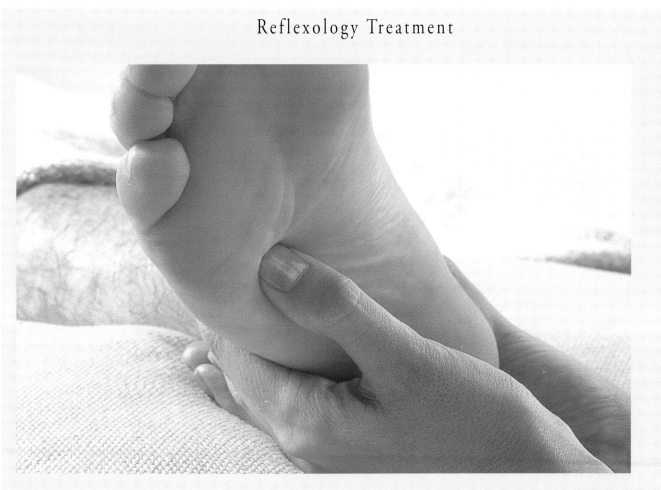

Liver

* Liver
* Gallbladder

GENITO-URINARY PROBLEMS

Women particularly can suffer from a whole host of conditions as the hormones are so easily unbalanced. Reflexology is excellent for relieving both the physical and emotional symptoms which can occur.

CYSTITIS

Cystitis is an inflammation of the inner lining of the bladder giving rise to frequent urination, burning or stinging sensations, low backache and a feeling of being run down.

Causes
- infection passing from the urethral opening into the bladder. The bacteria can come from the vagina or from the intestines via the anus
- stress often precedes an attack

NB always work FROM the kidney towards the bladder. NEVER go back up – otherwise you could transfer the infection. A kidney infection is much more serious than a bladder infection.

Other advice
- drink cranberry juice
- increase fluid intake to flush out the bladder

Reflexology Treatment

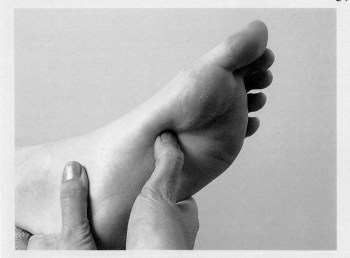

Adrenals

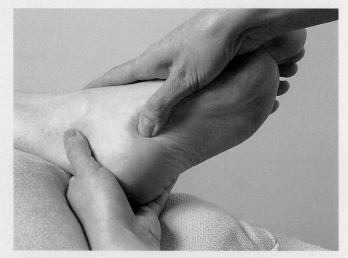

Bladder

- Kidneys
- Bladder – which will often and look raised and puffy where there is an infection
- Lower spine – for pain relief
- Adrenals – for inflammation

MENSTRUAL PROBLEMS

These include pre-menstrual tension (PMT), painful periods, absent or scanty periods and the menopause. Reflexology can correct hormonal imbalances, relax the body and mind, give pain relief from menstrual cramps and aid the elimination of excess fluid from the body.

Causes
- hormonal imbalances
- stress
- change in menstrual cycle

Other advice
- reduce salt which leads to fluid retention
- reduce sugar and caffeine which aggravate mood swings
- increase fibre
- take a B -complex supplement
- gentle exercise such as yoga and Tai Chi
- if menopausal increase calcium rich foods – e.g. fish especially sardines, sunflower, pumpkin, sesame seeds and nuts

Reflexology Treatment

Ovaries

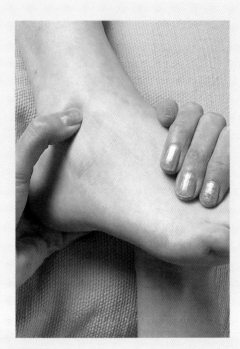

Fallopian Tubes

Breast area

- All reproductive areas:
  – Ovaries
  – Uterus
  – Fallopian tubes
- Kidneys – to remove excess fluid
- Breasts – to alleviate soreness
- Pituitary gland – to balance hormones
- Solar plexus – to relax
- Spine – to relieve back strain and cramps

HEAD AND NECK PROBLEMS

Common problems affecting this area include headaches, migraine and nasal problems such as catarrh, sinusitis and also hay fever.

HEADACHES/MIGRAINE

Most of us suffer from headaches at some time – the majority of which originate in the neck and shoulders. The really unlucky ones suffer from migraine, a one-sided headache characterised by intense pain and sometimes sickness and blurring of vision.

Causes
- anxiety
- tension in the neck
- hormonal imbalances
- irregular meals
- certain foods causing an allergic reaction
- tiredness and over use of the eyes

Other advice
- reduce stress
- if you suffer with migraine try avoiding chocolate, cheese, drinks with caffeine in especially coffee, alcohol especially red wine and food additives

Reflexology Treatment

Head and Brain

Spine

- Head and brain area
- Spine with emphasis on the neck area
- Pituitary gland – to balance the hormones
- Liver – to reduce toxicity and nausea (the entire digestive system may be worked to improve elimination)
- Eyes
- Solar plexus – to reduce stress and tension

NASAL PROBLEMS

Reflexology is excellent for nasal problems and in particular sinusitis and hay fever. Some sufferers find that regular treatment commencing a few months prior to the hay fever season is highly effective.

Causes

- infections and the after effects of a cold
- allergic responses e.g. to pollen/dust

Other advice

- avoid dairy foods which increase the production of mucus
- steam inhalations

Reflexology Treatment

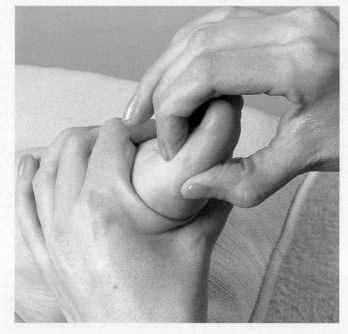

Face

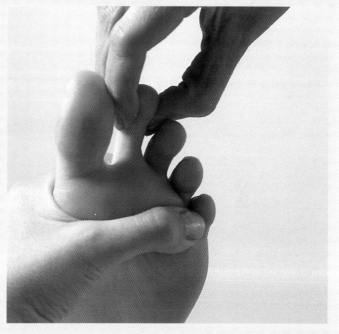

Sinuses

- Face area
- Sinuses
- Adrenals – to reduce inflammation
- Eyes
- Ears

MUSCULO-SKELETAL PROBLEMS

Reflexology has been enormously successful in providing relief for all muscular and skeletal conditions. It can provide pain relief, improve mobility, reduce inflammation and dispel toxins from the system. Sufferers find that they can often reduce their analgesics with regular reflexology.

It is interesting that stiffness in the foot represents stiffness in the body. As the feet are massaged so the muscles relax and the joints become more mobile.

ARTHRITIS

Osteoarthritis is the result of wear and tear of the joints and affects all of us to some extent particularly in later life.

Causes

*   getting older!
*   trauma to joints

Other advice

*   keep joints mobile with regular gentle exercise such as yoga or Tai Chi
*   eat a healthy diet as highly processed foods can lead to a build-up of toxic waste

Reflexology Treatment

Solar Plexus

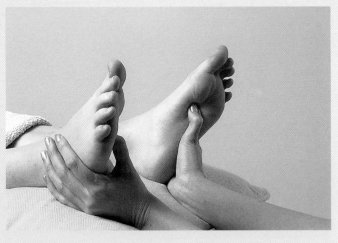

Adrenals

The whole foot should be worked as it is a general body condition. The following reflex points, however, should be emphasised.

*   Kidneys – to eliminate waste materials that accumulate around joints
*   Adrenals – to fight inflammation and give pain relief
*   Solar plexus – to release tension

    (plus any joints which are affected)

GENERAL ACHES AND PAINS

Where there are problems with the muscles and joints the painful
areas should be treated as described below.

Reflexology Treatment

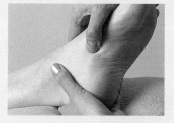

Spine

BACKACHE
- Length of the spine with particular concentration on the affected
area eg. cervical, thoracic or lumbar.

Sciatic line

SCIATICA
- Spine
- Sciatic line

Shoulder area

SHOULDER PAIN   E.G. FROZEN SHOULDER
- Shoulder area

Hip/Knee area

HIP PAIN
- Hip and knee area

Neck area

NECK PAIN
- Rotate the big toe
- Neck reflexes

ALSO
- work the adrenal reflex for pain relief and to reduce inflammation
- treat the top of the big toe (brain area) to block pain. This will stimulate the
release of endorphines which inhibit the transmission of pain impulses.

RESPIRATORY PROBLEMS

All respiratory problems including simple coughs and colds, asthma, bronchitis, emphysema and other chronic bronchial conditions respond well to the regular use of reflexology.

ASTHMA

Asthma is becoming more prevalent particularly amongst children. It is characterized by wheezing and is due to inflammation of air passages in the lungs, causing narrowing of the airways and reducing airflow in and out of the lungs.

Causes
- allergies such as pollen, house dust, fur, feathers, certain foods or pollutants
- stress and anxiety may precipitate an attack

Other advice
- avoid dairy foods which increase mucus production
- breathing exercises should be practiced daily. Most asthmatics breathe primarily from the chest while the lower portion of the lungs, which should be supplying 80% of the oxygen, is not used. Either sit up or lie down with one hand on your abdomen and one hand on your chest. Breathe in for approximately 6 counts and feel your abdomen fill with air and finally your chest. Hold the breath for two and then breathe out for 6 counts. The hand on the abdomen will move before the hand on the chest if you are performing this exercise properly

Reflexology Treatment

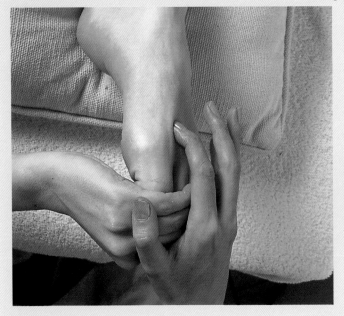

Lung/chest area

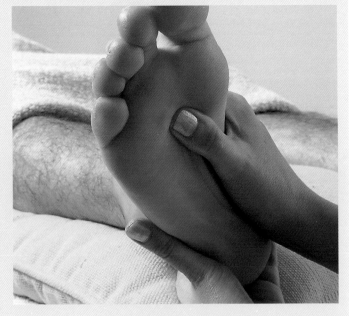

Solar plexus/diaphragm

- Lung/chest area
- Solar plexus/diaphragm – to release tension
- Adrenal glands – for allergies

COUGHS/COLDS/RESPIRATORY INFECTIONS

All of us will occasionally get a cold and reflexology is an excellent way of relieving the many symptoms and aiding the removal of mucus to prevent the occurrence of more serious conditions.

Causes

- exposure to viruses – schoolchildren have more coughs and colds due to exposure to lots of different germs and close proximity to each other

Other advice

- eat garlic which is known as 'nature's antibiotic'
- hot spices such as ginger will help to break down phlegm
- take vitamin C daily – at least 1 gram to prevent coughs and colds

Reflexology Treatment

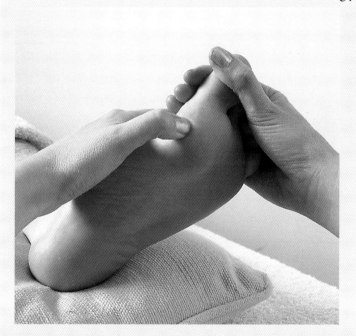

Thymus

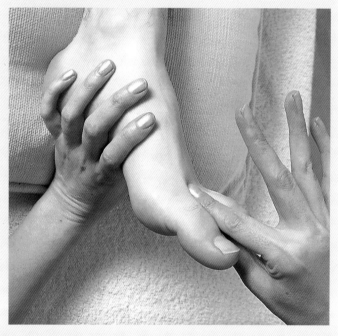

Lymph drainage

- Lung/chest area – to break up congestion
- Nose
- Throat
- Eyes
- Ears
- Thymus – to boost the immune system
- Lymph drainage – especially upper lymphatics

Hand Reflexology

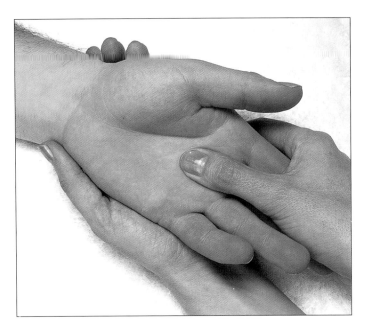

Reflex points in the hand mirror specific organs and structures of the body.

Hand reflexology is a method of applying pressure through the fingers and thumbs on the reflex areas of the hands. These reflex areas are found on all parts of the hands and they correspond to the organs, glands and structures of the body. The hands can be seen as a mirror of the body — the right hand reflects the right hand side of the body while the left hand reflects the left hand side.

Reflexology is a simple, non-invasive natural therapy, which stimulates the inner healing forces within the body, bringing about physical, mental and emotional well-being. Whether you have a specific health problem or are just looking for a way to relieve tension and promote optimum health, reflexology is of excellent therapeutic value.

Hand reflexology is completely safe provided that it is administered correctly. As long as a particular reflex is not overworked there is no danger of over-stimulation which can cause excessive elimination and unpleasant side-effects. It can be used on everyone from young babies to the elderly.

IMPORTANT:

- Reflexology should NEVER be used to diagnose medical conditions. A medical diagnosis should only be carried out by a qualified doctor.

- When giving a reflexology treatment, you must NEVER promise to 'cure' an ailment, nor should you use reflexology to give false hope. However, everyone WILL benefit from reflexology.

- Reflexology should NOT be used instead of orthodox medicine. The advice of a medically qualified doctor should always be sought. However, reflexology and orthodox medicine work well when used together.

- Reflexology should NOT be classed as a medical treatment.

- Reflexology is NOT like an acupuncture treatment. Acupuncturists talk about meridians whereas reflexologists use zones. Acupuncture is an extremely complex subject, which can take four years of full-time study. It can be very dangerous if not practised properly.

The Bony Structure of the Hands

There are 27 bones making up each hand and wrist. These are:

8 CARPALS (wrist bones) arranged in two rows. They are known as the trapezium (four-sided), trapezoid (four-sided), capitate, hamate (hook shaped), scaphoid (like a boat), lunate (resembles a crescent moon), triquetral, pisiform (pea-shaped).

5 METACARPALS, which form the palm of the hand. The heads of these bones make the knuckles.

14 PHALANGES, which are the finger and thumb bones. The thumb has two phalanges whereas the fingers have three.

The bones of the hand and wrist are held in place by an enormous number of muscles, tendons and ligaments. There is a rich supply of nerve endings in the hands, which make them very sensitive.

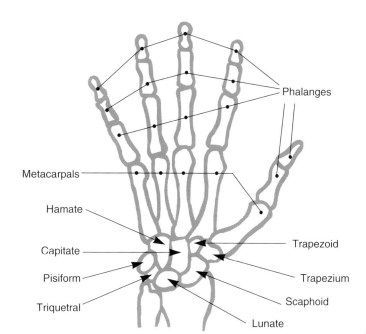

PRINCIPLES OF REFLEXOLOGY

Ten Longitudinal Zones

According to reflexology the body can be divided into ten longitudinal zones which run the length of body from the tips of the toes to the head and out to the fingertips and vice versa. If an imaginary line is drawn through the centre of the body there are five zones to the right of this mid-line and five zones to the left.

Zone one runs from the big toe, up the leg and centre of the body to the head and then down to the thumb.

Zone two runs from the second toe up to the head and then down to the index finger.

Zone three extends from the third toe up to the head, then down to the third finger and so on.

All organs and parts of the body, which lie within the same zone are related to each other. If any part of a zone is stimulated in the hand this will affect the entire zone throughout the body.

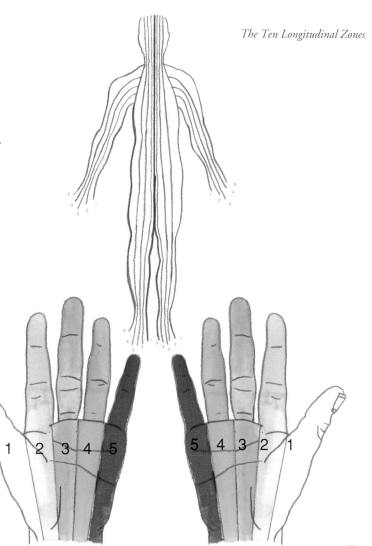

The Ten Longitudinal Zones

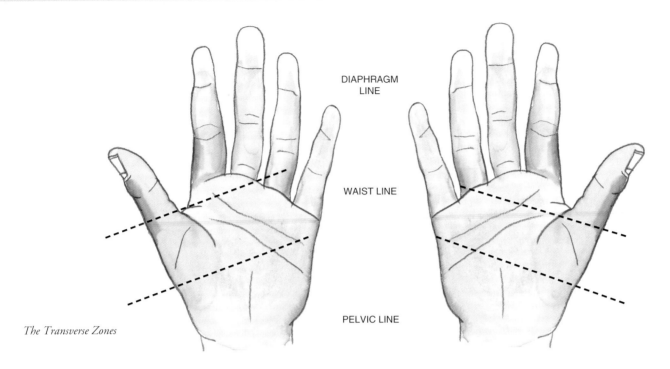

DIAPHRAGM
LINE

WAIST LINE

PELVIC LINE

The Transverse Zones

Transverse Zones

Reflexology also divides the hands (and feet) into transverse or horizontal sections.

1) The first transverse zone – the diaphragm line – on the hand is located just below the padded area beneath the fingers. All the organs above the diaphragm on the body are found here.

2) The second transverse zone – waist line – runs from the base of the web between the thumb and index finger where the thumb joins the hand across the hand.

3) The third transverse zone – pelvic line – circles the wrist.

The transverse zones and the longitudinal zones help us to describe the position of the reflexes on the hands.

Why Hand Reflexology?

Foot reflexology is the most popular form of reflexology and if you made an appointment to see a professional reflexologist the treatment would take place primarily on the feet. Hand reflexology is usually recommended as a self-help treatment to reinforce the work of the reflexologist.

However, times are changing and there is an increasing interest in the use of hand reflexology as the primary treatment. It has often been found that hand reflexology is a highly effective treatment, and sometimes patients have responded more quickly to hand reflexology than to foot reflexology. The best practices today generally use a combination of hand and foot reflexology and the results are excellent.

There are some occasions when it is impossible to administer foot reflexology and then working the hands becomes a necessity. Such circumstances include:
1) If the foot is injured — e.g. fractures; sprains etc.
2) If the foot is infected.
3) If the foot has been amputated.
4) If a person is too shy or embarrassed to expose his/her feet.
5) If the feet are extremely sensitive and cannot be touched without causing discomfort.
6) If the foot or part of the foot is very inflamed — e.g. gout in the big toe.
7) If foot reflexology has not previously worked, or progress is very slow.
8) If self-treatment is required.

Getting started

An oil burner can help provide soft lighting, as well as a calming aroma.

CREATING A SUITABLE ATMOSPHERE

Although the beauty of giving a hand reflexology treatment is that it can be carried out anywhere, if you create the right ambience you will achieve optimum results.

Ideally the surroundings should be as peaceful and calm as possible. Telephones ringing and children banging on the door to attract your attention ARE not conducive to relaxation, so remove as many distractions as possible, and ensure that you will not be disturbed. Some people enjoy silence during their treatment whilst others will prefer to listen to some soft relaxation music. It is up to the individual.

The room should be warm and inviting with soft and subdued lighting. Essential oils can be burned prior to the treatment. Particularly relaxing oils include lavender, chamomile, frankincense, sandalwood and ylang ylang. A vase of fresh flowers or some softly scented pot pourri will also enhance the environment.

The gentle scent of pot pourri can enhance the atmosphere.

A massage couch is a useful purchase for frequent treatments, but not essential.

POSITIONS FOR WORKING

Correct positioning of the receiver is an important factor in the success of your treatment. Whatever position you choose it is vital that it affords complete relaxation for both you and the receiver.

A professional reflexologist will undoubtedly have a massage couch. It is not essential for you to purchase one although you may decide to invest in one later on.

You may decide to work with the receiver lying on a bed. You would need to place pillows/ cushions under the head to support the neck and also to enable you to observe any facial expressions. Pillows/cushions can also be placed under the receiver's knees for comfort and it is a good idea to place a cushion under the hand you are about to treat. This provides a comfortable working position for you to work from. You will sit to one side facing the receiver. Towels or blankets are essential to cover up the receiver. This not only makes the receiver feel safe and secure but it also counteracts the loss of body heat, which will occur as the treatment progresses.

You may prefer to work on the floor and this is also acceptable. You will need a well-padded surface which can be made by placing a thick duvet, some blankets or sleeping bags on the floor. As before, for the receiver's comfort place pillows under the head and under the knees and cover them up. Put a cushion under your knees for your own comfort and a cushion under the hand which you are treating first.

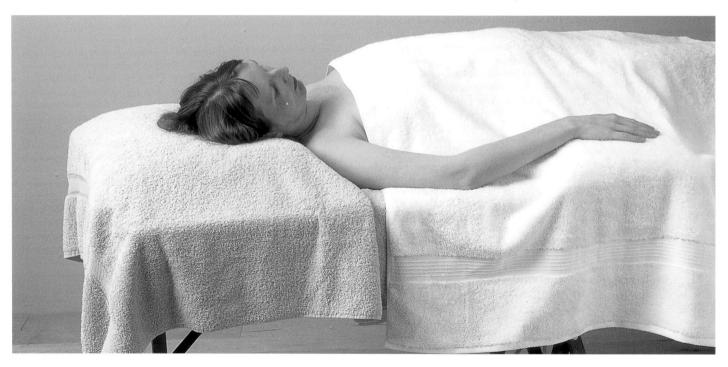

If using a couch or bed, ensure the receiver is warm and comfortable.

A supply of towels is essential to ensure the receiver stays warm and relaxed.

Some reflexologists work with the receiver sitting on a chair with their hand resting on a stool or table at the side but this position is potentially not as comfortable and seems to encourage conversation which is not conducive to complete relaxation.

Another possibility, is to sit facing the receiver with his/her hand resting on a cushion on a table or bench.

OTHER POINTS TO REMEMBER:

- Have extra towels/blankets on hand just in case the receiver feels cold.
- Remove all jewellery from your hands to avoid scratching.
- Ask the receiver to remove his/her jewellery so that the treatment is not impeded.
- Any restrictive clothing such as ties and belts may be loosened to maximise comfort.
- Clip your nails closely to avoid digging them in.
- Check your nails are clean!
- Wash your hands prior to a treatment.
- Do not use oils or creams during the reflexology session. Lubricants make it difficult to hold the hands properly, cause your fingers and thumbs to slip and decrease your sensitivity. You may use them at the end of the reflexology sequence.

Facing the receiver across a table or bench is a simple and effective reflexology position.

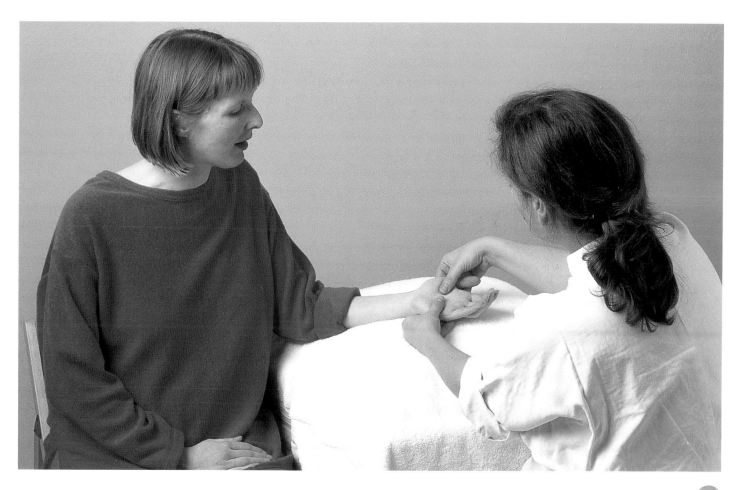

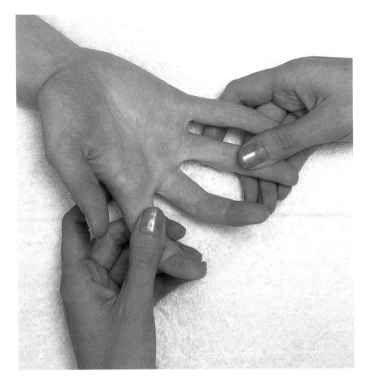

A visual examination of the hands is essential before starting a treatment.

EXAMINING THE HANDS

Prior to starting your treatment it is very enlightening to examine the hands visually. You will be amazed at what the hands can reveal. A healthy person will have hands that are a good colour with unblemished skin and good muscle tone. The hands should feel pleasantly warm but not excessively moist and clammy. Nails should have a strong and healthy appearance. Here are some points to observe:

- Infections of the hands and nails
- Calluses and hard skin
- Thin skin
- Blisters
- Cracks and crevices
- Warts
- Scars
- Cuts
- Spots and rashes
- Colour – too pale, too red, yellow, purple or mottled.

- Nails – split, flaked, broken. Are they hardened, thickened, ridged, spotted or a peculiar shape? (Spoon-shaped nails are sometimes seen in iron-deficiency anaemia)
- Shape of the fingers and thumbs – are they bent or straight and or puffy?

Any of these abnormalities indicate an imbalance of a reflex zone or zones. It is not relevant what the abnormality is–what is important is the SITE. For instance if there is a wart or some hard skin located on the outer aspect of the thumb this could indicate that there is a neck problem.

Puffiness around the wrist would indicate an imbalance of the lymphatic system as the pelvic lymphatic reflex area is located around the wrist.

You will now look at your hands in a new light.

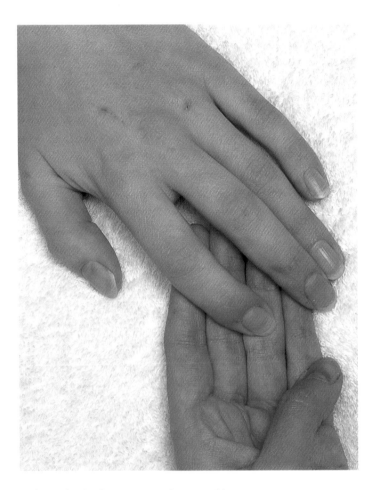

A deviated index finger may signify sinus problems.

hand relaxation
Techniques

Creams and oils should only be used after treatment.

The first contact between your hands and the receiver's hands is so important. The relaxation techniques will help to put both of you at ease and build up a sense of trust.

You will find that it will feel very natural to you to work on someone's hands and any initial nervousness and hesitation will disappear. These techniques will be enjoyable for both of you.

As your confidence grows do be creative and develop your own new techniques. Any movements that feel good to you will feel wonderful to the receiver.

Relaxation techniques should always begin and end a hand reflexology treatment. You will need to spend about ten minutes at the beginning of a session and a few minutes at the end. You can also include a few during your reflexology procedure.

Perform all the relaxation techniques on one hand before moving onto the other hand.

Ideally no creams or oils should be used for your preliminary relaxation sequence otherwise when you try to carry out the reflexology procedure the hands will be too slippery to apply sufficient pressure to the reflexology points. However, at the end of the treatment a small amount of oil or cream can be used. If the hands do feel at all greasy at the end of the relaxation session then just wipe them gently with a towel.

If you do not have time to give a hand reflexology treatment then this relaxation routine on its own can be very beneficial. Our hands are in constant use throughout the day and they really appreciate a massage! Massage them everyday with creams or oil to thoroughly moisturise the skin and keep them soft and smooth. A hand massage can be given any time, any place, anywhere. Before you start remember to remove all watches and jewellery.

GREETING THE HANDS

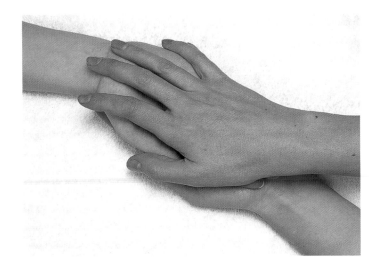

This initial contact will help to relax and reassure the receiver. Take hold of the receiver's right hand between both of your hands and gently clasp it for a few minutes Work with your eyes closed to heighten your sensitivity. Try to become aware of any tension and imagine it flowing out through your hands.

STROKING THE HANDS AND LOWER ARM

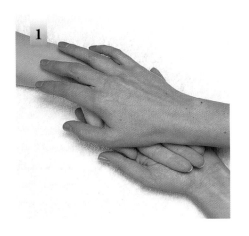
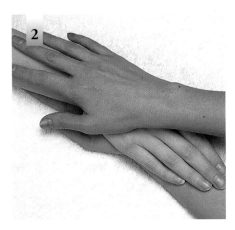

Support the forearm with your left hand and gently stroke up the hand and arm with your right hand (1). As you reach the elbow glide lightly back with no pressure down the arm and hand (2). The receiver will experience a deep sense of well-being and relaxation as the nerves are soothed and the tension melts away. You will feel the hand warm up as you help to stimulate the circulation and aid the elimination of toxins.

STROKING THE HANDS

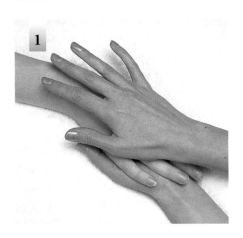
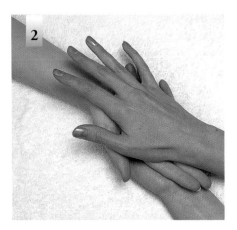

Supporting their right wrist with your left hand, stroke up to the top of the hand only. Repeat this movement several times. (1)

Now turn their hand over and repeat on the palm of their hand. (2)

For a deeper movement, stroke the palm with the heel of your hand.

OPENING THE HANDS I

Take the right hand in both of yours with the palm uppermost. Start at the wrist with your thumbs parallel and touching in the centre of the palm. (1)

Slide your thumbs out to the side gently opening up the palm of the hand. Repeat this movement in rows until you reach the base of the fingers. (2)

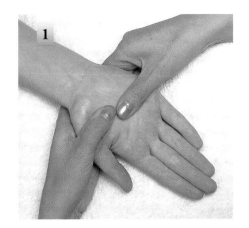
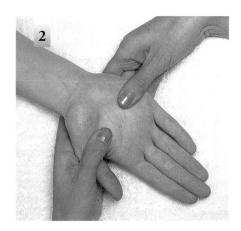

OPENING THE HANDS – II

Turn the hand over and repeat the movements above on the top of the hand.

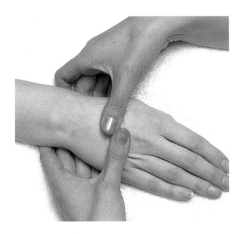
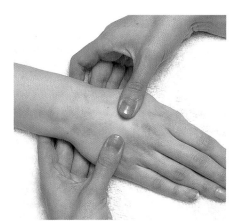

WORKING THE PALM OF THE HAND

With the palm uppermost interlock your little fingers with the receiver's right hand – one with the little finger, one with the thumb. (1)

Bring your thumbs round onto the palm and work into the palm with small round outward circular movements. (2)

You can work quite firmly into the palm of the hand. If your own hands are not very flexible then try the next technique.

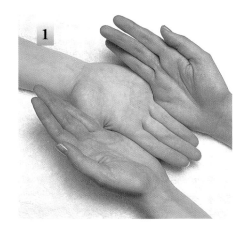
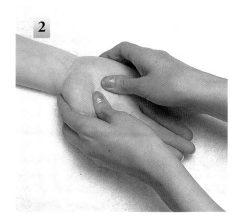

KNUCKLING THE PALM OF THE HAND

Make a fist with your right hand and support the receiver's hand, palm uppermost, with your other hand. Work into the palm of their hand with circular movements using your knuckles. This movement helps to loosen muscles, joints and tendons. It also increases the flexibility of your own hands.

STROKING BETWEEN THE BONES

Hold the receiver's hand with one hand to give support. Use the thumb of your free hand to work along each of the furrows between the bones of the hand. Start between the knuckles and stroke down towards the wrist.(1)

Now use your index finger to perform the same movement. (2)

 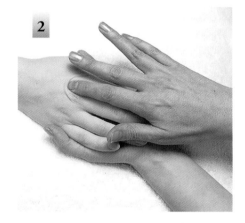

LOOSENING THE WRIST

Support the hand with your fingers. Use your thumbs to work in small circles all around the inside of the wrist. (1)

Now turn the hand over and work in the same way on the other side of the wrist.(2)

 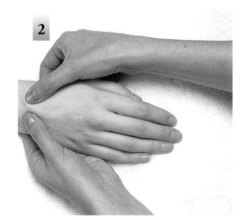

MOVING THE WRIST

Interlock your fingers with the receiver and then bend the wrist SLOWLY and GENTLY, first forwards (1) and backwards. (2)

Then bend the wrist from side to side. (3)

Finally, rotate clockwise and anti-clockwise (4)

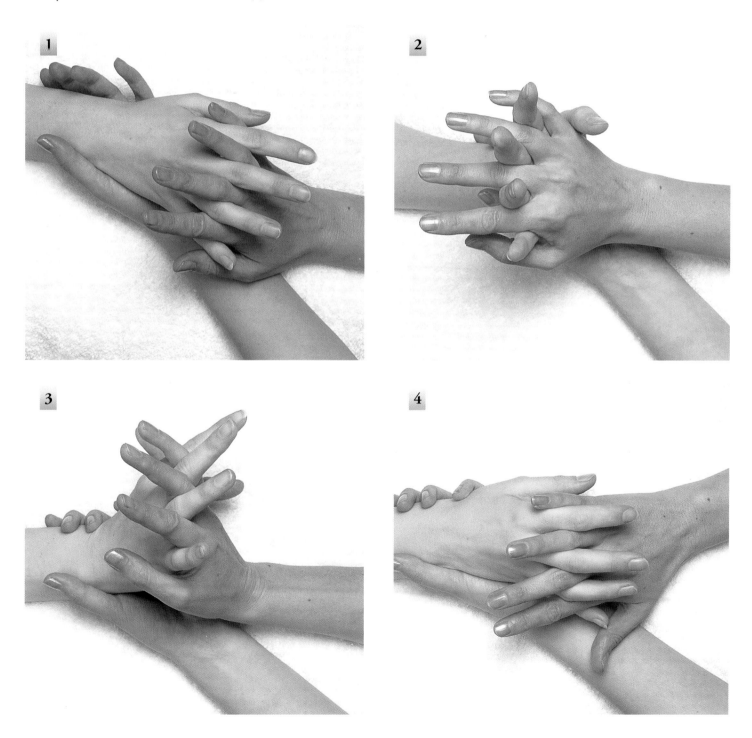

WRIST ROLLING

This technique is really invigorating. Leave the upper arm down on the couch and lift up the forearm. Place your palms on the sides of your partner's wrist. Move your hands rapidly back and forth. Your partner's hand should flop and move loosely as you perform this movement.(1)

If you prefer you may slot your thumbs in between the thumbs and little finger to perform this movement. (2)

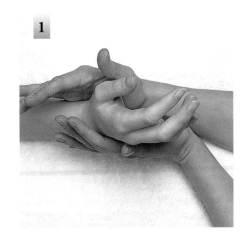 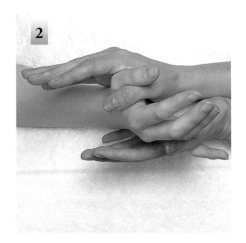

STRETCH AND SQUEEZE THE FINGERS AND THUMB

Hold your partner's wrist to support the hand. Gently and slowly stretch and squeeze each finger individually working from the knuckle to the tip.

 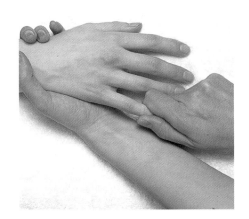

LOOSEN THE FINGERS AND THUMB

Make circular pressures around each joint using your thumb and index finger.

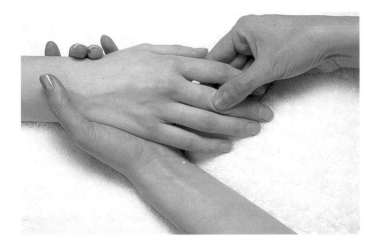

BENDING THE FINGERS AND THUMB

Gently flex and extend each finger and thumb joint with your thumb and index finger. (There are 2 joints in the thumb, 3 in the fingers).

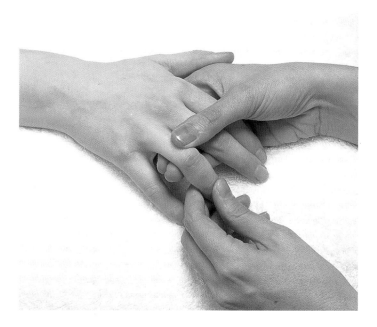
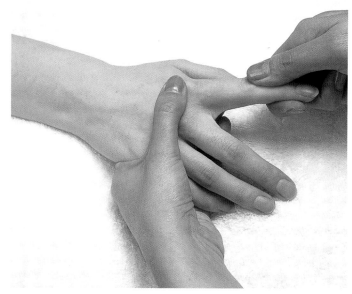

CIRCLING

Circle the thumb and fingers individually both clockwise (1) and anti-clockwise. (2)

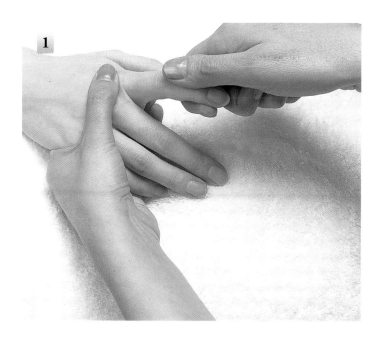
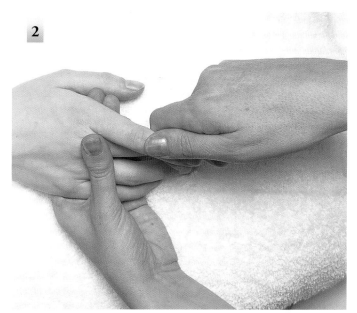

SOLAR PLEXUS RELEASE

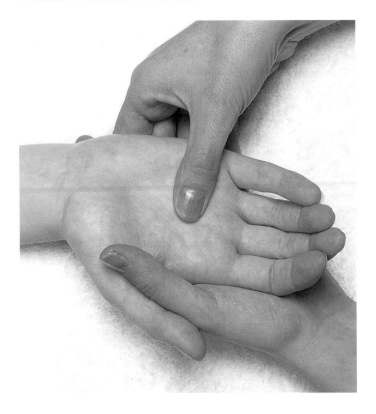

To release any remaining tension place your thumb on the solar plexus reflex which is found almost in the centre of the palm and press slowly and gently into it.

FINGERTIP STROKING

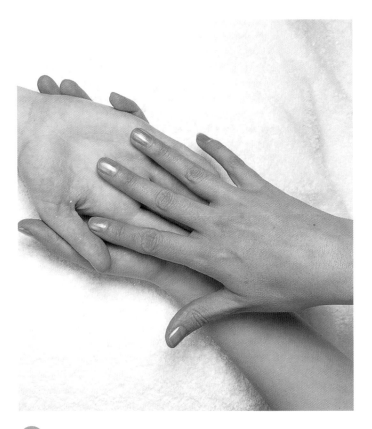

To end your relaxation routine sandwich your partner's hand between your palm and using your fingertips stroke the hand slowly from the wrist to the tips.

Now practise all these relaxation techniques on the other hand.

basic hand reflexology
Techniques

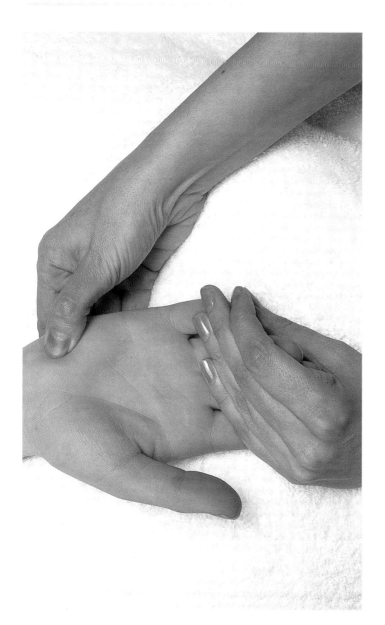

Now that you have mastered the relaxation techniques, you are going to learn how to treat the reflex areas in the hand. The reflex points are tiny and the thumb is the main tool used for applying pressure although on certain areas of the hand the fingers are used.

Please note the following before you begin:

1) Keep fingernails short – a nail digging into the skin is very painful.

2) You and the receiver should remove all watches, bracelets and rings.

3) Use only the flat pads of your fingers and thumbs to prevent even short nails from scratching or digging in.

4) Do not apply too much pressure – reflexology should not be uncomfortable.

5) Do not use oil or cream on the receiver's hands for the preliminary relaxation movements or for the step by step procedure. If the hands are sticky or slippery then you will not be able to make good contact with the reflex points. Oils also decrease your sensitivity making it difficult for you to pinpoint any abnormal areas. Oils and creams may be used for the final relaxation movements.

HOLDING TECHNIQUE

It is very important to support the hands properly during the treatment so that you have full control and exude an air of confidence. You also need to be able to reach and pinpoint the reflex zones easily and effectively.

Never grip the hand that you are working on too tightly or pull the skin taut otherwise your partner will feel tense and uncomfortable.

Remember to place a pillow or cushion under the receiver's hand, which should be covered with a towel to protect it if you are intending to use oils at the end of the session.

For most of the treatment the receiver's hand, palm uppermost, will be cupped in the palm of your hand with your thumb steadying on the palmar side.

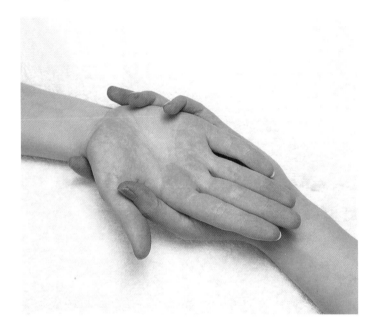

If you are working on the top (dorsal side), hold the hand by supporting the wrist from underneath in a 'handshake' position.

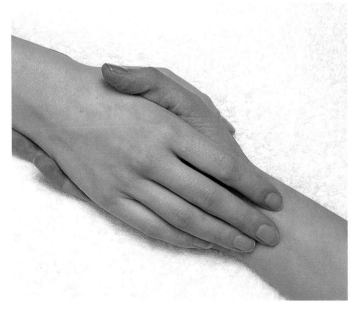

THUMB WALKING/CATERPILLAR WALKING TECHNIQUE

This technique is used for working large areas of the hand. Place the flat pad part of your thumb on the area to be treated and then bend the first joint SLIGHTLY and then unbend the thumb slightly so that you move forward a little.

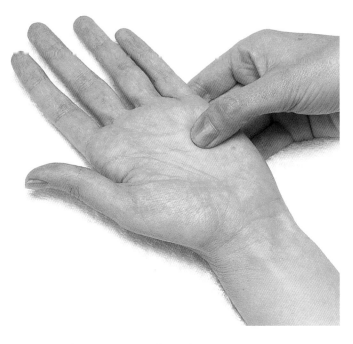
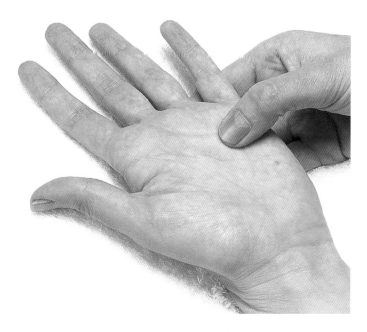

Continue in this way moving forward in tiny creeping movements like a caterpillar without losing contact with the hand. It is impossible to walk with a straight thumb and if you bend the thumb too much your nail will dig into the skin. Try this technique on the palm of your own hand.

Whilst your thumb is walking your other fingers should rest gently around the hand. Try to maintain a constant and even pressure always working in a forward direction. Do not worry if your movements feel somewhat jerky and clumsy at first. Persevere and you will achieve a smooth, consistent pressure.

REMEMBER

Thumb too arched (incorrect)

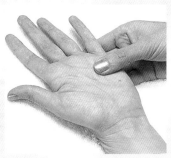

Thumb too flat (incorrect)

- Do not dig in with your nails
- Bend only the first joint of the thumb
- Bend the thumb slightly – it should be neither too bent nor too straight
- Take very small steps
- Movements are always forwards never backwards
- Pressure should be steady
- Pressure should be firm yet not hard enough to induce pain

PRESSURE CIRCLES

Pressure circles may be performed with the pad of the thumb or a finger. They can be used for working specific reflex points or to relieve the sensitivity of tender reflexes.

Place your thumb or finger on to a reflex point and press gently into the area. Keeping this pressure constant, circle gently over the point several times.

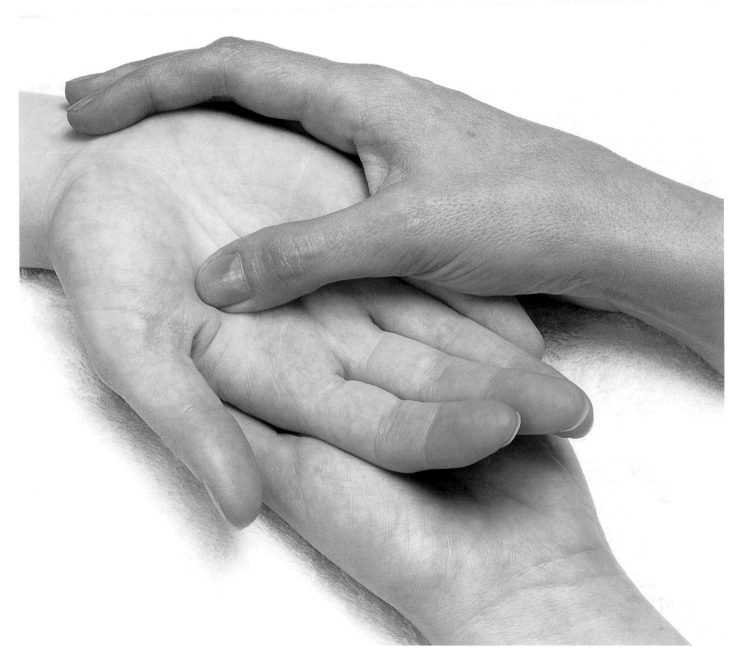

Pressure circles on the kidney point.

FINGER WALKING

The finger walking technique is almost the same as thumb walking. The object is the same – to exert a constant steady pressure, which is comfortable and effective for the receiver. Use finger walking in preference to thumb walking on bony or sensitive areas such as the top surface of the hand.

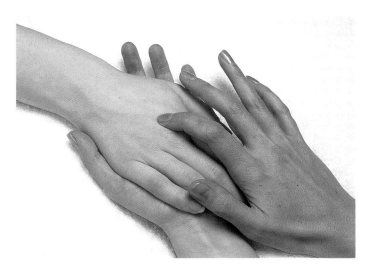 

Practice SINGLE finger walking first. Place the tip of your index finger on the area to be treated. Bend the first joint of the finger slightly and then unbend it a little to move the fingertip in a forward direction. Try this technique on the back of the hand, walking from the knuckles towards your wrist and remember to take the smallest possible steps.

Now try MULTIPLE finger walking using two or more fingers, once again working down the top surface of the hand.

If you are working on top of the hand walking downwards, place your fist under the palm of the hand to support it. Practise with one, two or three fingers to see which is most comfortable for you and the receiver.

 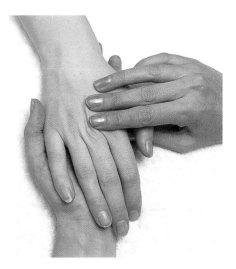

REMEMBER

- Maintain a steady even pressure

- Move only in a forward direction

- Take care not to dig your nails in

- Take only very small steps

- Use very gentle pressure — finger walking is specifically designed for bony and sensitive areas

You may also work sideways across the top (dorsal surface) of the hand. When working sideways your thumb will be placed under the palm of the hand to support it while your fingers walk across the top.

PRESS AND RELEASE

This technique is particularly effective for relieving pain and you may perform it with either your thumb or finger. Press into a tender point for about several seconds (here the ovary is illustrated).

Release the pressure and repeat several times until the sensitivity decreases.

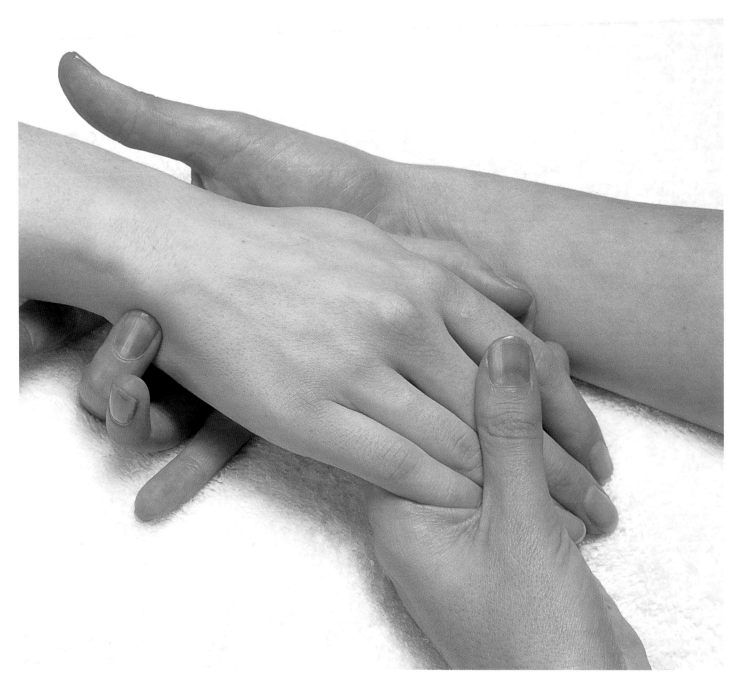

Press and release on the ovary area.

ROTATION ON A POINT

This technique involves pinpointing an area to be treated and rotating the hand around it. Thus the term – 'rotating on a point'. Place the pad of your thumb or finger on the relevant reflex point. (Here the right ovary is illustrated).

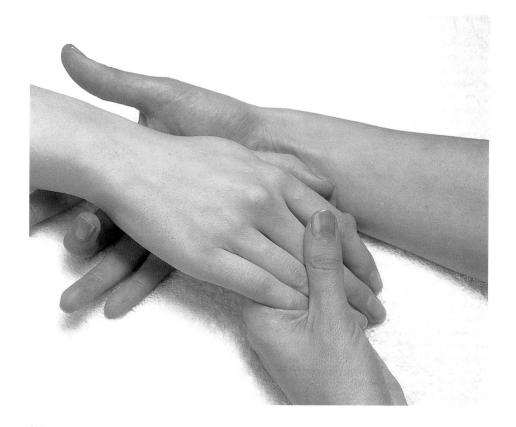

Use your other hand to rotate the receiver's hand around the point several times.

HOOK IN AND BACK-UP

To access specific points requiring greater accuracy, this technique is excellent. It would never be used for covering a large area – thumb or finger walking would be much more appropriate.

Press your thumb into your chosen point and apply pressure (hook in) and then pull back across the point (back-up).

RIGHT HAND

RELAXATION TECHNIQUES

- Greeting the hand
- Stroking hand and lower arm
- Stroking hand – palm up/palm down
- Opening the hand
- Knuckling the palm
- Loosening the wrist
- Moving the wrist
- Wrist rolling
- Loosening the fingers and thumb
- Moving the fingers and thumb
- Solar plexus release
- Fingertip stroking

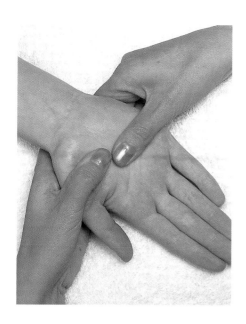

STEP BY STEP SEQUENCE

- Head and brain – thumb walk back and sides of thumb
- Pituitary gland – hook in and back – up on centre of thumb
- Face – thumb or finger walk front of thumb
- Neck – rotate base of thumb
- Neck/thyroid – thumb walk across back of base of thumb
- Neck/thyroid – finger walk across front of base of thumb
- Sinuses – walk down the back, sides and top of the fingers
- Teeth – walk down the front of the fingers
- Upper lymphatics – gently squeeze the webbing between each of the fingers
- Spine/sciatic line – caterpillar walk down the inside (thumb side) of the hand (spine) and above the wrist (sciatic line)
- Right eye and ear – thumb walk across ridge at base of fingers. Ear point (between fingers 4 and 5); eustachian tube (between fingers 3 and 4); eye point (between index and middle finger).
- Right lung – thumb walk upper third of palm of hand (to diaphragm line).
- Right lung/breast/mammary glands – finger walk down front of hand from base of fingers to diaphragm line

- Liver/gallbladder – thumb walk zones 5 - 3 between diaphragm line and waistline.
  Hook in and back-up technique on gallbladder reflex.
- Stomach/pancreas/duodenum – thumb walk zones 1 - 3 between diaphragm line and waistline
- Right adrenal gland – hook in and back-up
- Right kidney/ureter tube/bladder – pressure circles over kidney point, turn thumb and walk down towards inside of hand to bladder.
- Small intestines – thumb walk zones 1 - 4
- Ileocaecal valve/ascending/transverse colon – hook in and back-up on ileocaecal valve, walk up the ascending colon and across transverse colon
- Joints – right shoulder/elbow/hip/knee/ – thumb walk down outer edge of hand
- Right ovary – rotate on reflex point on outside of the wrist
- Uterus/prostate – rotate on reflex point on inside of wrist
- Right fallopian tube/vas deferens/lymph nodes of groin – thumb walk across back and front of wrist
- Stroke right hand

LEFT HAND

STEP BY STEP SEQUENCE

RELAXATION TECHNIQUES

- Greeting the hand
- Stroking hand and lower arm
- Stroking hand – palm up/palm down
- Opening the hand
- Knuckling the palm
- Loosening the wrist
- Moving the wrist
- Wrist rolling
- Loosening the fingers and thumb
- Moving the fingers and thumb
- Fingertip stroking
- Solar plexus release

- Head and brain – thumb walk back and sides of thumb
- Pituitary gland – hook in and back-up on centre of thumb
- Face – thumb/finger walk front of thumb
- Neck – rotate base of thumb
- Neck/thyroid – thumb walk across back of base of thumb
- Neck/thyroid – Walk across front of base of thumb
- Sinuses – walk down the back, sides and top of the fingers
- Teeth – walk down the front of the fingers
- Upper lymphatics – gently squeeze the webbing between each of the fingers
- Spine/sciatic line – caterpillar walk down the inside (thumb side) of the hand (spine) and above the wrist (sciatic line)
- Right eye and ear – thumb walk across ridge at base of fingers. Eye point (between index and middle finger), eustachian tube (between fingers 3 and 4), ear point (between fingers 4 and 5)
- Left lung – thumb walk upper third of palm of hand (to diaphragm line)
- Left lung/breast/mammary glands – finger walk down front of upper third of hand from base of fingers to diaphragm line

- Heart area – pressure circles on cardiac area and circular massage
- Stomach/pancreas/duodenum – thumb walk zones 1 - 3 between diaphragm line and waistline
- Spleen – thumb walk zones 5 - 4
- Left adrenal gland – hook in and back-up
- Left kidney/ureter tube/bladder – pressure circles over kidney point, turn thumb and work down towards inside of hand to bladder
- Small intestines – thumb walk zones 1 - 4
- Transverse/descending/sigmoid colon/rectum – walk across waistline zones 1 - 5, change hands to walk down descending colon, turn thumb 90° to walk across sigmoid colon and in to the rectum.
- Joints – left shoulder/elbow/hip/ankle – thumb walk down outer edge of hand
- Left ovary – rotate on reflex point on outside of wrist
- Uterus/prostate – rotate on reflex point on inside of wrist
- Left fallopian tube/vas deferens/lymph nodes of groin – thumb walk across back and front of wrist
- Stroke left hand

CLOSING MOVEMENTS

- Return to any areas which were sensitive
- Perform any of your favourite relaxation techniques – use oil/cream if desired
- Run fingertips lightly over both hands
- Clasp both hands gently
- Cover up hands and allow the receiver to relax
- Offer a glass of water for and encourage receiver to drink 6 - 8 glasses over the next 24 hour

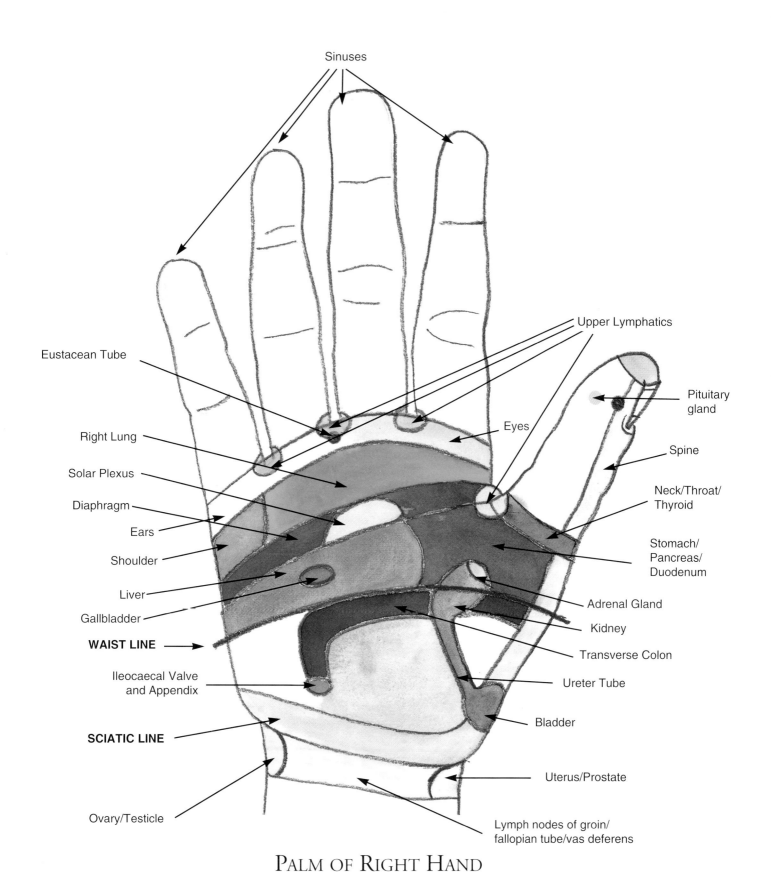

Sinuses

Upper Lymphatics

Eustacean Tube

Pituitary gland

Eyes

Right Lung

Spine

Solar Plexus

Neck/Throat/ Thyroid

Diaphragm

Ears

Stomach/ Pancreas/ Duodenum

Shoulder

Liver

Adrenal Gland

Gallbladder

Kidney

WAIST LINE

Transverse Colon

Ileocaecal Valve and Appendix

Ureter Tube

SCIATIC LINE

Bladder

Uterus/Prostate

Ovary/Testicle

Lymph nodes of groin/ fallopian tube/vas deferens

PALM OF RIGHT HAND

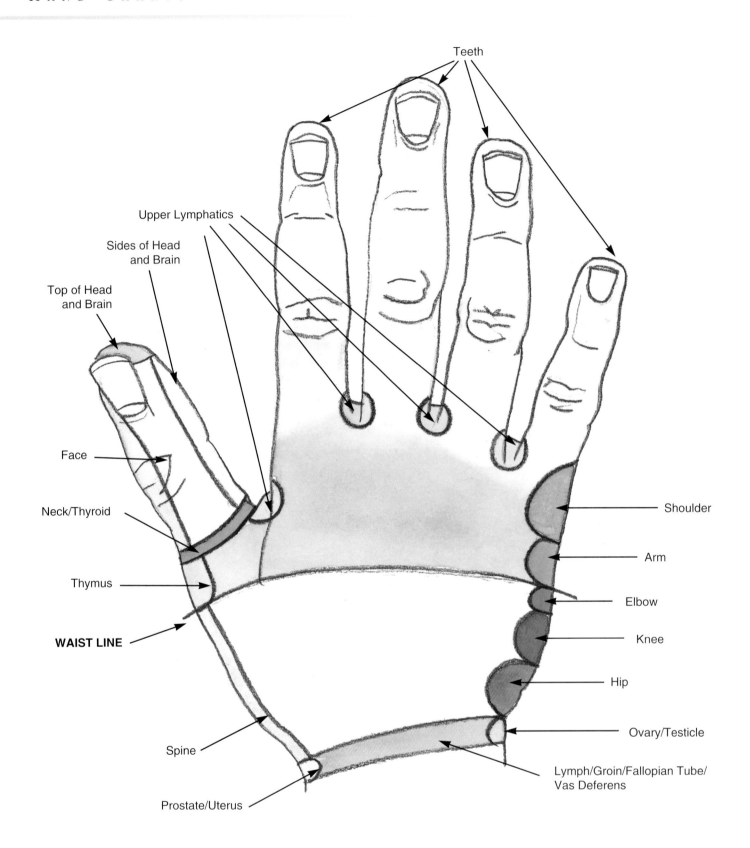

Teeth

Upper Lymphatics

Sides of Head
and Brain

Top of Head
and Brain

Face

Neck/Thyroid

Thymus

WAIST LINE

Spine

Prostate/Uterus

Shoulder

Arm

Elbow

Knee

Hip

Ovary/Testicle

Lymph/Groin/Fallopian Tube/
Vas Deferens

BACK OF THE RIGHT HAND

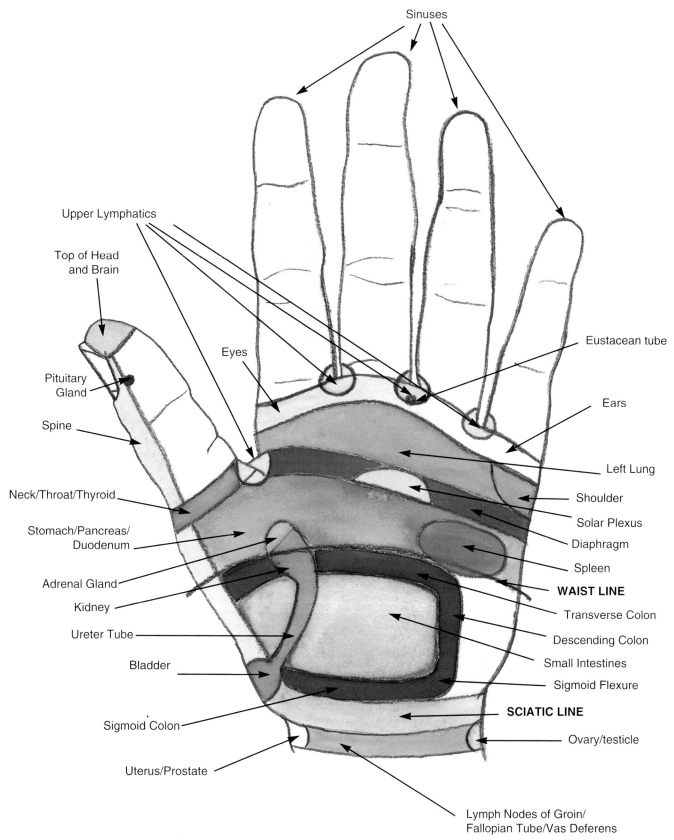

Sinuses

Upper Lymphatics

Top of Head
and Brain

Eyes

Eustacean tube

Pituitary
Gland

Ears

Spine

Left Lung

Neck/Throat/Thyroid

Shoulder

Solar Plexus

Stomach/Pancreas/
Duodenum

Diaphragm

Spleen

Adrenal Gland

WAIST LINE

Kidney

Transverse Colon

Ureter Tube

Descending Colon

Small Intestines

Bladder

Sigmoid Flexure

SCIATIC LINE

Sigmoid Colon

Ovary/testicle

Uterus/Prostate

Lymph Nodes of Groin/
Fallopian Tube/Vas Deferens

PALM OF LEFT HAND

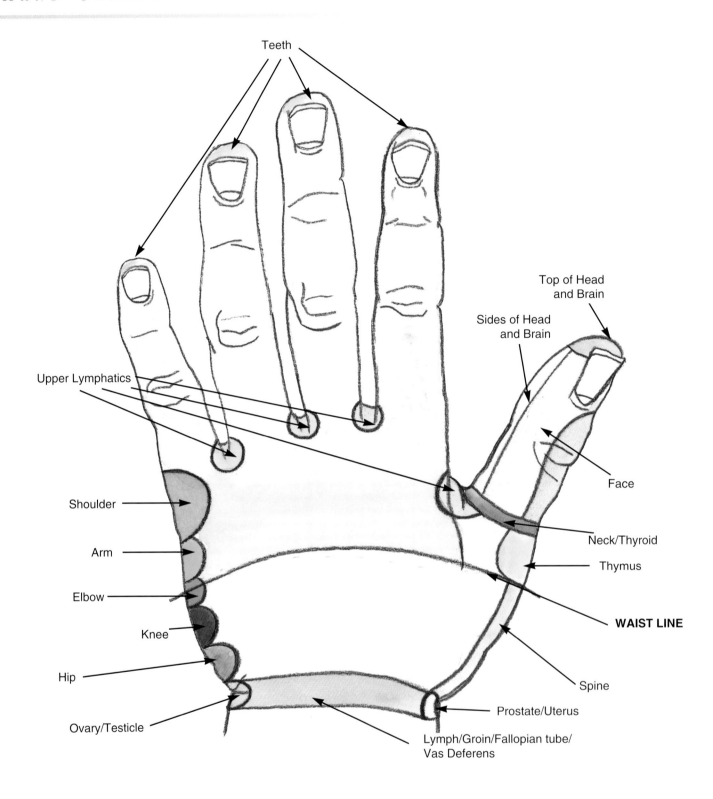

Teeth

Top of Head
and Brain

Sides of Head
and Brain

Upper Lymphatics

Face

Shoulder

Neck/Thyroid

Arm

Thymus

Elbow

WAIST LINE

Knee

Hip

Spine

Prostate/Uterus

Ovary/Testicle

Lymph/Groin/Fallopian tube/
Vas Deferens

BACK OF THE LEFT HAND

hand reflexology for
Common Ailments

In the course of a hand reflexology treatment, disorders may show up as tender areas.

IMPORTANT:
All medical conditions should be checked by a fully qualified medical doctor.

It is always much more beneficial to carry out a complete reflexology treatment on both hands and then give additional attention to the tender reflex points. However, if time is short then it will be beneficial to concentrate on the areas indicated.

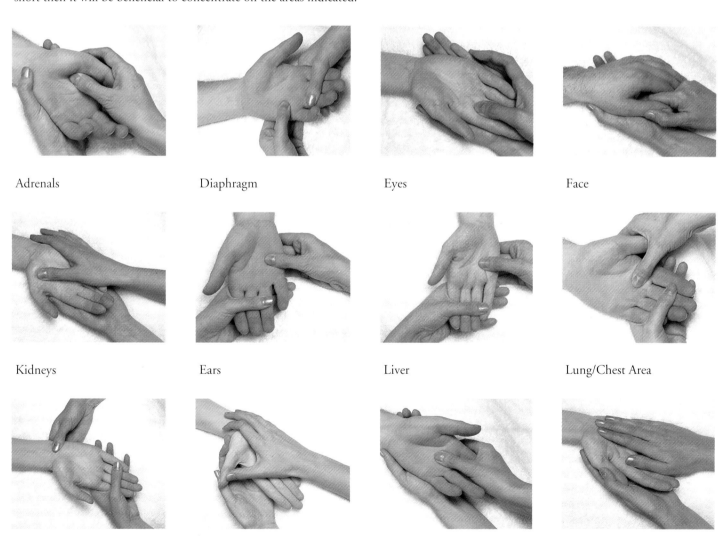

Adrenals   Diaphragm   Eyes   Face

Kidneys   Ears   Liver   Lung/Chest Area

Lymphatics (Grain)   Pituitary gland   Solar Plexus   Spine

BLADDER PROBLEMS

CYSTITIS

This is an inflammation of the inner lining of the bladder usually caused by an infection entering the bladder via the urethral opening. The bacteria can come from the vagina or from the intestines via the anus. The symptoms include a frequent desire to urinate, often with a burning sensation. The urine may be stained with blood and there may be a fever.

General advice
• Drink lots of fluid to flush out the bladder. Cranberry juice is particularly helpful.

Reflexology Treatment

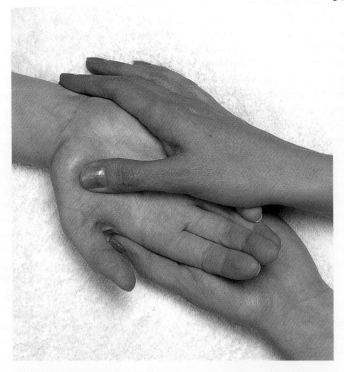

Kidney

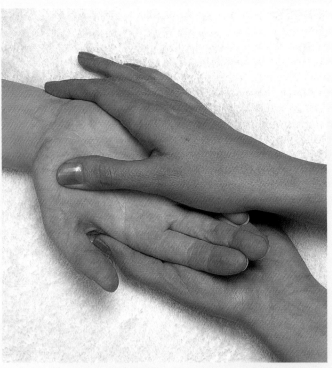

Working down the ureter tube towards the bladder

• Bladder
• Kidneys
• Ureter tubes
• Lymphatics

NB – always work from the kidney to the bladder and NEVER from the bladder to the kidney to avoid the risk of transferring a bladder infection into a kidney infection, which is far more serious.

DIGESTIVE PROBLEMS

CONSTIPATION

Constipation is commonly caused by a diet low in fibre; inadequate intake of water; lack of exercise; anxiety and certain medications such as excessive laxatives which make the bowel lazy; pain killers and antibiotics. It is characterised by the infrequent passage of hard stools usually with some discomfort.

General advice
- Eat a healthy, high-fibre diet to increase the frequency and quantity of bowel movements
- Avoid stress
- Do not ignore the urge to move your bowels
- Avoid laxatives

Reflexology Treatment

- Ileocaecal valve – which controls movement between the small and large intestines
- Small intestines
- Large intestines
- Adrenal glands
- Solar plexus – to reduce tension

Small intestines

INDIGESTION / HEARTBURN

This is a very common problem giving symptoms of a taste of acid in the mouth and pain in the chest sometimes with nausea. It is caused by eating the wrong foods such as cakes and biscuits; fatty foods; hot and spicy foods; rich or dairy foods. Rushing or not chewing food properly and stress will also exacerbate acidity.

General advice
- Avoid stress and learn to relax
- Reduce acid – forming foods
- Chew food slowly in pleasant surroundings

Reflexology Treatment

- Stomach/pancreas/ duodenum
- Solar plexus – to reduce stress
- Adrenal glands – to reduce inflammation
- Liver/gallbladder – where there is nausea

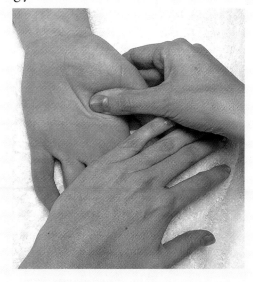

Stomach/pancreas/duodenum

FEMALE PROBLEMS

Ailments falling into this category include pre-menstrual tension (PMT); painful, absent or scanty periods; menopause; fibroids in the uterus; ovarian cysts and infertility problems.

General advice

- Eat a healthy diet
- Reduce sugar and caffeine, which aggravate mood swings
- Take vitamin B complex
- Take regular, gentle exercise such as yoga and Tai Chi
- If menopausal eat foods rich in calcium – e.g. fish where the bones are eaten, such as sardines, nuts and seeds.

Reflexology Treatment

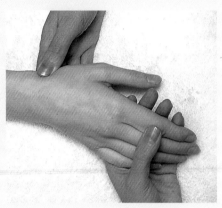

Ovaries

Uterus

- Ovaries (illustrated using index finger)
- Uterus (illustrated using thumb)
- Fallopian tubes
- Kidneys – where there is excessive fluid

- Breasts – where there is soreness
- Pituitary gland – to balance hormones
- Solar plexus – to relax
- Spine – for back pain

HEAD

HEADACHES/MIGRAINE

Headaches are usually caused by stress. Problems with the vertebrae in the neck arising from old whiplash injuries or poor posture are also frequently responsible. If headaches persist then medical advice should always be sought in case there is an underlying disorder. It may well be worth consulting an osteopath for spinal realignment.

Migraines are extremely painful, one-sided headaches usually accompanied by vomiting and an aversion to bright lights. Visual disturbances are also common. Sensitivity to certain foods such as cheese, chocolate and red wine; missed meals; tiredness and hormonal imbalances may also be contributory factors.

General advice

- Avoid stress and learn to relax
- Eat regularly
- Migraine sufferers should avoid substances suspected of inducing an attack
- Ensure that you have sufficient sleep

Reflexology Treatment

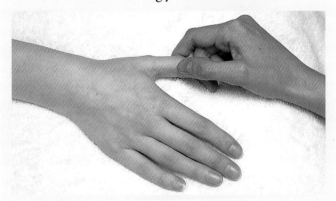

Head and brain

- Head and brain area
- Spine especially the neck
- Pituitary gland – to balance the hormones
- Solar plexus – to reduce stress
- Liver – to reduce nausea. The entire digestive system should be worked to encourage elimination
- Eyes

HEART PROBLEMS

ANGINA

Angina is caused by a lack of oxygen reaching the heart muscle due to coronary heart disease, high blood pressure or diseased heart valves. The symptoms are chest pain, which can radiate to the throat, upper jaw and left arm. Difficulty in breathing, sweating and dizziness may be experienced.

General advice

- Eat a healthy diet free from junk food, sugar, salt, fried foods and saturated animal fats. Increase your intake of fresh fruit, salads, vegetables, fibre and virgin olive oil
- Try to cut down on stress
- Take regular, gentle, physical exercise – e.g. Tai Chi, yoga or a 20 minute walk daily
- Give up smoking

Reflexology Treatment

- Heart area
- Lungs
- Diaphragm
- Solar plexus
- Adrenals

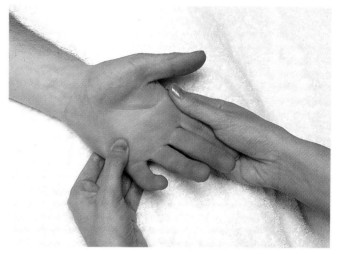

Heart

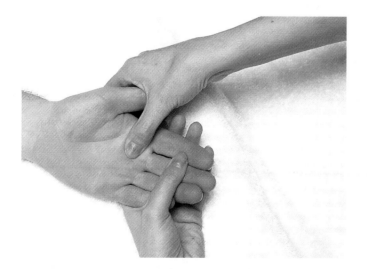

Lungs

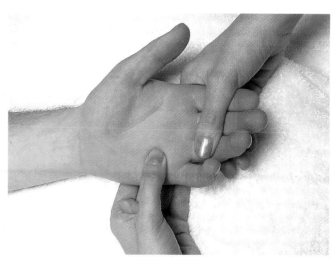

Diaphragm

RESPIRATORY PROBLEMS

ASTHMA

The causes of asthma are varied and include allergies such as pollen, house dust, fur, feathers, certain foods or pollutants. Stress often precipitates an attack.

General advice
- Yoga is very beneficial as it encourages deeper breathing as well as reducing stress
- Avoid irritating substances

Reflexology Treatment

- Lung/chest area
- Solar plexus
- Diaphragm
- Adrenal glands – for allergies

Lung/chest

COUGHS AND COLDS

Reflexology is not only an excellent way of relieving the symptoms of the common cold and speeding up recovery time but it is also remarkably effective at boosting the immune system. Regular reflexology greatly reduces the likelihood of catching a cold.

General advice
- Eat garlic, which is 'nature's antibiotic'
- Take at least one gram of vitamin C daily. Increase the dosage if you have a cold
- Eat ginger which helps to break down phlegm

Reflexology Treatment

- Lung/chest area – to break up the congestion and expel mucus
- Nose
- Throat
- Ears
- Eustacian tube
- Eyes
- Thymus – to boost the immune system
- Upper lymphatics

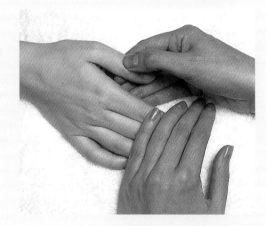

Nose

NASAL PROBLEMS

Nasal problems include acute or chronic catarrh, hay fever and sinusitis. Reflexology is renowned for its success with these problems. The most common causes are infections, allergies or the after effects of a cold.

General advice
- Avoid dairy foods, which encourage the production of mucus
- Steam inhalation with the addition of essential oils such as eucalyptus and cajeput

Reflexology Treatment

- Face area
- Sinuses
- Adrenals – to to counteract allergic responses
- Eyes and ears

Sinuses

SKIN PROBLEMS

Skin problems include acne, eczema and psoriasis and the causes are debatable. Hormonal imbalances, stress and certain foods appear to play a major part.

General advice

- Eat a healthy diet with plenty of fresh fruit and vegetables
- Drink 6 – 8 glasses of water daily
- Avoid stress and learn to relax
- Avoid perfumed products. Use pure organic skin creams

Reflexology Treatment

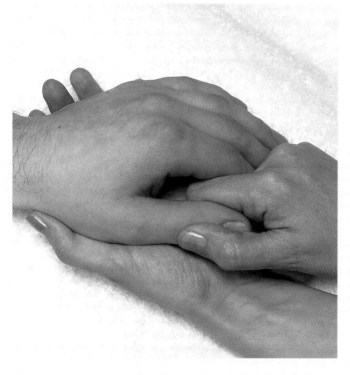

Face

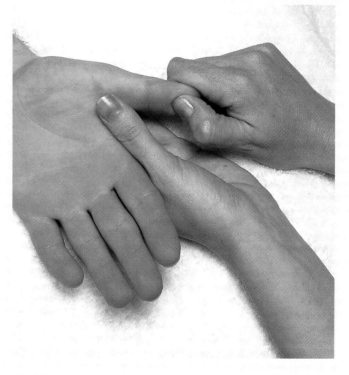

Pituitary Gland

- Reflex zones relating to the areas of the body affected e.g. face
- Pituitary gland – to balance the hormones
- Solar plexus – to relieve stress
- Adrenal glands – for stress and to counteract redness and itching
- Kidneys – to speed up elimination
- Lymphatics – to detoxify
- Digestive system – to encourage elimination

Index

Credits

The material in this publication previously appeared in:
Aromatherapy, Sandra White
Therapeutic Massage, Denise Whichello Brown
Sensual Massage, Denise Whichello Brown
Reflexology, Denise Whichello Brown
Hand Reflexology, Denise Whichello Brown

Quantum Publishing would like to thank Rod Teasdale for jacket design.